Thirty years ago the British Government ordered the rapid development of nuclear weapons. Deprived of US secrets from the Manhattan project, British scientists worked ceaselessly to develop first the atomic and then the hydrogen bomb. Today the speed with which they successfully completed their task is regarded by some as an heroic achievement. But for those servicemen who took part in the tests in Australia and at Christmas Island the memory is a different one: they look back on a time of ignorance and carelessness, which many believe has given them a deadly legacy of cancer. They remember taking part in a series of devastating nuclear experiments. Many now suspect they were deliberately placed close to the explosions as guinea-pigs.

The documents uncovered by the Australian Government's Royal Commission seem to confirm many of the veterans' worst fears. They show that the tests were carried out hastily and often in the wrong conditions: that servicemen and civilians were exposed to radiation; and that large parts of Australia were polluted — some for thousands of years — by the fallout.

This book brings together the mass of evidence and anecdote about the tests in Australia and the Pacific. It examines the claims of the ex-servicemen who say that they are now suffering from the radioactive poisoning they received at the time, and the British Government which says that no one suffered. The authors, who first broke the story, impartially recount the evidence of hundreds of the men who participated in the tests. Much of the material has never been revealed before. It shows a British Government prepared to admit in private that some men did suffer from the tests, but determined to avoid the payment of compensation; and it shows that the dying embers of British imperialism led to a 'shoestring and chewing gum affair' on the other side of the world, for which many people may still be paying with their lives.

ALSO IN COUNTERPOINT

FIELDS OF THUNDER
Testing Britain's Bomb

Denys Blakeway & Sue Lloyd-Roberts

COUNTERPOINT

London
UNWIN PAPERBACKS
Sydney   Boston

This edition first published in Great Britain
and Australia by Unwin Paperbacks 1985
This book is copyright under the Berne Convention. No reproduction
without permission. All rights reserved.

Unwin ® Paperbacks
40 Museum Street, London WC1A 1LU, UK

Unwin Paperbacks
Park Lane, Hemel Hempstead, Herts HP2 4TE, UK

Allen & Unwin Inc.
8 Winchester Place, Winchester, MA 01890, USA

George Allen & Unwin Australia Pty Ltd
8 Napier Street, North Sydney, NSW 2060, Australia

George Allen & Unwin with the
Port Nicholson Press
PO Box 11-838 Wellington, New Zealand

ISBN 0 0-341034 0 (PB)
ISBN 0 0-341029 4 (HB)

National Library of Australia
Cataloguing-in-Publication entry:
Blakeway, Denys.
  Fields of thunder.
  Bibliography.
  Includes index.
  ISBN 0 86861 816 0.
  ISBN 0 86861 808 X (pbk.).
  1. Radioactive fallout – Australia.   2. Radioactive
  fallout – Christmas Island (Indian Ocean).   3. Atomic
  weapons testing victims – Australia.   4. Atomic weapons
  – Testing.   I. Lloyd-Roberts, Sue.   II. Title.
363.1'79

Set in 11 on 13 point Garamond by Mathematical Composition Setters Limited
Salisbury, Wiltshire
and printed by
Singapore National Printers (Pte) Ltd.

CONTENTS

ACKNOWLEDGEMENTS

We should like to thank Harry Crosbie of the Australian Nuclear Veterans' Association, Ken McGinley of the British Nuclear Test Veterans Association, Mark Mildred, solicitor acting for the British Veterans, and Denise Johnstone-Burt for help and guidance with the text; and the BBC for giving Denys Blakeway permission to write the book.

Chapter One

FALL IN FOR FALLOUT

On 3 January 1985, Australia created a new landmark in her relations with her former colonial masters and a legal precedent in the history of the Commonwealth. The Australian Royal Commission which had been established to investigate the conduct of the British atomic bomb test series in Australia opened its hearings in London. British Government employees, scientists and servicemen were to be cross-examined in their own country during a judicial inquiry instigated by another government.

There was little doubt in the minds of those who witnessed the scene that the Australians relished their task. In his opening address the Commissioner, Mr Justice James McClelland, upbraided the British Government for 'dragging its feet' over the Australian investigation. He accused Britain of being a 'proud country' and of using secrecy about nuclear weapons as a 'convenient alibi for failure of disclosure'. Later he charged the man responsible for agreeing to British nuclear tests in Australia, Robert Menzies, with being a 'lickspittle of the British'. As far as this former Australian Prime Minister was concerned, it had been a question of 'ask and thou shalt receive'.

The bench of Australian lawyers sitting with the Commission in London enjoyed the outburst. Back home, Mr Justice 'Diamond Jim' McClelland was known as a rebel and admired for his outspokenness. They had expected something like this. The more sober British lawyers, the Treasury solicitors acting for Her

1

Majesty's Government, were taken aback and embarrassed. They had not expected to be harangued by a Commonwealth judge. Members of the Australian and British press were delighted. The speech made excellent copy and a dramatic start to the Commission.

The members of the British Nuclear Test Veterans' Association who had travelled to London for the first day's hearings felt that they were rewarded at last. The British Government had steadfastly refused to hold its own inquiry and the Australian judge's call for Britain to 'come clean' on the tests would provide ample ammunition for their cause. Representatives of the British forces who had served in Australia were being asked to come forward to testify; the Commission had already received hundreds of submissions from veterans in Australia. The British veterans regretted only that the Commission's brief did not extend to an examination of the servicemen who had taken part in the Pacific 'H' bomb tests on Christmas Island.

About twenty thousand British servicemen and two thousand British civilians took part in the twenty-one atmospheric nuclear tests in Australia and Christmas Island between 1952 and 1958. Fifteen thousand Australians were involved in the atomic bomb tests held on the Australian mainland and on the Monte Bello Islands. The majority of the men involved were conscripts, many of them teenagers. A few hundred Australian and British servicemen also took part in the so-called 'minor trials' – experiments with radioactive and toxic materials held at the Maralinga testing range in South Australia during the late fifties and early sixties. One of the purposes of the six hundred minor trials was to discover the effects of fire and chemical explosions on the materials that make up nuclear bombs. They may also have been a way of circumventing the international moratorium on atmospheric testing to which Britain became a party in 1958.

The procedure for witnessing the tests did not vary greatly between 1952 and 1958. The men were assembled in groups on the decks of their ships, in the scrub of the Australian bush or on the beaches of Christmas Island, which would give them a grandstand view of the explosion, sometimes no further than seven miles away. Each test was awaited with excitement and fear by the servicemen: the extraordinary sight of an atomic or hydrogen explosion from so close was often the one event of interest in an extremely uncomfortable and tedious tour of duty.

As the moment of detonation approached, orders were called out over tannoys to the assembled men, and the countdown was broadcast simultaneously. Apart from the selected few in the 'indoctrination force' who stood within a few thousand yards of ground zero (the point immediately below the explosion), the majority of men did not wear protective clothing. Later, for the seven hydrogen bomb tests at Christmas Island, the men were issued with 'zoot suits', white anti-flash gear with over-arm and over-head protectors and, in some cases, welder's goggles to protect the eyes from the blinding flash at the instant of detonation.

Whether dressed in protective clothing or not, all the men were ordered to take up the same position shortly after the countdown had begun. Turning their backs to ground zero, they flattened their hands and pressed their palms hard into their eye sockets. With the cry of 'zero' at the end of the countdown, a brilliant flash of blue-white light split through the heads of the witnesses. It was so bright that they could see quite clearly the bones of their hands pressed into their eyes, as if highlighted by X-ray. This flash was followed by a wave of intense heat – 'like standing against an open oven'. Seconds later, the men were told to turn to view the explosion and brace themselves for the shock wave. The hydrogen bombs were so powerful that the force of the blast often knocked men over who were watching twenty-five or more miles away.

The sight of the H bombs, burst several thousand feet up in the atmosphere, was especially beautiful and terrible. Shaped like an enormous billowing halo; and coloured orange, white and red by chemical reactions, the clouds rose rapidly into the upper atmosphere. As each ascended a white plume formed underneath which slowly grew until the explosion took on the familiar mushroom shape. The Australian atomic bombs were mostly burst at ground or sea level; only two were exploded in the air. The ground bursts sucked up huge quantities of earth and water, and lacked the immediate beauty of the H bombs. They were black and oily clouds, often misshapen by the tonnage of debris raised – which was later to fall back to earth as radioactive fallout.

Each of the twelve major atomic bomb tests in Australia has had questions raised about its safety. After the first detonation in 1952, on the Monte Bello Islands off the north-western coast, men claim that they were sent into the forward areas to collect radioactive samples without sufficient protection or monitoring procedures. The following year the tests were held at Emu near the Woomera rocket range in South Australia. One of the bombs was fired in unsafe weather conditions and produced the 'black mist' that passed over Aboriginal settlements, allegedly causing death from radiation sickness. The Mosaic tests which followed in 1956, once more on the Monte Bello Islands, contaminated the Australian mainland.

The Buffalo tests in the same year on the permanent test range at Maralinga were used to measure the effects of nuclear weapons on the morale and operational capacity of troops: members of the 'indoctrination force' stood within a few thousand yards of the detonation. The Antler test series in Maralinga in 1957 again raised doubts about the safety of Aborigines, and the so-called 'minor trials' on the range held between 1957 and 1963 spread quantities of radioactive materials including plutonium across the bush. The frequent dust storms in the Australian bush have been blowing potentially lethal carcinogens hither and thither now for nearly three decades.

Recent investigations into the monitoring procedures, both close in and at long range, have shown them to be inadequate.

It may never be known how much radioactive material was deposited over Australia. Fallout clouds were not properly traced and sampling stations were few and inefficient. Servicemen in Britain and Australia now claim that they were being used as 'guinea-pigs' in an experiment to discover the effects of radiation.

Although the British hydrogen bomb tests in the Pacific did not produce local fallout, the same lackadaisical attitudes to the safety of those exposed to radiation are reported. The crews who flew their aircraft through the H bomb clouds were exposed to even higher doses of radiation than the men in Australia, and those who decontaminated the planes on the ground were liable to be sprayed with radioactive water. Men wandered, out of curiosity, into areas with known radioactive hazards.

In Australia there are now ten thousand test veterans who have joined organizations fighting for compensation. A former Australian serviceman or his widow may claim compensation for damages against the Government under the Commonwealth Employees Act, and six veterans or their widows have so far received awards under this scheme. Five more are holding out for larger sums by sueing their Government under common law. The thirteen hundred members of the British Nuclear Test Veterans' Association are also dedicated to the fight for compensation but in Britain an Act of Parliament makes it impossible for an ex-serviceman to claim compensation for injuries received as a result of service in the armed forces. A test ex-serviceman or his widow may only apply for the small discretionary disability pension which is made available to members of the armed forces instead of compensation.

The different legal positions in the two countries mean that an Australian veteran who served alongside a British serviceman in the same tests may today be given compensation for his injuries while his British colleague receives nothing. As a British MP remarked to the House of Commons, 'It is ironic that while Britain and Australia should share the same sovereign, each nation is applying different ground rules to the atom test controversy.'

The British Government has always denied that there is any truth in the claims that negligence in the conduct of the tests had led men to suffer radiation-induced illnesses. The number of test veterans developing cancer, it says, is no higher than normal, and nor is the number of their offspring with birth defects. To prove this, the British Government has commissioned the National Radiological Protection Board to survey the health records of test participants. Indeed, the British Defence Minister, Adam Butler, has publicly cast doubt on the wisdom of the Australian Government in setting up the Royal Commission. In the House of Commons in December 1984, he questioned the benefit of collecting anecdotal evidence from test veterans and test planners. The report by the National Radiological Protection Board would, he said, be 'statistical and objective. That is the importance as compared with the work of the Royal Commission.'

Despite the evidence emerging from the Australian Royal Commission, the British Ministry of Defence and the Atomic Weapons Research Establishment (AWRE) – the Government bodies that supervised the test programme – dismiss the allegations by ex-servicemen that the tests took place without proper safeguards. They point out that radiation safety procedures followed well-established practice and conformed to international standards of the day. However, an examination of the veterans' anecdotes dismissed by the British authorities raises many doubts. Most veterans agree that there were strict procedures and rules on the test ranges but that 'all the rules laid down were not enforced and some were broken outright'. Many of them remember sharing a light-hearted, even contemptuous, attitude to radiation precautions and few of them recall being properly briefed about the hazards.

There is, furthermore, evidence that servicemen were subjected to radiation in order to increase contemporary knowledge about its effects: the Ministry of Defence wanted to establish the operational usefulness of the armed forces in the event of nuclear war. Servicemen were told to 'march, crawl and lie' in radioactive dust. A ship was instructed to sail into a fallout area. An RAF Canberra flew into the atomic cloud four minutes after each detonation. The British authorities argue, however, that most of the men involved in the tests did not even experience radiation exposures above the levels of everyday life. Those who did receive higher doses were within the 'prescribed limits' and were 'given appropriate protection'. If this is the case, the authorities have behaved very strangely about revealing all the test details.

For six months the Australian Royal Commission asked the British Ministry of Defence for details of individual radiation doses received by servicemen. They were consistently refused. Many British veterans tell stories which suggest official attempts to stifle the truth. One man, for example, told the Royal Commission that his medical records had been stripped of all the details relating to his life in the services and that doctors had told him his files were classified. In another instance, a former RAF man was denied a body scan by the Government nuclear establishment at Harwell 'in case he should use the results in proceedings against the Government', and a widow of a test veteran related that when she had contacted the Ministry of Defence about her husband's death, she was told that the bomb tests in Australia had never taken place.

There has been as much anger in Australia about the permanent scars left on the country by the bomb tests as there has been about injuries to veterans. Although the British 'cleaned up' after they left the ranges, and even returned in 1979 to retrieve half a kilo of plutonium, some 800 kilos of radioactive materials remain buried at the test sites and in recent years surveyors have found particles of plutonium scattered over the bush area. The Australian Government is unlikely to wish to finance and carry out further clean-ups, the cost of which could run into billions of Australian dollars, if, as is quite possible, the topsoil of large areas of the Australian bush needs to be removed to rid it of contamination. Britain, however, is equally unlikely to want to take on the cost and difficulties of tracing and removing every piece of radioactive rubbish strewn over the Australian bush. As a result, relations between the two Governments may be strained far more by the recommendations of the Royal Commission than they were by its inception.

The Australian people have always been sensitive to what they consider to be the patronising behaviour of their old colonial rulers and the nuclear tests are a classic example of the attitudes they have grown to resent so deeply. The initial agreement to the use of Australian locations as atomic bomb test sites was gained within a few days of a telegrammed request from Clement Attlee to Robert Menzies, and the first tests took place without any formal consultation. When dissident voices were raised among members of the Australian Labor Party, the Minister for Supply, Howard Beale, issued a statement proclaiming: 'The whole project is a striking example of inter-Commonwealth co-operation on the grand scale. England has the bomb and the know-how; we have the open spaces, much technical skill and a great willingness to help the Motherland.' The Australian people are thus not merely concerned with Britain's conduct of the tests but with the behaviour of their own authorities; particularly of such men as Sir Ernest Titterton, the physicist on the Australian Weapons Test Safety Committee whose job it was to protect the interests of the Australian people during the test programme, and Sir Howard Beale, the Minister responsible.

The indifference that Britain showed towards the welfare of Australia during the fifties still appears to prevail today, judging by the British press, whose coverage of the Royal Commission hearings in London was largely confined to the judge's outburst and dramatic stories from British veterans. There was little interest in the contamination in Australia caused by the tests, although when, on the last day of the hearings, it was revealed that Britain's nuclear scientists had considered holding some of the 'minor trials' in Scotland, on the north-east coast at Wick, the press woke up to a sensational story. Articles entitled 'Rain saved Scotland from atom tests' and 'A-test story horrifies Wick' commanded more column inches than the previous three months' hearings. Nonetheless, members of all British political parties have urged that the British Government should make amends. Britons still believe that Commonwealth ties are important and their opinions were echoed in the London *Times* on the day the Royal Commission returned to Australia: 'We owe Australia a considerable debt which, it turns out, is being paid in slow instalments. Although Britain may have already fulfilled its formal liabilities to the land and people affected by the tests, it will not pay us to quibble mean-mindedly over reasonable requests for reparation.'

The men who took part in Britain's H bomb programme believe that they were just as much the victims of the nuclear tests as their Australian counterparts. Instead of a Royal Commission, however, they have to make do with their own collection of anecdotes as evidence and await the NRPB's statistical survey, the results of which are expected in 1986. It is no surprise that they feel frustrated by the weight of evidence available about the Australian trials while their own case is ignored. Yet the action of the Australian Royal Commission in gaining access to so many documents about Britain's tests may benefit all the veterans. As the documents are read and understood, so the tide of public feeling in support of the British veterans' case grows, for while it is no doubt true that the majority of the men who witnessed the tests thirty years ago were not put at any great risk, the evidence shows that the tests were carried out in a spirit of complacency and with frequent dangerous disregard for the safety of servicemen. These men may now be paying the price of their loyal service in the successful development of Britain's independent nuclear deterrent with their health and even with their lives.

Chapter Two

COUNTING THE RISKS

The British Government's public statements of confidence that all was well with the nuclear tests in Australia and at Christmas Island have appeared increasingly misplaced as revelation after revelation of incompetence and mismanagement has been made. The confidence comes from a tradition of bureaucratic indifference and scientific arrogance whereby only those with inside knowledge of the facts are supposed able to make judgments, which are not open to explanation or questioning. It was an indication of the early confidence in the safety of nuclear trials that in 1955 the government even considered holding them in the crowded island of Britain, a proposal only rejected by the chief British scientist, William Penney, after fears were raised that fallout might get into the local water supply. The United Kingdom thus narrowly escaped the long-lasting radioactive pollution from which the Australians may suffer for thousands of years.

When the plans to use Scotland for atomic tests were brought out during the 1985 Commission, the Ministry of Defence explained it, as so many issues raised by the tests, in ambiguous scientific terms which could mean little to the layman. According to an official: 'There was a proposal to carry out experiments in the Wick area involving the release of short-life radioactive material; this was polonium which had a half-life of 138 days'. To the Scots the news that their country had been a possible test site was another example of English colonial attitudes. The Scottish National Party leader, Gordon Wilson, said that 'the view from Whitehall obviously was that the Scottish natives, like the Australian Aborigines, were totally expendable.'

The Government's claim that the tests were quite safe is most clearly debatable when the plight of the Aborigines in the outback, close to the test ranges, is considered. Even some of the Government's own scientists now accept that they got it wrong. David Barnes, a senior AWRE scientist, told the Australian Royal Commission: 'If you are asking me whether we did it properly at that time, I have to say no. Speaking now, we might well have taken more account of the Aborigine population.' It is, of course, in Whitehall's interest to maintain that all aspects of the tests were safe. The nature of radiation is so complex and so little understood that a single admission of negligence could lead to a flood of compensation claims both in Britain and Australia against which there would be little defence.

As the risks of the nuclear tests are highlighted through the Australian Royal Commission, the fact that they often involved little or no risk to the majority of participants is forgotten. Many of the test veterans, not understanding the nature of the explosions which they witnessed because it was never explained to them, conclude that if Aborigines were exposed to many times the permitted level of radiation, so too were they. In fact, however, many of the test participants were quite safe. By denying that anything went wrong at the tests, the Ministry of Defence blurs the distinction between areas of risk and safety, and needless anxiety and public embarrassment are caused.

Had the test veterans understood better the nature of radiation and the various types of British nuclear explosions in the atmosphere, they might have attached less significance to cases like that of Kenneth Measures and more to those cases where there had been a real risk of dangerous exposure to radiation. As a Chief Petty Officer on HMS *Warrior* in 1957, Kenneth Measures had witnessed H bomb tests and taken part in decontamination drills in the Central Pacific. In the same way as many servicemen who took part in British atmospheric tests in the fifties, he had been ordered to stand on the flight deck of his ship and turn away at the point of explosion – a few miles away – crouching with his hands pressed tightly into his eye sockets. A short while after detonation he had been commanded to turn and watch the fireball racing up into the higher atmosphere. A non-smoker, he died in 1984 of a very rare form of lung cancer. A year later a coroner's court in Penzance held an inquest into his death, which had been built up as a test case in the veterans' campaign for compensation and recognition. In this it failed utterly. The jury, after only fifteen minutes, returned a verdict of death by natural causes.

For many of the test servicemen today it seems inconceivable that witnessing a nuclear weapon from close quarters in the way that Kenneth Measures did, usually wearing no more than standard white anti-flash gear, could have been safe. The mere fact that they were able to see the bones of their hands through their flesh at the instant of detonation seems, in retrospect, to confirm their worst fears of radiation exposure. Ministry of Defence Officials have, however, always said that the majority of servicemen were never in any danger. They point out that the men were too far from the bombs to have been exposed to radiation and even if they did receive a dose, the levels would have been far too low to have done any damage. They insist that the tests were carried out safely and that decontamination and clean-up operations afterwards were effective.

Certainly, Kenneth Measures had no record of radiation exposure. He was built into a test case after his death because many of the veterans both in Britain and Australia believe that all the men in the tests were deliberately placed at risk: they see themselves as the innocent victims of a deliberate policy of using servicemen as guinea pigs. Their case is extremely difficult to prove. It is often based more on emotion than on a basic knowledge of the nature and effects of radiation, without which it is not possible to make any judgment about the safety of the nuclear tests.

Since 1945 there has been little argument about the effects of very high doses of radiation. The two atomic bombs over Hiroshima and Nagasaki in Japan showed decisively that radiation produced a unique and terrible condition, called 'radiation sickness', at doses above fifty rads or so (see end of chapter for definition of radiation measurements). It is also generally accepted that a dose of about 450 rads causes death in roughly half those unfortunate enough to receive it. The effect is to kill or damage individual cells in the body, particularly in areas where cells are multiplying quickly: the bone marrow, the reproductive organs and the stomach and intestines are all highly sensitive. At very high dose levels the central nervous system is disturbed, with symptoms of alternating stupor and hyperactivity; death follows within a few days. Potentially lethal doses produce symptoms such as nausea, persistent vomiting, bloody diarrhoea and hair loss, and may result in death in a few days or weeks.

RADIATION

Radiation may be divided into two forms: ionising and non-ionising. Sunlight, radio waves and radar are all forms of non-ionising radiation and they normally do no harm. Ionising radiation, produced by nuclear reactions, is potentially much more dangerous and the fear that humans may have been exposed to damaging levels of it is the basis of the concern about the safety of the nuclear tests. A certain level of ionising radiation occurs naturally in the environment but it is thought that humans have evolved to withstand this 'background' radiation. It is, however, now generally accepted that there is no absolutely 'safe' level of exposure to radiation. Ionising radiation is potentially dangerous at all levels because it can cause 'ionisation' in atoms, which leads to permanent or temporary structural damage to the cells which they make up.

Ionisation is the process whereby the electrically neutral atom becomes charged. This occurs when the electrons surrounding the nucleus of the atom are knocked out of their position by the energy of the radiation passing through the body. The atom without electrons is called an 'ion' and is a charged particle. Ions can destroy a living cell's ability to replicate itself accurately and once this happens, and distorted cells multiply, cancer may occur. This effect is not immediate. Cancer caused by radiation has a 'latent period' which may be as long as, or even longer than, thirty years after exposure.

Radiation produced by nuclear weapon explosions consists of:

ALPHA PARTICLES (the nuclei of helium atoms).
These particles are not very penetrating and are easily stopped by the skin, but radioactive elements, like plutonium, which emit alpha particles are dangerous when ingested by swallowing or breathing, or if they enter the body through a cut. In minute quantities they give off high energy, which can cause great harm to the parts of the body where they lodge and they can only be traced in the body with the greatest difficulty.

BETA PARTICLES (electrons)
These particles are more penetrating than alpha particles and are a hazard as 'external' radiation. They can be stopped by protective clothing.

GAMMA RADIATION (electro magnetic radiations similar to light and radio waves)
Gamma rays are highly penetrating and can pass through several inches of steel. They can only be screened by a very thick layer of steel or concrete, or similar material.

NEUTRONS (neutral particles present in all nuclei except hydrogen)
Neutrons are basic particles out of which atomic nuclei are made. They are highly penetrating and can only be screen-

ed by a thick layer of concrete or by deep water. If a neutron is absorbed in the nucleus of another atom, it can make that atom unstable and radioactive.

RADIATION MEASUREMENT

There are a bewildering variety of units which measure ionising radiation, but those used here are the Roentgen, Rad and Rem.

The ROENTGEN (R or r) measures ionising radiation in the air.

The RAD – Radiation Absorbed Dose – measures a specific amount of radiation absorbed by human or animal tissue.

The REM – Radiation Equivalent Man – measures the biological damage done to tissue by a specific amount of radiation. Different sorts of radiation do different amounts of harm to living tissue, and this is taken account of by the Rem. The British test scientists also used a similar unit called the REP.

For beta and gamma radiations, one rad equals one rem. For neutron and alpha particles, one rad may equal up to twenty rems, depending on the energy of the particles. A low dose of radiation is usually considered to be several rems or less, and a high dose approximately 100 rems or more.

A high dose can cause directly observed effects: radiation sickness, hair loss and changes in blood cells. Under 25 rems no physical changes are observed, but a low dose of radiation may lead to increased risks of cancer and possible birth defects in the offspring of the exposed person.

There is no firm evidence that the servicemen involved in the 1950s tests suffered from such effects. It is quite possible, however, that Aborigines were exposed to doses high enough to produce the symptoms of radiation sickness and even to cause death. Those Aborigines found in the bomb craters or wandering on test sites after explosions are likely to have received very high doses; and those exposed to the 'black mist' of fallout from the Totem One test in 1953 may also have suffered radiation sickness and death.

Before the atomic bombs, ignorance about the hazards of radiation was reflected in the high dose levels allowed for radiation workers: up to ten times the maximum annual dose permitted today. It was also believed that there was a threshold level of exposure below which radiation caused no harm at all, a belief which continued for some time after the war. High doses of radiation have never been considered safe, however. In the early 1900s, as the use of X-rays in medicine grew, the harmful effects of high exposure became known when radiographers showed a tendency to contract skin cancers and leukaemia. In recognition of these emerging dangers an international regulatory body, the International Commission on Radiological Protection (ICRP), was set up in 1928 to establish 'safe' radiation doses. The self-appointed ICRP has continued in existence and determined among other things the dose levels used as a basis by the British authorities, in consultation with the Medical Research Council, for their nuclear tests.

Clear proof of the past exposure of humans to very high doses of radiation is now possible because of more sensitive detection techniques. One such technique, known as a 'cyto-genetic test', has been used on ex-servicemen who suffer from various cancers known to be linked with radiation. It can detect chromosomal damage after twenty-five years or so, which, if extensive, shows beyond reasonable doubt that an individual has suffered a high dose of radiation – about two or three hundred rads. This is a very high dose indeed, about ten times the highest level officially permitted at the tests, and not one of the British nuclear test veterans examined has yet presented sufficient chromosomal damage to confirm such a high dose of radiation. This does not establish beyond doubt, however, that the test veterans are not suffering as the result of exposure to radiation. The arguments about safety still remain but in the complex area of the effects of low doses of radiation to which servicemen may have been negligently exposed in ways not appreciated by the authorities at the time.

Although radiation produced by nuclear reactions has probably been studied more than any other environmental hazard, there is still considerable ignorance and argument about its effects, especially at levels as low as those possibly received by test servicemen. It is known that low doses can lead to cancer, and animal studies have shown that they may cause birth defects, but these are problems which are not caused by radiation alone. Humans are exposed to cancer-causing agents throughout their lives; many of which are still unknown. As a result it is not easy to differentiate between a cancer caused by radiation and one caused by any other agent. About twenty-two per cent of deaths in Britain and the Western world each year result from cancer, which means that of the twenty thousand British test participants more than four thousand can be expected to die of cancer irrespective of their having been exposed to radiation.

The only way to show that the test veterans were exposed to damaging radiation is to establish that they suffer from more cases of cancer than a similar group who were not at any nuclear tests. This is the purpose of the government-sponsored study of British ex-servicemen, being carried out by the National Radiological Protection Board, which is comparing the number of deaths from cancer among test veterans with those in a group of ex-servicemen with the same age range and background who did not witness any tests. A similar type of survey of Aborigines is being carried out in Australia.

The statistical surveys will not be able to allay an individual's fears that he or she has suffered as a result of the nuclear tests, since to establish proof of any one person's exposure to damaging low doses of radiation is almost impossible. All that can be said is that if a comparatively high number of cancer cases are found among test veterans, there is a possibility that radiation from the tests brought about an individual's cancer.

The belief that low doses of radiation can harm humans does not rest on direct physical evidence. No specific illness is suffered immediately after exposure, and there are no observable physical changes in the body. Most modern understanding of low levels of radiation is based on the experience in Hiroshima and Nagasaki, where victims of the two A-bombs were exposed to a very wide range of doses, from the very high to the very low. Studies of those who survived high radiation doses showed that they later developed a higher than average number of cancers, starting with leukaemias in the early years and going on to a wide range of other cancers as time passed.

Based on the assumption that the effects of radiation are proportional to dose, and extrapolating from the evidence of effects at high doses, the excess number of cancers which would occur in a population exposed to low doses of radiation has been calculated. This method of working out the effects of low doses is called the 'linear hypothesis', and it tends to be confirmed by the evidence from victims of Hiroshima and Nagasaki, which shows that the number of cancers among the survivors declined as their radiation dose decreased. There is much debate about the adequacy of the data on which the hypothesis is based but if it is correct, it follows that there is no dose of radiation without a corresponding risk of cancer. According to Professor Edward Radford, one of the leading authorities on the effects of low doses, 'there is no threshold below which no effect occurs; an effect will occur at any level of radiation exposure, no matter how small.'

There has been no consensus of opinion about the risks of low doses of radiation since the crucial year of 1945; only a general decrease in the maximum permissible levels set by the ICRP. During the fifties nuclear tests, standards were changing as the theory of a threshold level below which exposure was safe lost ground. Between 1934 and 1950 the ICRP had recommended a maximum 'tolerance dose' – the threshold level – of 0.2R a day, with 1R per week as the maximum permissible external exposure. These 'tolerance doses' were applied to the limited number of workers, mainly in the medical field, who came into contact with radiation when using X-rays and radium. It was considered that no harm could arise from such doses.

After the war the development of nuclear weapons and nuclear energy meant that much larger numbers of people were exposed to radiation. Fears of long-term genetic damage prompted the ICRP in 1950 to make new recommendations, which were used, according to the physicist William Penney, as the bible for the early and middle part of the test series in Australia, code-named Hurricane and Totem. The new maximum permitted dose was 15R a year, with a permissible dose of 0.3R a week measured 'in free air' or 0.5R on the body. The ICRP document setting out the levels still recognized the existence of 'tolerance doses' but it made clear the dangers and warned that exposure should be kept as low as possible: 'While the values proposed for maximum permissible exposures are such as to involve a risk which is small compared to the other hazards of life, nevertheless in view of the unsatisfactory nature of much of the evidence on which our judgments must be based, coupled with the knowledge that certain radiation effects are irreversible and cumulative, it is strongly recommended that every effort be made to reduce exposures to all types of ionising radiations to the lowest possible level'.

Despite the ICRP's caveat, the authorities who set the levels for the early tests were confident that there were doses below which no harm would arise. As late as May 1953 the health physicists – the experts in radiation safety – in charge of the decontamination procedures at the Australian tests stated: 'The body can of course tolerate a certain amount of radioactivity without injury, but above a certain level of activity there arises a real danger to health'. Such statements were made despite

British Medical Research Council work as early as 1947 showing that there was no threshold level below which genetic damage could be prevented.

In 1954 the concept of a threshold dose was finally and totally rejected by ICRP: 'Since no radiation level higher than the natural background can be regarded as absolutely safe, the problem is to choose a practical level that, in the light of present knowledge, involves a negligible risk.' In the same same document the ICRP recommended that exposure to the public be a tenth of that of radiation workers and suggested dose limits for specific organs of the body. It also lowered the daily dose levels and recommended the limitation of 'temporary' exposure to high doses to those whom it was thought would be unlikely to work again with radiation. The new 'rad' and 'rem' measurements were introduced.

These recommendations were meant to be used as a basis for the Mosaic and Maralinga tests, but the dose limit of only 0.5R per week during the tests was too low for the successful operation of the programme. Many essential jobs, such as flying through the nuclear cloud or retrieving instruments from radioactive areas, could not be carried out at all if the ICRP limits were followed. To get round the problem, the British authorities introduced 'specially planned exposures' where a small number of servicemen were allowed temporary doses many times the ICRP's normal levels. These were called 'integrated doses' and were permitted on the assumption that radiation effects are cumulative. Single operations, using up six weeks or more of a serviceman's weekly radiation dose level in one 'integrated' go, were allowed on the understanding that the individual concerned would not be exposed again within a specified period. For example, the 'lower integrated dose' of 3R used up six weeks' dose allowance of 0.5R per week. A man receiving that dose would not be allowed any further exposure for six weeks.

Since the servicemen involved were unlikely to be exposed to radiation in their work after the tests, it was later considered acceptable to expose them to an integrated dose which would use up a lifetime's allowance in one exposure. At first, however, the integrated doses allowed were between 3 and 10R, and it was only for tests after Hurricane and Totem that the higher level of 25R was introduced, which was meant to be the 'once in a lifetime dose'. According to the Ministry of Defence such planned exposures, 'vital to the success of the tests', were allowed by the ICRP but in fact the ICRP recommended in 1954 that such 'temporary exposures' 'should not be permitted'.

The health physicists at the early tests differentiated between gamma rays and beta particles when setting dose allowances, because beta radiation was considered safer, being less penetrating. Such differentiation between types of radiation, with the consequent possible increase in dose levels, was unheard of at American nuclear tests taking place at the same time. The British then used a unit called the 'rep' which is similar to the more frequently used 'rem', and test regulations laid down the combined beta and gamma maximum exposures as 50 rep, of which the gamma component should not exceed 10R. All the official British figures now refer only to the gamma component and take no account of beta radiation, which is partly due to poor beta monitoring at the time of the tests but also because, according to official accounts, 'in practice exposure was almost always limited by gamma rather than beta exposure'. The official published dose levels may not, therefore, reflect the total exposure permitted during the tests and recorded at the time.

By the end of Britain's bomb testing in 1958, the maximum permitted dose was reduced again by the ICRP to 5 rem a year, with a quarterly limit of 3 rem and no weekly dose allowances. A distinction between doses permitted to radiation workers, who chose to expose themselves, and members of the public, who did not, was also introduced. This allowed a dose of only 0.5 rem to a member of the public in any year, which was a level which had previously been exceeded at settlements near the Australian test ranges on several occasions. The new lower levels – which were applied to the last Christmas Island tests and the later experiments in Australia – have remained in force to this day, despite many calls for their reduction.

The doses permitted at the tests were relatively high by today's standards but apart from the exposures of Aborigines and other members of the public they would not breach the letter of present ICRP regulations. Furthermore it was official policy that 'the actual dosage received must be kept to a minimum', and this policy was, if monitoring records from the time can be trusted, quite successful. These records were kept only for those considered at risk of radiation exposure – some five thousand British servicemen and civilians, and one and a half thousand Australians.

On 19 December 1984 Adam Butler, the Minister in Charge of Defence Procurement (formerly the Ministry of Supply), stated that according to government records only fifty British participants in the tests were exposed to levels of radiation of any significance. Of these fifty, thirty men received doses higher than 7 rem. These were the 'special higher integrated doses for cases of extreme necessity'. Fewer than one hundred and fifty men received doses between 2 and 7 rem; about five hundred were exposed to between 0.35 and 2 rem, and one and a half thousand or so had measured exposure of less than 0.5 rem. The remaining four thousand British men monitored were exposed to levels too low to be distinguished from naturally occurring background radiation. According to the Australian Ionising Radiation Advisory Council only four Australians received doses above today's annual limit of 5 rem. The majority, 969 men, are recorded as having nil exposure, and the remainder of 527 men received doses between 0 and 5 rem.

The test veterans' associations reject such figures. They claim that the doses were more widespread and that the monitoring facilities were insufficient to take account of the reality of the doses. They say that the tests were unlike the controlled exposures of radiation workers today, which can be efficiently supervised and where there is much greater control over the nuclear reactions. They also argue that the risks of low levels of radiation were not, and are not, properly understood and that the participants were in much greater danger than was recognized at the time.

The Ministry of Defence and the Atomic Weapons Research Establishment (AWRE), however, have no fears about the risks raised by the nuclear tests, even if there is no such thing as a totally 'safe' dose of radiation. They believe that the risks arising from the doses recorded were negligible, and that the calculated and small risks taken were fully justified by the national importance of the nuclear tests. Nevertheless, some experts in radiation safety are now convinced that new evidence shows that the tests involved the participants in dangerous exposures to radiation even if the exposures were considered to have been within ICRP levels. If their fears are justified, the government-sponsored survey of the British nuclear test participants may show a significant excess of cancer deaths among them.

In the last decade a number of studies have been published which cast doubt on current ICRP safety limits. In 1977 the preliminary results of one of the most wide-ranging and controversial studies of the effects of low doses of ionising radiation were published in the United States by the University of Pittsburgh. The authors, Dr Thomas Mancuso and Drs Alice Stewart and George Kneale, had surveyed the records of 24,939 workers from the Hanford nuclear reprocessing plant in Washington between 1944 and 1977. The plant had been working since 1944, when it was made operational for the manufacture of the first atomic bombs, and as the workers had often been exposed to low doses of radiation, and had been monitored constantly for such exposure, they made an appropriate study population.

Even before the survey was published it aroused controversy. Its director, Thomas Mancuso, claimed that his funds had been cut off by the United States government when the survey started to show results which indicated that low doses of radiation could cause more harm that expected. The US government's Atomic Energy Commission, on the other hand, claimed that his funding had been cut because of the length of time the survey was taking. The results, when eventually published, showed a high incidence of two types of cancer: multiple myeloma (a cancer of the bone marrow) and cancer of the pancreas. This indicated, according to the authors, that the risk of cancer being caused by radiation could be ten to twenty times greater than that estimated from the experience of Japanese A-bomb survivors, on which ICRP figures are based.

The survey's methods were, however, widely criticized, and some of its claims about the effects of low level radiation were dismissed, even by scientists known for their opposition to current dose levels. Nevertheless the excess in the two types of cancer is still accepted as statistically 'significant', though it is not possible to say categorically whether they were caused by radiation from the plant or by other environmental agents. One of the principal doubts about the survey was that it found a lower incidence than normal of leukaemia, whereas the surveys of the victims of Hiroshima and Nagasaki had suggested an association between above-average numbers of blood cancers and radiation at low doses. The study's supporters argued, however, that leukaemia may only occur in excess after high doses, or where people are placed in highly traumatic situations such as the experience of an atomic bomb from close quarters. They point out that the survey is an indication that the Hiroshima-Nagasaki cancer survey cannot be relied upon alone to provide evidence of the effects of low levels of radiation.

More evidence that the risks from low levels of radiation may be greater than those officially accepted has recently emerged from other studies of radiation workers in the United States.

Unpublished documents from the US Department of Energy, as revealed in the *New Scientist* in October 1984, show that cancer rates are higher than expected in the four nuclear facilities studied, despite adherence to standards in line with those of the ICRP. Unlike the Hanford study, the Deparment of Energy's Health and Mortality Study shows an increase in reported leukaemias. The 'major research result' was 'excess mortality due to site/type specific cancers (leukaemia, lung, brain, digestive tract, prostate, Hodgkin's disease) and excess non-malignant respiratory disease morbidity were found among workers exposed to uranium dusts and/or radiations from other internal and external sources'. At one plant, the Oak Ridge National Laboratory, there was a forty-nine per cent excess leukaemia mortality among the workers compared to the general public which showed a link between leukaemia and increased radiation doses received at the plant. This survey, which was kept secret for seven years, was carried out after the methods of analysis used by Mancuso, Stewart and Kneale had caused so much controversy.

Another survey, of 3224 soldiers who took part in a nuclear test code-named Smoky in the Nevada desert in 1957, lends weight to the argument that nuclear tests damage health despite the absence of records of high radiation doses. In the test, a medium-large 48-kiloton atomic bomb was detonated to discover, among other things, the 'physiological and psychological' effects on the men. The aim of measuring how servicemen would function militarily when close to nuclear bomb detonations was similar to that of the British test, Marcoo, which was part of the Buffalo series in 1956.

The radiation from the Smoky test was minimal and within ICRP levels, according to the monitoring devices – film badge 'dosemeters' – worn by the men who took part. Yet a survey of the participants in 1980 showed 9 cases of leukaemia where only 3.5 would normally be expected; which was the first indication from the United States that nuclear testing may cause more damage than the authorities expected. A more recent study, published in 1984, of the Smoky test participants also shows an excess of a very rare type of bood cancer, polycythaemia vera: three cases of the disease where only one would be a rarity. The researchers who carried out the study are, however, not yet convinced by the evidence. They still believe there is insufficient data to day that the results of the Smoky tests prove a link between nuclear tests, low radiation doses and subsequent cancers.

A significant development in the controversy about the effects of low radiation doses has been the recent reassessment of the Nagasaki-Hiroshima bomb data on which the ICRP has based its dose level recommendations. In 1981, scientists working at the US Lawrence Livermore National Laboratory showed that there were significant errors in the calculation of the doses received by the victims of the two bombs; in some cases the dose estimates were wrong by a factor of ten. Previous estimates had, according to this study, assumed too high doses of neutron radiation and too little shielding of the survivors from gamma radiation. The cancer rates observed in the survivors must, therefore, have been caused by much lower doses. The implications of this discovery have been investigated by a senior group of scientists at the Radiation Effects Foundation at Hiroshima and Nagasaki, and it is likely that their conclusions will lead to a cut, perhaps even a tenfold reduction, in the annual dose limits set by the ICRP.

In the light of the discovery that radiation doses at Hiroshima and Nagasaki were much lower than had been thought, and to 'put the importance of the bomb data into perspective', Professor Patricia Lindop and Mr M. W. Charles decided to look at the available evidence of the effects of radiation specifically excluding any data from Hiroshima and Nagasaki. They found that cancer deaths among groups exposed to radiation, such as people treated with high doses of X-rays, appeared to be two to three times higher than would be expected from the old estimates of radiation doses for A-bomb survivors, which confirmed that a rethink of the present safety limits is called for.

Perhaps the most disturbing evidence of our ignorance of the causes of cancer, and the lack of knowledge of the effects of radiation, comes from the public debate about the various 'clusters' of leukaemia near nuclear power stations in the United Kingdom. These clusters or outbreaks of leukaemia much in excess of the national average have been reported near Sizewell, Berkeley, Winfrith and Sellafield – formerly known as Windscale. In late 1983, after a Yorkshire television programme 'Windscale, the Nuclear Laundry', the Minister of Health commissioned an independent inquiry into the increased incidence of cancer in the area close to the Sellafield (Windscale) site. The inquiry was headed by Sir Douglas Black and concluded that background radiation alone could not explain the high incidence of deaths from leukaemia in under twenty-year-olds in the area. It did not conclude, however, that low doses of radiation were necessarily responsible for the excess. Instead it called for more studies to be carried out in the hope that a cause might be found. Sir Douglas Black's critics have called the report a 'whitewash'. They say that the high incidence of cancers is a clear indication of radiation exposure; that it is, indeed, a very sensitive method of recording exposure to radiation – far more responsive than any of the monitoring and recording that has been carried out over the years.

The same arguments could, of course, apply to any excess of cancers found by statistical studies of the nuclear test participants and Aborigines. Without firm evidence of high doses, those involved will never have clear and unequivocal proof that they have suffered as a result of the tests. The arguments about the effects of low doses are complex and the results of the surveys concerning them as yet only tentative. To win their case the test veterans must establish not only that low doses of radiation may be much more dangerous than the authorities understood in the fifties but also how it was that men, like Kenneth Measures, with no record of exposure could have accidentally come into contract with radiation. The British Government is confident that the majority of test veterans were never exposed at all and were at no risk from the bombs but judging by the precautions taken at the tests, and the hair-raising incidents individuals have reported, that official confidence may well be misplaced.

Chapter Three

CALLING THE SHOTS

The British authorities were determined to use the tests of the fifties to discover as much as possible about the effects of nuclear weapons. As a circular issued in May 1953 by the Defence Research Policy Committee to the Chiefs of Staff stated: 'Many of these tests are of the highest importance to departments, since on their results depend the design of equipment, changes in organisation and administration, and offensive and defensive tactics'. In particular, it went on, the army 'must discover the effects of various types of explosions on equipment, stores and men with and without various types of protection'. Ministry of Defence Officials have argued that such information was gained by the use of instruments and not by the deliberate exposure of men to radiation. The evidence, however, points to servicemen being used at every possible opportunity to discover the nature and effects of nuclear warfare. If they were exposed to radiation, the 'fortuitous' occurrence was used as a chance to establish the workings of this little known but revolutionary new ingredient in the services' armory.

The tests were not merely a scientific experiment. They were an opportunity for the military and civil defence forces to learn about a completely new form of warfare. Men were exposed to nuclear bombs in order that monitoring and decontamination exercises could be assessed, and their ability to function as disciplined troops could be studied by military strategists. Although there is no firm evidence of deliberate exposure of men to high doses of radiation, there is no doubt that the servicemen at the tests were part of an experiment from which the authorities were determined to learn everything they could.

Early in 1985 the Prime Minister, Margaret Thatcher, categorically denied that there was any truth in the allegations that that servicemen were used as 'guinea pigs'. No British servicemen, she said, were 'exposed unnecessarily to levels of ionising radiation in excess of the prescribed limits'. The distinction between a serviceman being exposed to high doses of radiation as a guinea pig and his being in necessary, carefully monitored contact with radiation and nuclear weapons in order to benefit scientific and military knowledge is clearly a fine one.

When a nuclear weapon is detonated, the resulting fireball almost instantaneously reaches a temperature nearly as high as that of the sun's interior, and causes an enormous radiation of heat and light energy. This flash of heat, which lasts about twenty seconds, can cause burns and start fires at considerable distances. Some of the energy produced within the first minute of the explosion takes the form of intense 'ionising' radiation, made up of penetrating gamma waves and a stream of fast neutrons, and is called 'prompt' or 'initial' radiation. Both the gamma rays and neutron particles of this initial radiation are rapidly absorbed in the atmosphere and the range within which they may damage humans is quite limited: even for the largest bombs no harmful effects of prompt radiation are expected beyond a radius of four miles. It was thus a simple matter for those in charge of the tests to ensure protection against this initial radiation by placing the men at a safe distance.

The vast majority of servicemen were placed well beyond the danger zone during the tests but in the autumn of 1956, selected servicemen from Australia and Britain were placed as close as possible to two nuclear explosions as part of a programme of 'indoctrination'. At the first explosion the programme required the 'exposure of the indoctrinees to the flash, heat and blast effects at a distance of about four and a half miles'. There was no mention of exposure to radiation and at a range of four and a half miles the men were not in danger of any damage from initial radiation. At the second 'indoctrination' test, the men were placed much closer to a very low yield weapon of 1.75 kilotons (a 'trigger' device for a Christmas Island H bomb). According to the Australian Ionising Radiation Advisory Council (AIRAC) 'UK scientists and service personnel were included at locations about 2.5 km and 4 km respectively from ground zero', which would still not have put the men in range of dangerous initial radiation. The group nearest the detonation were placed under cover. It is now known that the AIRAC report is mistaken, and the men were in fact closer: 2000 and 3000 yards respectively. At such close ranges the men would have been at risk of exposure to low doses of prompt or initial radiation. It is stated in the AIRAC report that their recorded doses averaged less than 0.5R, though higher than average doses would probably have been received by the men who took cover in slit trenches, since in all the tests these men were the most likely to be closest to a blast and thus to have been exposed to initial radiation.

As well as the pulse of initial radiation emitted within a minute of the explosion, energy is also released in the form of 'residual' radiation one minute or more afterwards. This can be a deadly hazard, either as fallout or as 'induced radioactivity'. The latter occurs when the stream of neutrons which are part of the initial radiation make naturally occurring minerals in the area around the explosion radioactive. After all the tests in Australia and at Christmas Island, anyone going into areas close to the sites of the nuclear explosions would have been at risk of exposure to this form of residual radioactivity. All such areas were therefore meant to be clearly marked out of bounds and only those in suitable protective clothing under the direction of health physicists permitted access.

Almost all the nuclear devices detonated in Australia were exploded on, or near, the surface of the earth, causing an added hazard of residual radiation in the form of fallout, both locally and at longer ranges. Local fallout could not be avoided in the early days of weapon testing because the technology for preventing it by dropping the bombs from RAF aircraft did not exist. The devices were too large and the bombers too small. The first successful air-drop was in 1956, code-named Kite. Before then the nuclear weapons were either placed in ships or mounted on towers about thirty feet from the ground. These tests were, of necessity, 'groundbursts', i.e. their fireballs touched the surface of the earth.

When the intensely hot and swirling gases of the fireball touch the ground, the heat is so great that a giant crater is formed, and huge quantities of earth and rock are sucked up by the fireball as it rises. The heat causes the millions of tons of debris to vaporize and be drawn up through the radioactive cloud. As the fireball cools and takes the form of a mushroom-shaped cloud, the debris becomes incorporated with, and contaminated by, the radioactive products of the explosion, and it slowly falls back to earth as dust, made up of millions of particles of highly radioactive fallout. Most of the fallout from a groundburst is deposited around the crater of the bomb but if the mushroom cloud drifts downwind, it can be deposited over a broad area, extending several hundred miles. This sort of fallout is called 'local'.

All the tests at Christmas Island and Malden in the Central Pacific were 'airbursts'. Their fireballs were not meant to touch the ground at all and therefore local fallout would be avoided completely. The only danger from radioactivity to those nearby during airbursts was thought to be from induced radioactivity and prompt radiation. However, traces of induced radioactivity at Christmas Island remain to this day in the areas directly beneath the airbursts, and although local fallout was avoided, there was little understanding of the dangers of 'global' fallout resulting from airbursts. This comes from the vaporized bomb casings and the uranium or plutonium that has not been used up in the chain reaction of the atomic explosion and it stays in the high atmosphere for months or years before coming down to earth as global fallout.

The residual radiation caused by local fallout from ground-bursts was a major hazard of the tests in Australia. Made up of alpha particles, beta particles and gamma rays, it presented two separate hazards: the gamma rays could irradiate the whole body, and the alpha and beta particles if ingested, or lodged in the skin and hair, could give a high dose to a specific part of the body. The greatest danger was in the immediate vicinity of the explosion, and although all areas where such 'local' fallout occurred were patrolled and signposted and, as with the induced radioactivity areas, entrance unless supervised was strictly prohibited, almost all the rules and regulations appear to have been breached in some way or other at each of the tests. Men working in conditions of extreme heat are reported to have removed their protective clothing in desperate attempts to cool themselves and see what they were doing. Others, merely inquisitive, claim to have wandered into controlled areas in order to satisfy their curiosity. And Aborigines, unable to understand the warning signs, are said to have been found even in the bomb craters, where there would have been both fallout and considerable induced radioactivity.

Fallout comes down locally within twenty-four hours and contains half the total radioactivity of the bomb. Just where it lands depends on weather conditions: the wind direction, which carries it in a 'plume' from ground zero, and rain, which can bring down fallout rapidly and in strong concentrations called 'hot spots'. Because of the danger of the 'plume' and 'hot spots', a safety zone was extended a hundred miles around the Emu and Maralinga testing ranges and all Aborigines were meant to be cleared from these areas, their ancient tribal lands. The nearest Aboriginal settlements were just on the edge of the hundred mile limit; there were thirteen within two hundred miles. The authorities at first believed that the risks of any delayed fallout contaminating the Aboriginal settlements outside the safety zones were zero. In this they were wrong, and on one occasion at least, after the Totem 1 test in 1953 at Emu, it is feared that freak weather conditions deposited dangerous levels of fallout at a settlement beyond the limit. Despite recommendations that the safety zone be extended to 240 miles because of the vulnerability of the Aborigines living in the open, the hundred mile limit remained.

The radioactive particles which are too light to come down as local fallout are carried to great heights with the fireball as it rises into the troposphere and stratosphere. They come down days or weeks later as 'delayed' or 'long range' fallout, the time and position being dependent on wind and rain conditions. Delayed fallout after the passage of weeks or even months is not such a risk to health as local fallout, but if it is brought down relatively rapidly by rain or other weather conditions, it can pose a significant hazard. The safety of a nuclear test depended, therefore, on accurate weather forecasting and responsible decisions based on the calculated risk of wind changes and rain. It was recognized by the Australian Atomic Weapon Trials Safety Committee after the first two blasts that the meteorological measurements before and after the first two blasts were not satisfactory. Despite improvements, weather conditions seem to have continued to be inaccurately forecast before tests, or else dangerous risks were knowingly taken. Both in Australia and at Christmas Island it has been alleged that weather conditions brought about substantial unexpected contamination.

The monitoring of the pattern of fallout clouds after tests has also been dismissed as inadequate. This involved the Royal Air Force and Royal Australian Air Force in flying through the mushroom clouds to collect samples of airborne fallout or following the clouds to monitor the direction in which they travelled. Scientists on the ground were thus able to estimate the size and nature of the blast, and the direction of travel of the fallout cloud. The modified aeroplanes, often called 'sniffers', used for the cloud sampling operations had ducts fitted to the wings into which baskets with filter bags were placed. After a mission, the baskets in which the samples had collected were removed from the ducts by men wielding long-handled calipers; who placed them in lead-lined boxes. The samples were then taken away for radiochemical analysis.

In the early days of the tests the aircraft were highly polished in the vain hope that radioactive particles would not stick to the bodywork. Later the jets were painted white and, before each mission through the nuclear cloud, covered with a waxy barrier paint to which any fallout particles were supposed to adhere. After a mission, once the samples had been removed, the aircraft was immediately taxied to a washdown pad where the barrier paint was washed off. The radioactive paint and water were then meant to flow into a soak-away. All those who took part in this procedure – and during every test the cloud sampling and fallout monitoring procedures were put into action – were exposed to radiation.

Fallout is radioactive because it contains the 'fission products' of a nuclear reaction. 'Fission' is the process whereby the nucleus of heavy elements, uranium or plutonium, is split into two fragments with a tremendous release of energy. Both fragments are unstable and tend to disintegrate or 'decay', giving off radiation in the form of gamma rays, alpha or beta particles as they do so. These fission products are called 'radioisotopes'. There are about three hundred of them, each decaying over a different period called a 'half-life'. At first the greatest hazard from the fallout during the Australian groundburst tests came from the beta and gamma rays emitted from fission products with short half-lives in the local fallout. This danger decreased rapidly, however, and the lesser but nevertheless significant hazards of the longer-lasting radioactive fission products remained. Many pollute the test sites to this day.

The half-lives of the fission products scattered across the Australian desert and the Monte Bello Islands varied considerably. Some lasted only a fraction of a second; others will remain radioactive for many millions of years. Plutonium 239 was one of the most insidiously toxic and long-lasting of the fission products produced and experimented with in the British nuclear testing programme. It did not extend beyond some 3000 yards from the firing zones, but it lingers to this day at many of Britain's nuclear test sites: at Monte Bello, at Maralinga and, in minute quantities, at Christmas Island.

Although plutonium is an 'alpha emitter' and therefore produces radiation which is not highly penetrating (it can be stopped by a thick pair of trousers), it is one of the most lethal carcinogens known to man. Particles of plutonium weighing only one millionth of a gramme may produce cancer if inhaled or ingested. Such tiny quantities can only be detected by the most powerful and sensitive radiation monitors soon after entry into the body. Over the years, lodged in the body, the particles can produce powerful local doses of radiation without being traced and it is only at autopsy that they are found.

Other hazardous fallout particles in the firing areas included uranium and beryllium – a non-radioactive carcinogen. In some tests the danger of fallout was increased by the 'salting' of weapons: the process whereby certain chemicals were added to nuclear bombs in order to discover the effects of fission on them. In 1957, for example, non-radioactive cobalt was added to the ingredients of an atomic bomb in order to assess its lethal potential. At the time the possibility of a cobalt bomb as the ultimate 'doomsday' weapon was being considered, for although ordinary cobalt is non-radioactive, when it is bombarded with neutrons in an atomic reaction its nucleus is changed and it becomes a highly energetic gamma ray emitter called cobalt 60. It has a half-life of 5.3 years, much longer than most gamma emitters in fallout. In 1957 the cobalt 'induced' by neutrons into a radioactive form was scattered in pellets over the testing range. Most but not all of these were collected and buried in a later clean-up operation.

Because gamma rays are so penetrating, the special clothing

issued to those servicemen and scientists who entered the fallout zone after the explosion gave them little protection. Indeed irradiation from gamma rays represented the greatest hazard after each of the weapons trials. Most of the gamma activity fell off quite rapidly, however, and it was only a danger for those entering fallout zones very quickly after explosions. There are records of high doses received by survey parties who entered the zones within the first twenty-four hours of a detonation. After the Totem trial the first entries were made only twenty minutes after detonation.

As the fallout fission products decayed in Australia it became safer to enter the contaminated areas to collect the instruments and objects left behind for experimental purposes (anything from food for the civil defence experts, to tanks and aeroplanes for the military). A danger remained from the fission products with longer half-lives but as these tended to be less penetrating, it was thought that adequate protection could be provided by protective clothing, respirators and subsequent decontamination. The precautionary measures would combat the radioactivity in the form of tiny particles of alpha- and beta-emitting fission products which could be hazardous if inhaled, ingested or allowed to remain on the skin. The problem was that while the test servicemen could be adequately protected if all the rules were followed, no such precautions could be taken for the Aborigines. They are known to have wandered across the firing ranges barefoot and almost naked shortly after the explosions, and for years after the tests the ranges were not fenced off or guarded. It seems that the dangers were not recognized at all. Long-lasting fission products, re-suspended in dust storms and blown hither and thither by the wind, still pose a problem to the Australians today.

As weapon technology developed, bringing a reduction in the weight of the bombs and improvements in the aeroplanes that carried them, it became possible for the British to detonate the bombs high above the ground. Two of the tests in Australia and all the Christmas Island trials were airbursts, which should have produced no local fallout. Prompt radiation and induced radioactivity remained a danger from airbursts close to ground zero but these were far smaller hazards than those created in groundbursts by the dispersal of fission products across wide areas of Australia. Unless the mushroom clouds interacted with a rain cloud, and fission products were brought down by rainfall, there would be little danger from residual radioactivity to the people who witnessed airbursts and never went near ground zero.

The greater energy of the hydrogen bomb, tested by the British at Christmas Island, is derived from fusion: the coming together of light nuclei to form a heavier nucleus. In an atomic explosion, on the other hand, the energy is derived from fission: the splitting of a heavy nucleus. In order to achieve the intense heat for fusion to occur, a 'trigger' for an H bomb is necessary. This trigger is a small fission device − a low-yield atomic bomb. Fusion does not produce radiation and it is the fission process that produces the bulk of the radioactivity in a conventional H bomb. The fission devices which triggered the first H bombs at Christmas Island were so low in yield that they did not produce great quantities of radioactivity and were referred to by the scientists who controlled the experiments as 'clean' bombs. A number of the fission trigger devices were tested in Australia in 1956 and 1957, as well as at Christmas Island.

When the H bombs were exploded in airbursts above the Central Pacific by the British in 1957 and 1958, the dangers from 'global' delayed fallout were only just understood. The contaminated particles from the explosions − the vaporized bomb casing, the fission products of the trigger device, and any plutonium or uranium which escaped fission − were blown high into the stratosphere, to remain there for months, even years, before being brought down to earth by rainfall. When such delayed fallout eventually comes down to earth, only the longer-lived radioisotopes are still active: mainly iodine 131, strontium 90 and caesium 137. These pose a hazard to humans if they enter the food chain and are ingested. For example, although iodine 131 decays quite quickly, it enters the food chain rapidly, and milk with concentrations of this radioactive iodine was found thousands of miles from test areas within only four weeks of the explosions. Strontium 90 and caesium 137 – with thirty-year half-lives – pose longer-term hazards: if ingested by humans, they lodge in various parts of the body, giving off radiation for three decades. The danger of these radioisotopes was only just realized as the nuclear testing took place in the late 1950s, at which time it was the British Government's avowed policy to seek an end to atmospheric testing on the basis of the health hazard of global fallout. The danger was a main reason for the decision by the USA and USSR to agree to a temporary halt to atmospheric nuclear explosions in 1958.

It is now possible to calculate the number of deaths worldwide which may result from the general release of radiation in global fallout after a large nuclear weapon is detonated in the atmosphere. According to the United States Government agency, the Office of Technology Assessment, the global fallout from a one-megaton airburst would cause between two hundred and two thousand cancer deaths if exploded in the northern hemisphere. This estimate is based on fairly conservative estimates of the risks of radiation. If the OTA's assessment is correct, it would follow that a number of deaths were caused by the global fallout from Britian's seven hydrogen bomb tests, which took place in the northern hemisphere very close to the equator. Few surveys have been carried out to investigate this assumption but some researchers believe that atmospheric testing has produced an increase of certain forms of cancer, especially among young people born at the time of the nuclear explosions.

A survey in East Anglia published in 1984, for example, has shown a dramatic rise in the incidence of testicular cancer among men who were babies when global fallout reached a peak in the late 1950s and early 1960s. According to the reseacher responsible, Dr Karol Sikora of the University of Cambridge, a time-lag between exposure and subsequent cancer of about twenty years would be expected, and he found that testicular cancer was now the commonest form of cancer among young men, and that its incidence had increased threefold among those aged between thirty and thirty-four between 1975 and 1980. Overall, testicular cancer now affects one man in 25,000, and the figures in the East Anglia study match those of other regions in the United Kingdom.

Fears increased as the British tests progressed that nuclear explosions in the atmosphere would lead to cancer and genetic defects, and caused worldwide revulsion and protest. Under pressure both at home and from abroad, the British tests in Australia and on Christmas Island took place as quickly as possible and her main testing programme was ended in late 1958. The same year the three big nuclear powers signed an agreement for a 'moratorium' on nuclear testing and Britain never exploded a device in the open again. Her contribution to global fallout had been small: the United States and the Soviet Union between them had exploded thousands of weapons of all types in the atmosphere. As a result of the moratorium and later partial Test Ban Treaty in 1963, global fallout has been decreasing in strength since its peak in the late 1950s. It now contributes only 0.5 per cent of our total background radiation exposure.

Global fallout from British nuclear tests was confined to the H bombs exploded at high altitudes. The groundbursts in Australia produced long-range fallout, consisting of the finer radioactive particles taken into the troposphere by the fireball. Because they are not carried as high as the stratosphere, they are more likely to mix with clouds than global fallout and be brought down by rain over a smaller part of the earth's surface. There has been considerable controversy about the records of this delayed fallout in Australia. It is now alleged that the monitoring was inadequate and that the existing evidence of contamination was tampered with by the British authorities in order not to raise public fears in Australia.

At first the monitoring methods for contamination were undoubtedly rudimentary. At the early tests it was not even considered necessary to monitor some of the men who flew through the nuclear cloud to follow the fallout pattern: as a result some high doses were not recorded. However, decontaminating techniques and exposure measurement were improved. As men were 'fortuitously' exposed to fallout particles, the success or failure of the various methods used to wash them clean was carefully assessed and by the time of the Christmas Island tests, scrubbing contamination off men had reached a peak of sophistication. In the same way the progress of radioisotopes through the body and their excretion rate through urine were observed with keen interest by the atomic weapon scientists.

The equipment used to monitor the men also increased in sophistication as the tests progressed, although the procedures remained much the same from 1952 to 1958. For dangerous operations, men were accompanied by health physicists carrying geiger counters and personal dosemeters. The most common way of recording personal radiation doses was, however, by a 'film badge' worn on the lapel. This was a light-proof plastic device containing unexposed film: gamma radiation would penetrate the plastic and expose the film according to the strength of dose. The film badges worn by the test participants did not, however, record exposure to radiation from alpha particles, and only a rudimentary measurement of beta particles was possible with them. Nor could they detect any internal radiation caused by the ingestion of radioisotopes. It was the duty of the health physicists to monitor these types of radiation with their more sensitive apparatus.

The reliability of film badges is now a matter of debate. It is possible that in the conditions of a nuclear test, they do not record all the radiation that strikes the body, and they may also be inherently unreliable. In the United States, the Nuclear Regulatory Commission allows for a fifty per cent inaccuracy on individual film badges. When the Commission ordered a study of 23,000 badges in 1980 from the University of Michigan, doses were reported which were ninety per cent above or below the correct dose. The Commission concluded that 'a significant percentage of personal dosimetry processors [film badges] may not be performing with an appropriate degree of accuracy'. The processors in the study did not differ much from the film badges worn by servicemen in the tests in the 1950s. A further indication that film badges were unsuitable for recording the doses of test participants is given by the evidence of excess cancers among the participants in the Smoky test in Nevada. No significant radiation doses were recorded after the troops had marched around fallout areas and it seems likely that the film badges failed to record the true exposures.

The individual dose records of the men exposed to radiation at the tests have not been released by the Ministry of Defence and without them, even if they are not wholly accurate, it is difficult to judge the adequacy of the protection for those known to be at risk. If the British Government's figures are correct, however, the men should have little to fear. The same goes for the majority who were never monitored. They may never have been at risk at all: they were never close enough to a test to suffer from prompt radiation, however terrifying the sight may have been; they never entered a fallout zone; and they never handled contaminated material. Their fears should be laid to rest. But the minority who were exposed to radiation through ignorance or carelessness may well have been placed in danger.

Chapter Four

A BOMB FOR BRITAIN

Britain has been committed to the manufacture of nuclear weapons for longer than any other nation. American political nerve and technical skill may have been behind the atomic bombs that fell on Japan in August 1945 but their inspiration was British. It was partly because British scientists had conceived the idea of the atomic bomb that British politicians became so determined that it should become part of Britain's armoury. More importantly, possession of the bomb was seen as the only way Britain could retain international authority after the war. Even though the wartime collaboration between America and Britain collapsed in the years afterwards, Britain continued her nuclear weapons development. The bomb tests that this entailed were an assertion of Britain's nuclear independence and of her determination to remain among the decision makers in the post-war world.

Winston Churchill's wartime Cabinet had discussed the possibility of a uranium bomb in 1940, after the Danish physicist, Neils Bohr, had published his work on uranium fission. Scientists in Britain began exploring the possibility of developing an explosive whose power would be beyond the imagination of current weapon manufacturers. Churchill was doubtful, however, that the bomb would contribute to this war and warned his Cabinet that the results of these discoveries, however great their scientific interest and perhaps ultimately their practical importance, were incapable of being put into operation on a large scale for several years.

He underestimated the enthusiasm and ingenuity of two refugee scientists from Nazism, the Austrian Otto Frisch and the German Rudolf Peierls, who were working at the University of Birmingham. In 1940, they published a report claiming that uranium 235 could be separated from uranium 238 and initiate the fast chain reaction necessary for an atomic bomb. They deduced that material weighing just five kilos could equal the explosive power of several thousand tons of dynamite. Their conclusion, questioning the moral implications of a weapon whose effects would be fatal to generations long after the explosion, was ignored by the British Cabinet in its haste to act immediately on the new information. It was known that scientists in Germany were working along the same lines and urgent arrangements were made to remove stocks of uranium on the Continent that might fall into Nazi hands. In Britain, the 'Maud' Committee of scientists was set up to build on the foundations laid by Frisch and Peierls.

It was at this early stage that the idea of Britain's nuclear deterrent was born, the idea that committed Britain to her own nuclear weapons supplies and to the bomb test programme. In their first report to the Cabinet, the Maud Committee echoed Churchill's caution but said: 'Even if the war should end before the bombs are ready, the effort would not be wasted, except in the unlikely event of complete disarmament, since no nation would care to risk being caught without a weapon of such decisive possibilities.'

The Americans agreed. When American scientists read the first Maud report on how and why an atomic bomb was necessary, they were impressed not just by how technically advanced their British colleagues were but also by how far ahead Britain was in her perception of the post-war implications of the bomb. They persuaded Roosevelt to set up the Manhattan bomb project and to write to Churchill proposing joint collaboration. Britain's lofty and even hostile reply to the proposal appears ironic in the light of the frantic efforts in later years to get and keep America's technical cooperation on nuclear matters. But Britain was worried about America's ability to keep a secret (this too seems ironic in view of the number of post-war British atomic spies). In the short term, British politicians felt uneasy about America's still neutral position in the war. Above all, in the long term, Britain was reluctant to surrender her nuclear secrets, which many politicians and scientists believed would give Britain the power to police the post-war world.

Six months later, the British and American roles had reversed. The Japanese attack on Pearl Harbor committed America to the war and to the bomb. The American Government poured money, materials and manpower into the atomic project and the Manhattan team forged ahead. War-torn Britain could not compete. Sir John Anderson, the minister in charge of atomic energy, called on Churchill to persuade him to seek collaboration with the Americans: 'I make this recommendation with some reluctance, as I should like to see the work carried forward in this country. We must, however, face the fact that the pioneer work done in this country is a dwindling asset and that, unless we capitalise it quickly, we shall be outstripped. We now have a real contribution to a merger. Soon we shall have little or none.'

It was almost too late. It took all Churchill's diplomatic skill to persuade Roosevelt to sign the Quebec agreement of 1943, giving British scientists the chance of joining the Americans at the 'bomb headquarters' at Los Alamos in the desperate bid to build the bomb before the end of the war.

So how much did Britain, now the junior partner, get out of the wartime arrangement? General Groves, the tough and forthright army officer in charge of the bomb project, was determined to protect America's current and post-war military and commercial interest. British scientists were 'compartmentalized', confined to reseach essential only to their specific part in the bomb work and prevented from getting an overall view. He insisted that all exchange of information should be restricted to 'use-in-current-war' only and that America should get more from the British scientists than she gave away. After the war, Groves concluded that the British had been 'helpful but not vital' and yet he could not 'escape the feeling that without active and continuing British interest there would probably have been no atomic bomb to drop on Hiroshima'.

As for the British, the official historian of Britain's atomic past, Margaret Gowing, believes that the 'United Kingdom emerged from the war possessing the theory and the technological knowledge of the atom bomb, as well as the fundamental concepts of the hydrogen bomb'. Lord Chadwick, chairman of the post-war atomic committee reporting to the Ministry of Supply, observed that British scientists could not be expected 'to take amnesia tablets before returning home'. British scientists were able to pool their knowledge and put together a working manual that would attempt to duplicate the American atomic bomb without repeating all the work that had been done at Los Alamos. Nonetheless, there were substantial gaps in the Britons' knowledge, in areas such as the fabrication of electric detonators, plutonium metallurgy, exterior ballistics, arming and fusing. It was to take Britain seven years to fill those gaps and assemble the raw materials necessary to produce her own bomb.

The British Labour party had not been invited to play a part in the wartime decisions over the atomic bomb and, on taking over in 1946, the Labour Prime Minister Clement Attlee was duly impressed by the progress made by Churchill's Government on the bomb project and by the new political responsibility that it involved. In a letter to the newly elected President Truman, Attlee sought a political and and moral understanding with the Americans in addition to the technical cooperation the scientists were so anxious for. 'Thoughtful people aready realize that there must be a revaluation of policies and a re-adjustment of international relations. There is widespread anxiety as to whether the new power will be used to serve or to destroy civilization. . . . Am I to plan for a peaceful or a warlike world? If the latter, I ought to direct all our people to live like troglodytes underground as being the only hope of survival, and that by no means certain.' Attlee set in motion the immediate post-war production of fissile material in Britain for a nuclear weapon building programme. By the end of 1945, a plan for building large-scale reactors to produce plutonium for the atomic bomb was agreed.

Attlee was soon to discover that his relationship with Truman was destined to be less cosy and 'special' than that between Churchill and Roosevelt. Despite Attlee's overtures to the new American President, the mood in America was isolationist. A wartime agreement, the Hyde Park memorandum, signed by Churchill and Roosevelt in 1944 and promising full atomic collaboration after the defeat of Japan, was conveniently 'lost' and forgotten. Although Truman himself was sympathetic to Attlee, his closest advisers and the majority of Congressmen had little time for the pleas of a poor relation. They were suspicious of a socialist government and, so long as Britain continued to help America in obtaining uranium supplies, they saw no political advantage in the continued sharing of atomic secrets.

Less than a year after the war, the McMahon Bill passed through Congress, and was the death blow to British hopes of US collaboration. It ignored the wartime Quebec and Hyde Park agreements and made it illegal for Americans to pass any information to another country, Britain included, under penalties of life imprisonment and even death. Attlee was outraged and hurt, and in a telegram to Truman he made one last frantic plea 'that our continuing co-operation over raw materials shall be balanced by an exchange of information which will give us, with all proper precautions with regard to security, that full information to which we believe we are entitled, both by the documents and by the history of our common efforts in the past'. Truman did not even acknowledge the telegram.

Britain was thus on her own in the bomb-making business. It was a position turned to immediate advantage by the chief protagonists. 'We could not afford to acquiesce in an American monopoly of this new development', said Foreign Secretary, Ernest Bevin, years later. Similarly Attlee, in an interview well after he retired from politics, confided: 'It had become essential [to build the bomb]. We had to hold up our own position vis à vis the Americans. We couldn't allow ourselves to be wholly in their hands and the position wasn't awfully clear always. There was the possibility of their withdrawing and becoming isolationist once again. The manufacture of a British bomb was therefore at this stage essential to our defence.'

The decision to go ahead with bomb production was taken by a small ad hoc British Cabinet committee known as Gen. 163 in January 1947. The project bore the deceptive title, 'High Explosive Research' (HER) and was put under the control of the scientist William Penney, a brilliant mathematician and physicist whom the Americans had wanted to stay with their bomb team after the Los Alamos test and the end of the war. Through HER, he was to supervise the entire British bomb test programme and after the first detonation at Monte Bello, affectionately dubbed 'Penney's Fizzer', he was knighted by Churchill. In 1985, now Lord Penney, he was the key witness in the Australian Royal Commission hearings in London.

Britain did not determine to build her bomb alone without another attempt at persuading the Americans to share their nuclear know-how. When, in 1948, negotiations reopened with the United States, Britain was forced to surrender the clause in the wartime Quebec agreement that said that neither country would use atomic weapons without the other's consent. This clause was revoked at a time when American B29 bombers, with a nuclear capacity, were based in Britain, leaving Britain apparently vulnerable to a terrible retaliation from the Soviet Union without the guarantee of consultation. In these 1948 negotiations, called the 'modus operandi', Britain made available to America two-thirds of the considerable uranium stocks controlled by the United Kingdom, but there was no guarantee of nuclear information in exchange.

The Government insisted that all matters concerning the bomb programme should be shrouded in secrecy and ironically, it was in order to safeguard the secret that the matter was first made public. The Government wanted to place a D notice on the press – a 'voluntary' undertaking not to publish information of military importance – to prevent speculation about the nature, locations and personnel of HER, but they could not get the agreement of the Services' Press Committee, which issues the notices, because they allegedly knew nothing about it. Accordingly, in May 1948, the Ministry of Defence 'planted' the information in a discreet parliamentary question. When George Jaeger MP asked the Minister of Defence whether he was 'satisfied that adequate progress was being made in the development of the most modern types of weapons', the reply was: 'Yes, sir. As we made clear in the statement relating to Defence 1948 ... research and development continue to receive the highest priority in the defence field, and all types of weapons, including atomic weapons, are being developed.' Thus the momentous decision that Britain was about to become the world's second nuclear power (as was then thought) was made public and a D notice was promptly applied.

Having legitimized the project, the next step was to justify and quantify it. Who was to be the enemy? How many devices would it take to deter him? The decision to build one plutonium-producing reactor with a view to nuclear bomb manufacture had been taken in 1945, but because of the sensitivities of those on the left in the Labour Government, it had been thought wiser not to identify the most likely enemy. However, by 1948, after the Berlin blockade and with the onset of the Cold War, the Chiefs of Staff could afford to be forthright about naming the enemy. The Soviet Union was known to be developing her own weapons and the only means of defence against this new threat would be, it was agreed, nuclear retaliation. 'We believe', wrote the Chiefs of Staff in their submission to the Government in 1948, 'the knowledge that we possessed weapons of mass destruction and were prepared to use them would be the most effective deterrent to war itself.'

It was also assumed that the American supply of nuclear weapons would be used as part of the common defence against an attack on Europe. Since the Berlin episode, the United States had based sixty B29 bombers in East Anglia, giving the impression that there did indeed exist between Britain and America a special relationship in strategic nuclear weapons. For all-out war, the British Chiefs of Staff estimated a minimum requirement of six hundred bombs by 1957, of which two thirds would be American, leaving Britain with the task of producing two hundred. In order to meet this target, ministers authorized a third reactor at Windscale, in addition to the two further air-cooled reactors that had been authorized in May 1947.

All of these paper calculations went up in smoke with the news of the first Russian atomic explosion in August 1949. The event took politicians and scientists on both sides of the Atlantic by surprise. In 1945, General Groves had estimated that it would take Russia fifteen to twenty years to build the bomb and British defence experts had been sure they were ahead, as the cool calculations made by the Chiefs of Staff in 1948 demonstrated. The Government, the military top brass and the scientific fraternity alike shared a deep sense of outrage and shame that, despite the lessons learned at Los Alamos, the British had been beaten in the atomic race by a nation that had virtually to start from scratch.

The Russian success led to a period of agonizing doubt and revaluation by those involved in the bomb project. Sir Henry Tizard, chief scientific adviser at the Ministry of Defence, questioned whether there was any point in continuing with the notion of an independent deterrent and queried the basic psychology behind Britain's nuclear aims. 'We persist in regarding ourselves as a great power, capable of everything and only temporarily handicapped by economic difficulties. We are not a great power and never will be again. We are a great nation, but if we continue to behave like a great power we shall cease to be a great nation. Let us take a warning from the fate of the great powers in the past and not burst ourselves with pride.' Tizard argued that the nuclear programme should be scrapped in favour of building up conventional forces and strategic air defence. He was appalled by the money being spent on atomic weapon development, estimated to exceed £154 million by 1955, and which involved the employment of some fifteen hundred scientists and engineers.

Lord Portal, on the other hand, argued that with the money already invested in nuclear reactors, cancellation would waste more money than it would save. He was, predictably, backed by the Chiefs of Staff and Lord Cockcroft, the head of the Atomic Research Establishment at Harwell and Churchill's scientific and general adviser. 'If we are unable to make the bomb ourselves', Cockcroft wrote, 'and have to rely entirely on the United States for this vital weapon, we shall sink to the rank of a second-class nation, only permitted to supply auxiliary troops, like the native levies who were allowed small arms but not artillery.'

Certainly the desire to retain great power status was uppermost in the minds of the decision makers of the early 1950s. But the decision to go ahead with a British independent deterrent was not simply the posturing of nostalgic neo-imperialists. Penney, who was by now working full-time on developing Britain's first atomic device, was perhaps the most reluctant weapon manufacturer of all and was frequently heard questioning whether Britain should spend so much on atomic bombs in such a depressed economic situation. And yet, as he told the authors, 'it is essential to place the bomb tests in the political context of the time. The development of the Russian nuclear weapon, the events in Korea and the memory of the Berlin airlift made the development of the British atomic bomb appear imperative at the time.' The threat of nuclear attack from Russia loomed large and this prompted a sense of urgency throughout the bomb test series. Scientists and senior officers saw it as their duty to hasten the bomb-making programme for the defence of the nation and, as a result, short cuts were taken during the weapons testing.

Also, by 1949, attitudes in America had if anything hardened. In February, Truman declared, 'We have got to protect our information and we must certainly try and see that the British do not have the information to build atomic weapons in England because they might be captured.' One British diplomat in Washington at the time, Roger Makins, now Lord Sherfield, concluded that there was in America an 'ill-defined and almost unconscious feeling that atomic energy is and should remain an American monopoly, both for military and industrial purposes'. It soon became clear to the British that America was in a completely different league in atomic weapon development and production. America regarded the atomic bomb as her 'sacred trust' and believed that Britain should have no share in it. The arrest in 1950 of Klaus Fuchs, the British-naturalized spy who had worked at Los Alamos, gave the Americans the excuse they wanted and talks broke down irrevocably.

Churchill was astonished and impressed when he returned to power at the end of 1951 by how far the Attlee Government had progressed and by how much had been spent on the atomic programme with so little publicity. He even took pains to appear offended that he had not been taken into the previous Government's confidence: 'The Conservative Opposition would certainly have supported the Government, as we did on so many other of their measures of defence, and their majority would no doubt have been overwhelming. Nevertheless, they preferred to conceal this vast operation and its finances from the scrutiny of the House, not even obtaining a vote on the principle involved.' Nonetheless, Churchill did not hesitate to follow exactly the same policy. Figures spent on the atomic programme continued to be carefully hidden in the estimates of the Ministry of Supply. When, in October 1952, Emrys Hughes asked the Prime Minister, 'In view of the fact that well over £100 million has been disbursed on atomic research without Parliament being made aware of it, what steps is he taking to ensure that there will be a greater measure of public control and parliamentary discussion on such expenditure?' Churchill replied, 'For the present, I am content to be guided by the precedent created by the previous Government on this matter.'

In the summer of 1952, the Chiefs of Staff met again to discuss Britain's defence strategy. On Britain's nuclear role, the Chiefs admitted that the only existing deterrent was American, and that America could not be trusted to take on an enemy that did not threaten her directly. Furthermore, Britain had to possess a nuclear weapon if she wanted to be consulted in another war: 'We feel that to have no share in what is recognized as the main deterrent in the Cold War would mean that in war the United Kingdom would have no claim to share in the policy or planning of the offensive.' For the first time the Chiefs of Staff recognized the importance of delivery technology and called for an urgent programme to build up the bomber force. And, while acknowledging Britain's economic problems, they called for the doubling of Britain's plutonium output to increase the stocks of fissile material available for bomb production.

It was a statement of faith in Britain's pursuit of an independent deterrent. Churchill had been no more successful than his predecessor in his attempts to rekindle the special relationship with America, and Lord Cherwell, now Paymaster General, persuaded him to abandon any hope of depending on the Americans and to pursue an independent policy. It was becoming clear to everyone, Churchill included, that without the bomb, Britain lacked clout. The priority must be to explode an atomic device as soon as possible. Penney and his team were now almost ready with the hardware. The fissile material would be available by the end of the summer. It was up to the Government now to find a test site.

The choice lay between using one of the American test sites or building a new site in one of the Commonwealth countries. It might appear strange that Britain was still prepared to go cap in hand to America on the question of a site after America's intransigence on technical help, but to the British Government there seemed little sense in the two 'allies' exploding test bombs simultaneously but separately in the Pacific and Indian oceans. This absurdity was lost on the Americans, who remained as obdurate as ever. Penney made several frantic visits to the United States where he received a friendly reception from his erstwhile colleagues on the Manhattan project, but the Administration remained hostile. The British Joint Services Mission in Washington concluded in their advisory memorandum to the British Cabinet, 'Supposing the British did choose the American alternative ... when the British team arrived over here they would be subjected to so many petty restrictions and there would be so much red tape that in effect the Americans would explode our weapon for us and let us have only those results which they felt they could safely divulge.'

Penney began exploring possible sites in Canada and Australia. The test team required an isolated area, with no human habitation within one hundred miles downwind of a detonation and where prevailing winds would blow contamination over the sea but not into shipping lanes. Furthermore, the area needed to be big enough to accommodate about a dozen tests, each of which would have to be distanced from another test by at least three miles because each would cause severe contamination in the immediate area. For the first test, Penney was particularly anxious to find out the effects of a weapon in shallow water and the otherwise best suited Canadian site, near Churchill, Manitoba, on the west coast of Hudson Bay, was ruled out because the sea was too shallow for ships to get near the shore.

As far back as 1950, the Australian Prime Minister, Robert Menzies, had readily agreed to a British Admiralty survey of the Monte Bello Islands, a group of uninhabited islands off Australia's north-western coast, as a possible bomb test site. Unlike the Americans, the Australians could not have been more obliging. Britain's High Commissioner in Melbourne reported back to London: 'On reading Mr Attlee's message, Mr Menzies at once said that any special facilities which Australia might possess for this or similar purposes would of course be made available.' As in the United Kingdom, bomb business was settled at prime ministerial level, without need for further consultation.

By the end of 1951, a decision had to be made on the test site if the October 1952 deadline for Britain's first atomic detonation was to be met. Australia was looking distinctly the better option. The survey of the Monte Bello islands had been successful and fears that the cost of transporting men and equipment half way around the world would be prohibitive had been scotched by a Government estimate claiming that the tests could be carried out on the Monte Bello Islands for well under £1 million, 'reinforcing the point that there might be little advantage in the American offer from a purely financial point of view'. On a more practical note, Lord Cherwell urged Churchill to choose Australia because there was always the chance that something might go wrong with the test and 'it would be disastrous if this happens in full view of the United States newspapers!'. Above all, there was the political consideration. Even if the Australian option were the more expensive, the Defence Minister in the previous Administration, Emmanuel Shinwell, argued that it would demonstrate that Britain was 'not merely a satellite of the US'. Churchill's ministers were inclined to agree.

The Australian Government's enthusiasm for the tests to be held on the doorstep is partly explained by Australia's keenness at the time to start a nuclear energy programme of her own.

However, given that Australian scientists and politicians were anxious for any experience that might add to their nuclear know-how, it is surprising that the Australian Government missed the opportunity to strike a tough bargain with the British over technical collaboration in exchange for the testing site, although perhaps they realized that any such request would meet with a frosty response. Despite America's unfriendliness, Britain still felt bound by the wartime tripartite agreement between America, Britain and Canada which forbade the exchange of nuclear information beyond those three powers.

A key reason for Australia's enthusiasm for the tests, or at least the enthusiasm of her Prime Minister, was the pro-British sentiment of Robert Menzies. Thirty years later, Senator Walsh, Minister for Resources and Energy in the Labor Administration, called for an inquiry into how the tests came to be carried out in Australia and he told Parliament that the real villain was Sir Robert, 'the lickspittle empire royalist who regarded Australia as a colonial vassal of the British Crown'. Whatever the view of Menzies' political opponents today, it is true that he never took full advantage of Britain's predicament to press Australia's needs. That Britain was fairly desperate by 1952 is suggested in a memo written by Penney in March that year in which he said: 'If the Australians are not willing to let us do further trials in Australia [after the first one], I do not know where we should go.'

The new Conservative British Government finally decided in early 1952 that Britain's first atomic bomb test, code-named 'Hurricane', would take place on the Monte Bello Islands. The decision was taken by the select Cabinet committee who were privy to atomic secrets and who had concluded that Monte Bello was the only option given the time available. However, all that the public announcement from Downing Street on 18 February said was that a British atomic weapon would be tested at 'a site in Australia'. Not even Parliament was invited to inquire further. In July 1952, three months before the detonation, Sir

Waldron Smithers asked the Prime Minister 'if he can state the approximate date on which the first British atomic bomb will be exploded'. The Prime Minister's Office drafted the following answer: 'It would not be in the national interest to state the approximate date of the test of the United Kingdom atomic weapon', and added, 'Previous public statements have referred to the "United Kingdom atomic weapon" not to the "atomic bomb". This has led, as intended, to useful uncertainty about the exact nature of our test and it is considered that all public statements should keep to this wording.' To add to the confusion, it was put about that the test would take place at the Woomera rocket testing range.

The British Government immediately fell victim to the rule that 'useful uncertainty' can often cause more problems than it solves. The press assumed that the tests were to take place within fallout distance of a Central Aboriginal Reserve bordering on the Woomera range and this misunderstanding led to questioning of Government Ministers by the Labour Opposition about the safety of Aborigines, culminating in a question from Emrys Hughes: 'Is the Prime Minister aware that the Australian Aborigines who are converted to Christianity are now thinking of sending missionaries to this country because they think that the atom bomb can only have been invented by savages and barbarians?'

Robert Menzies' simultaneous announcement in Canberra on 18 February 1952 was equally vague about the time and the location: 'In the course of this year, the United Kingdom Government intends to test an atomic weapon. . . . The test will take place at a site in Australia. It will be conducted in conditions which will ensure that there will be no danger whatever from radioactivity to the health of the people or animals in the Commonwealth.' Menzies did not mention that he had been told by the British that the Monte Bello Islands would be badly contaminated for at least three years and out of bounds to the local pearl fishing industry. Nor did he mention that this first test was likely to mark the beginning of an ongoing atomic bomb programme by the British in Australia.

While the British and Australian Governments were occupied in deflecting questions about the tests in their respective Parliaments, the test organizers set to work on the many preparations necessary in the short time available. The barren and dispersed nature of the islands meant that everything from fresh water to recreational facilities would have to be transported. And there was the selection to be done in Britain of some two thousand servicemen and scientists for the expedition. Air Vice Marshal Davis, a member of the planning committee, believed there would be little problem in encouraging men to go; 'Any right-minded man would regard these trials as a grand experience combined with the fun of a picnic', and the sea voyage out and back would be a 'prolonged rest-cure'. Few of the men who went on that picnic would concur with the Air Vice Marshal's enthusiasm today.

Chapter Five

'ALL THE FUN OF A PICNIC'

Between February and June 1952, five Royal Navy ships of the 'special squadron' left Portsmouth on the thirteen-thousand-mile voyage to the Monte Bello Islands, off the north-west coast of Australia. To the outsider, there was nothing to suggest that the squadron was any different to any other about to embark on a summer exercise. There were few external signs of the elaborate conversions that had taken place inside to accommodate laboratories, decontamination units, weapons rooms and heavy engineering equipment – except on HMS *Plym*, the bomb carrier and so called 'target vessel'. A naval intelligence officer had come up with the witty idea of using the the initials 'TV' to disguise the ship as 'television vessel', and the frigate was hung with lookalike television antennae. Thus adorned, the *Plym*, carrying Britain's first atomic bomb, took the slow route to Australia, around the Cape. It was considered too risky to go through the Suez Canal.

A second look at the ships would have revealed another oddity about the 'special squadron'. They carried at least one hundred civilian scientists on board – not a happy arrangement as it turned out. Friction between the Navy professionals and the scientific contingent, known as 'the boffins', was apparent from the very start. As the flagship, HMS *Campania* sailed from Portsmouth with all naval hands on deck fallen in, the scientists, as one officer on board noted, were leaning over the side 'waving to mum'. They had all been made honorary members of the wardroom and yet, to the horror of the officers, they fraternized

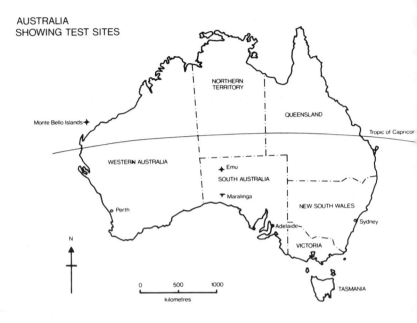

AUSTRALIA
SHOWING TEST SITES

NORTHERN
TERRITORY

QUEENSLAND

Monte Bello Islands

Tropic of Capricor

WESTERN AUSTRALIA

Emu

SOUTH AUSTRALIA

Maralinga

Perth

NEW SOUTH WALES

Adelaide

Sydney

N

VICTORIA

0   500   1000

kilometres

TASMANIA

with stewards and even seamen. Pettiness about protocol dogged the entire two-month voyage, culminating in the incident when the first lieutenant announced that ties should be worn at the Sunday evening film show. Most of the 'boffins' responded by wearing ties but no shirts.

Many of the ratings remember the voyage not as the 'rest cure' promised by the Air Vice Marshal but as a frenzy of unpacking equipment, checking, testing and then re-packing. Few of them knew the nature of the expedition before embarking. On board the *Campania*, Sidney Fletcher, now living in Liverpool, remembers a briefing about the bomb from the scientists. 'They told us quite frankly that they did not have a clue exactly what would happen and they could not say what would happen to future generations. As a result of this, one person tried to get off.' On board HMS *Tracker*, however, the ratings were given a series of lectures by an RAF officer. Raymond Jones, now living in South Australia, remembers being told that 'we would all be sterile for the next ten years as a result of the tests. No one complained because we were young and reckless then, and most lads thought that would be great because there were no family planning precautions in those days and they would all be in for a good time. It's funny, but when I think about it, there is ten years' difference between my oldest daughter and when my next child was born.'

On 8 August, the flagship *Campania* and 'TV' *Plym* sailed into the appointed lagoon exactly on schedule and docked off the western shore of the Monte Bello island of Trimouille. For the *Plym*, it was to be her last berth: she was to be vaporized in the explosion. But that was still two months away and there was a huge amount of work yet to be done. It soon became clear that the expedition had set off with too little planning and with too hurried a packing operation. The Royal Engineers, with the help of the RAAF, had done an extensive job in the two months before the main expedition arrived in constructing roads, jetties and essential buildings. Nonetheless, there were not enough boats for transport between the expedition ships and the shore. There were too few land vehicles and even a shortage of typewriters; moreover the VHF radio telephone links failed to work properly. It was something of a miracle that 'D' day was reached with everything in place.

The test, code-named Hurricane, was designed to fill the many gaps in Britain's knowledge of nuclear warfare. The testing of the prototype bomb, plutonium-based and similar to the 'fat man' of Nagasaki, was of course important, but Penney was just as anxious to study the effects of the weapon – its radioactivity, blast, shock waves – knowledge of which would be valuable for Britain's offensive strategy and civil defence.

Britain's needs were not the only consideration. The very nature of the detonation had been chosen to provide useful information to the Americans. In all America's twenty-six tests to date, the effects of placing a bomb in shallow water, as if in a *shallow water*

port, had not been examined. This is what Hurricane set out to do. In a memo from Lord Portal to the Chiefs of Staff in 1950, it was pointed out that 'this is the type of attack which presumably must be taken into account as a possible form of "bolt from the blue" but its effects have not yet been studied by the Americans'. The Monte Bello Islands were an ideal testing ground for an attack on, say the Port of London or on Pearl Harbor, and if successful the test would win Britain America's esteem.

Every British Government institution involved in military or civil defence had its 'sideshow' at the test. On Alpha Island, Ministry of Supply photographers built a site with remote-controlled cameras ready to record the test. On Trimouille, the Army's Mechanical Effects Division planted different types of gauges to measure the effect of blast; two hundred petrol cans and a row of toothpaste tubes featured among their props. The Thermal Effects Division placed thermometers, special paint samples and 144 different types of clothing to demonstrate the effects of heat, while air sampling equipment made from modified vacuum cleaner units and ionization chambers were set up by the Radiation Hazard Division. The Medical Research Council team would be testing the effects on agricultural products and servicemen would be delegated to catch fish and rats after the explosion to measure how much iodine and strontium they had absorbed.

Each experiment involved teams of scientists and servicemen whose jobs were to collect the materials after the explosion, examine them and pack or dispose of them, all of which involved risk to a varying degree. Dr Penney took advice from the Medical Research Council to establish 'safe' levels of radiation for the thousand or more men concerned, and the three maximum permissible levels of radiation suggested for Hurricane were: first, a 'low' dose of 0.1R a day for continuous work at limited exposure levels; second, 3R a day, restricted to a few exposures essential to the test programme; and third, 10R a day, in cases of extreme urgency, such as recovering vital records, after which there would be no exposure to radiation for at least twelve months. All these levels were considered 'safe' at the time, although subsequent scientific studies have suggested that there is no such thing as a safe dose of radiation (see Chapter 2).

Time and again during the Australian Government's Royal Commission hearings into the conduct of the tests held in London in 1985, Dr Penney, now Lord Penney, would answer with 'At that time, we did not know what we know today', or, 'May I remind you that at the time, health physics was not what it is today' and 'I took the best advice available at the time', and so on. But Penney himself *did* believe there was a slight risk, even in 1952. In his role as Chief Superintendant, Armament Research at the Ministry of Supply, he wrote to the Chiefs of Staff Committee in January 1951, pointing out a security problem that had arisen during the preparations for Hurricane: 'the provision of adequate insurance cover for the participating personnel, especially against radioactive hazards, without undue disclosure to insurance companies.'

Questioned about this during the Royal Commission hearings, Lord Penney explained that there were many risks to consider, such as aeroplanes crashing. 'These RAF planes were carrying people a long way and if they crashed there would be a calamity . . . and in naval ships there are steep ladders and the ship would be rocking and someone could fall off.' But, it was pointed out, these are the risks run by any serviceman. Pressed again on the specific reference to radiation in the document, Penney explained that 'some of our scientists were going right in. Some of them would say, "All right, I am sure I will be all right, but I would like some insurance." It was the scientists, the men who knew most about the risks, who were asking for the insurance cover.

The detonation itself went faultlessly, to the surprise of many of the scientists and officers, who had at times felt profoundly pessimistic during the two months of hectic preparation. Work on the final assembly of the bomb on board HMS *Plym*, anchored to the west of Trimouille, had been finished just before dawn on 'D' day, 3 October 1952. Ships of the Australian Royal Navy and RAAF Lincolns had searched the surrounding seas and skies to check that no civilian ships or commercial aircraft had strayed into the prohibited area. A final check on the task force was made to ensure there were no absentees. A team of scientists from Aldermaston, a support military group and the official photographers were under cover on Hermite Island, some seven miles from HMS *Plym*. It would be up to Ian Maddocks, one of the Aldermaston team and nicknamed the Count of Monte Bello, to start the countdown and detonate the bomb from the control room set up on the island. The ships of the task force withdrew to safe distances upwind of the expected direction of the fallout cloud, the nearest to the detonation being the health ship, HMS *Tracker*, positioned eleven miles from HMS *Plym*.

Ten seconds after the detonation at 9.15 am the photographers ran out from their cover to get to their cameras. It was an awesome and not very beautiful sight: the bomb had sucked up millions of tons of mud in a water column. The silence was unnerving. Twenty seconds later, the men heard the crash of the blast and felt a slight tremor. Eye witnesses were confused by the shape of the cloud. It was huge and billowing and was moving sideways. It was not the traditional mushroom cloud that they had seen on American films of atomic explosions. The uninformed believed that this was a new kind of atomic bomb developed by Penney and his team.

From fifty miles away on the mainland – the closest the press could get to the blast – a *Daily Telegraph* reporter made random notes as he watched: 'A brief lightning flash, a red glow like the top segment of the setting sun, a huge expanding cloud racing skywards. A heavy pressure smacked our eardrums. Simultaneously, there was a report like a clap of thunder, followed by a rumble best likened to a train roaring through a tunnel. One minute after the flash the cloud, white with purple shadows rising swiftly to about six thousand feet. After two minutes it is about ten thousand feet high. After three minutes, it is about a mile wide at the centre.'

Ratings on board the ships of the special squadron were mustered on deck and given the 'privilege' of watching the bomb from close range, their backs turned to the blast at the actual point of detonation. Harry Carter, who had sailed out on the *Plym*, believes he and his colleagues were positioned on land about five miles away as their ship was vaporized in the atomic explosion. 'At the end of the countdown, there was a blinding electric-blue light, of such intensity I had not seen before or since. I pressed my hands hard to my eyes, then realized my hands *were* covering my eyes and this terrific light power, or ray, was actually passing though the tarpaulin, through the towel and through my head and body, for what seemed ten or twelve seconds, it may have been longer. After that, the pressure wave, which gave a feeling such as when one is deep under water. This was then followed by a sort of vacuum suction wave, feeling as if one's whole body was billowing out like a balloon. I am sure we felt slightly incontinent for a second or two. However, all clear came from over the radio. At this point we removed our hands from our eyes, and the towels from our heads. The cloud was rising at speed, and spectacular of course, from where we were. We didn't look horizontally, but tilted our heads right back to view "Penny's Fizzer".' The next day Carter remembers feeling 'a bit rough'. Today, at sixty-two, he suffers from cataracts in both eyes, an affliction unusual in a man Carter's age and which has been associated with high doses of radiation.

The next operation facing the task force was the controlled re-entry into the contaminated area to take samples and to recover instruments and exposed materials, for which the scientists and military men involved wore protective clothing. Their 'booty' was then airlifted from the islands on to the waiting ships by helicopters or transported back to the laboratories by small boats. Acting Petty Officer Mabbutt, on board HMS *Zeebrugge*, remembers the canisters containing radioactive samples arriving and being winched down on to the upper deck. 'They were collected manually by the scientists and taken down to the laboratory. There were a large number of arrivals on the same day of the explosion. The Royal Marines who were stationed on HMS *Zeebrugge* were manning the landing and assault crafts which went ashore to pick up water and possibly solids from the "dirty areas". When they talked about their work, they told me that they would sometimes have their radiation instruments going off the scale because they were too close to highly contaminated areas and they had to retreat as fast as possible.'

All men going into radioactive areas were equipped with film badges or personal dosemeters and after returning from radioactive areas were monitored and then taken on board the health ship, HMS *Tracker*, for decontamination and re-monitoring. According to the official records, one per cent of these men remained contaminated after going through the *Tracker*'s decontamination procedures, which included numerous showers, scrubbing with nail brushes dipped in a solution of precipated chalk and mopping themselves with cotton wool soaked in potassium permanganate. Some of the worst examples of contamination were among a special party which went ashore on Trimouille to recover contaminated specimens from an experimental site. These men in their protective clothing each registered between 3 and 6R of gamma radiation – a relatively high dose but within the limits set by Penney for 'special operations'.

Blame for the contamination lay, we are told, with the loose-fitting protective overalls and the areas of the body left completely exposed by the clothing, such as the back and sides of the head. Another problem arose with rubber gloves and boots. Not enough of these had been provided because it was assumed that they could be easily decontaminated and reissued. Decontamination in fact proved particularly difficult, as the official records explain: 'It appears that, in the constant flexing of rubber surfaces, contamination becomes firmly fixed and virtually impossible to remove.' But the inadequate protection offered Britain's first test servicemen provided, the official reports say, valuable data for future tests and useful information on the contamination hazards of nuclear warfare. The most contaminated men, we are assured by test reports from Aldermaston, suffered no long-term effects.

The Medical Research Council were able to carry out biological experiments to test whether fission products could enter men's bodies by breathing. 'At various times, men entered the radioactive areas without respirators and it was possible to find traces of radioactivity in their urine within a few days. In an experiment designed to utilize a situation which arose fortuitously, it was possible to secure convincing evidence that such radioactivity in urine had been due to inhalation of fission products, rather than by other possible routes of entry. These results indicated that respirators were effective barriers against the inhalation of fission products from this atomic weapon. Although only traces of radioactivity were found in men exposed to the fall-out several days after the explosion, it would seem advisable to wear a respirator while the fallout settled.'

The records do not tell us how it came about that men entered the contaminated areas without respirators apparently 'fortuitously'. The reader is left to assume that there must have been some unforeseen event that sent men into the ground zero area without time to equip themselves properly and that every chance exposure was used to test the effect of radiation on men. In this way servicemen were indeed used as guinea pigs. As for the 'biological experiment', it is now well known that man can breathe in fission products. A millionth of a gramme of plutonium can cause lung cancer.

Hurricane, it must be remembered, was an operation conducted in great secrecy and urgency, involving thousands of conscripts whose education and preparation left them ignorant of the hazards involved. It is not surprising that their accounts of the expedition give an impression of lightheartedness and recklessness about possible contamination. Michael Stephens, a meteorological rating on board HMS *Campania* who was assigned to ferry scientists to and from the islands, remembers the strict procedures governing decontamination and how he was required to shower three times after one sortie. 'But the system was not foolproof. For years I retained a pair of sea boots which should have been destroyed, as a souvenir of the operation. Of course I would not have done this if I had known there was any radiation risk, but radioactivity was regarded as a joke by the crew and servicemen there. There was no education about any potential danger. In 1954 I developed a very bad skin complaint which lasted on and off for five years.'

Another veteran from the *Campania* who ferried scientists into contaminated areas remembers that they were issued with personal dosemeters when they went ashore and told that they should leave if the meters registered a certain high reading. But 'in common with the rest of my mates I never bothered to look because I did not understand how it worked and nobody else bothered with them'.

Derek Parker, an Able Seaman on board HMS *Narvik*, was issued with a film badge before sailing back into the 'parting pool' where the *Plym* had been anchored, a week after the detonation. His most vivid memory is of the huge quantity of dead fish washed up on the beaches, including shark and stingray and many smaller species. He remembers there were no markings on the plastic tag that contained his film badge and at the end of the expedition they were all thrown into a bucket and nothing more was seen or heard of them. Thirteen years ago, twenty years after the nuclear test, Parker began having blood circulation problems. He has been admitted to hospital five times and has had two major operations. 'On two separate occasions in hospital I have mentioned the fact that I had been involved in atomic tests and on both occasions the doctors have shown a great deal of interest. They have taken notes and gone away quite excited. A few days later they have pooh-poohed the whole idea that there could be any connection. I may have dreamed it but I distinctly got the impression that both times they had asked questions about the nuclear tests at some official source and had been very firmly told drop the whole question. Why else would they do an about turn in so short a time?' Mr Parker has polycaethaemia, a blood cancer associated with exposure to radiation.

It was not only British men who were involved in hazardous operations. Australian servicemen had helped build the test sites, their meteorologists had advised on weather conditions for firing, and their scientists were invited to witness Hurricane – after Penney had given strict instructions that they were not to be told any details about the weapon's make-up. For the first three detonations in the bomb test series, the decision to fire lay solely with the British. After the detonation, RAAF aircraft took part in cloud tracking operations and members of all three Australian services were involved in collecting nuclear debris.

A month after the blast, a former RAAF officer, Keith Park, now living in Brisbane, was sent to the Monte Bello Islands on HMAS *Hawkesbury* as a member of an interservice training unit of twelve men who were to be given practical experience in using atomic instruments and dealing with radiation hazards. For the 'training' they were given all the monitoring devices available: film badges, personal dosemeters and geiger counters. Peck remembers that the dosemeters did not agree with the film badges on the first or the second day. 'The other officer and I also had geiger counters which we carried around and which ticked and roared and buzzed. His instrument didn't read the same as mine even though we were walking side by side: he would have five hundred milliroentgens and I would have two hundred. ... We put two or three dosemeters in our pockets and walked around and they all had a different reading – some double the others – and they were in the same pockets. After three days, we asked the captain about a radioactive source – to 'zero' the geiger counters – to which he said, "I've got it but you can't have it. It's locked up in the safe and nobody's allowed to touch it."'

Peck also remembers that it was so hot wearing the protective overalls and kneeboots that the respirators filled up with perspiration. The men began suffering from rashes and after a while they just wore shorts and ordinary boots. They were told that their permitted level of radiation dose was 0.5R a day but they remember recording 2.5R a day. At first when their instruments recorded high levels of radiation, they would leave the area quickly but later, because they were told they had to get the job done, they took fewer precautions. 'We believed we were taking a calculated risk to complete the job. We were over-irradiated on five or six separate occasions and accepted over-exposure as an almost standard operating procedure.'

The men on the training course remember returning to HMAS *Hawkesbury* with every item of clothing irradiated and they were instructed to set up a base camp on the islands because the ship did not have enough fresh water to cope with their decontamination needs. A few weeks later, Peck was removed from duty, suffering from radiation sickness. 'It was diagnozed by the medical officers and scientists on the health ship *Tracker*. I had diarrhoea and bleeding from the gums. I used the lavatory of the *Hawkesbury* and that set an alarm bell going in the bridge.' He was transferred to Onslow where he was told that his red blood count was abnormally low. 'They said, "With a blood count like that if you had an ulcer it would rupture and you would die. You're just lucky you were physically fit before you got this."'

Safety precautions were just as lax for the RAAF crews involved in the Hurricane test. Five RAAF Lincolns flew from Amberley air base to take samples of airborne radioactivity up to five hundred miles from the explosion, and another five were fitted with filters to collect samples up to two thousand miles away. On the east coast of Australia, three planes from the New Zealand Air Force stood by to fly sampling missions from Townsville. No provisions were made to equip the aircrews with film badges or oxygen masks, and no one thought to advise the crews not to eat or drink during the flights through the contaminated clouds. Although the aircraft were all equipped with monitoring equipment to assist the crews in locating the cloud, there was no such equipment to indicate the radiation dose being received by the crews themselves. In fact the equipment that that they did have failed to work properly, so the crews could not be sure whether they had intercepted the cloud, whether they were in the thickest part of it or for how long they were flying through it. Nevertheless, each aircraft came back with filters loaded with radioactive material.

Just as the test planners had not worked out protective measures for the RAAF crews, so the ground crews waiting for the contaminated aircraft to return from their sorties found themselves similarly exposed. Colin Bird, from Brisbane, is currently suing his Government for negligence which he claims resulted in his suffering from cancer after his service at Amberley air base over thirty years ago. As an engine fitter, it was his job to unscrew the radioactive filters from the planes and give them to the British scientists, all of whom were wearing full protective clothing. Still wearing just shorts and shirt, he was then told to hose down the aircraft. He remembers 'the oil and the rubbish from the engines falling all over us. The engines were very high and the stuff fell on to our faces as we sprayed them from the ground. We were covered in highly radioactive material. Even after we showered, we were so radioactive that we had to be kept away from the other men. We had to have a special meal parade when no one else was in the mess.'

When we interviewed Colin Bird at his Mount Gravatt home in 1984, he was dying of cancer – of the throat and tongue. He has been given legal aid to sue his Government, and his challenge is being seen as a test case by the Australian Nuclear Veterans Association. 'We knew nothing about radiation,' Bird told us bitterly, 'we believed our officers when they told us that precautions were being taken. We were used as guinea pigs. They didn't give a damn whether we lived or died.'

With the wide range of experiments being carried out at the Hurricane test, huge amounts of nuclear waste necessarily accumulated. Radioactive samples had to be dumped before the special squadron left for home, an exercise that involved another kind of hazard. On the way to their first port of call at Freemantle, ships' crews had to throw the drums full of radio-active waste material overboard and the crew on board HMS *Zeebrugge* remember winching up to thirty drums from the laboratory on to the deck and then overboard; six to eight of the drums were seeping badly. One officer recalls: 'The davit would not swing properly because it was too small and the drum would catch in the scuppers. I then had to step forward and manually shove the drum clear of the ship's side. I did this because I was in charge of the operation. I remember getting splashed over the arms and legs by the seeping liquids from these drums. I can clearly remember a scientist who was observing these operations saying when he saw me being splashed, "One day, you may live to regret that." This raised a laugh among the ratings present.'

Among them was a Royal Navy Marine Harry Angwin: 'Some of the drums split and liquid splashed from them. I remember a joke being made by someone about us all possibly being sterile from being splashed with radioactive waste. I can't remember scientists being there at the time of our disposal of the drums.' He also recalls that on the way back to England, he slept in the boat that had been taken into the lagoon at Monte Bello. On arrival at Plymouth, the marines were told that their ship could not help out with the recent flood disaster on the East coast because it was too radioactive. In his account of his test service submitted to the Royal Commission, Angwin tells of a malignant tumour 'as big as a man's head' being removed from his thigh in 1980. He was optimistic then that his cancer was cured, but he died of it in December 1984.

As far as the test planners and the weapons people at Aldermaston were concerned, there was little cause for complaint and plenty for congratulation. The weapon had worked and the retrieval of scientific information had been successful. Winston Churchill sent a suitably florid telegram to the Monte Bello team, bestowing an honour on Britain's bomb maker: 'Well done, Sir William . . . and to all those concerned at Monte Bello and at home . . . the thanks of Her Majesty's Government for all their toil and skill which have carried this great enterprise to fruition.'

News of the atomic explosion was released in Canberra and London simultaneously on 3 October, the day of the detonation. Considering the strict press censorship, the reports were confused and contradictory. Five months before, the *New York Times* had compared the British secrecy about their tests unfavourably with the openness of the American ventures. 'No reporters, photographers, radio or television men, parliamentary observers and definitely no women' were being invited to the British show. Little wonder that the British and Australian press exaggerated when they tried to imagine what Penney and his team were actually up to. Eye-witnesses on the western coast of Australia had been further confused by the unfamiliar formation of the cloud. Some newspapermen said 'Penney's Fizzer' had been the first hydrogen bomb or, said *The Times* in London, 'it may be some kind of guided missile'. At least, all agreed, it must be 'a new type of weapon'. They were no doubt disappointed to discover that, although Penney claimed twenty per cent greater efficiency than the American weapons tested at the end of the war, the Hurricane device was built on the same fundamental principles with little innovation.

The average MP in Westminster was as bewildered as the press about what was going on. If they inquired, they were met with a lofty put-down from the select few ministers 'in the know'. When one MP tabled a parliamentary question in November 1952 – 'How far will the recent experiments culminating in the explosion of the British atomic bomb at Monte Bello have provided data other than of exclusive military significance?' – officials at the Ministry of Supply suggested that the Minister should reply: 'The explosion enabled us to determine accurately certain nuclear constants whose precise values will be useful in future work on the civil use of atomic energy'. If the MP should pursue this, the suggested response was: 'If the Honourable Member is interested in nuclear constants he may find it convenient to consult one of the elementary textbooks on nuclear physics.'

Although wishing to remain quiet about the test's non-military significance, could the Government honestly say that it had achieved its military intention? The detonation was supposed to give Britain a new status, especially in her relationship with America. As Penney put it in 1951, the propaganda put out by the Americans and the Russians about their atomic weapons 'has placed us in the position of either having to produce the atomic weapon or admit that for one reason or another we cannot do it. The discriminative test for a first-class power is whether it has made an atomic bomb, and we have either got to pass the test or suffer a serious loss in prestige both inside this country and internationally.' Britain had apparently 'passed the test' – but she had failed to impress the Americans. When US Congressmen were asked whether they should reconsider atomic collaboration with Britain, one Congressman said, 'We would be trading a horse for a rabbit.' And only a month after the Monte Bello test, America exploded her first hydrogen bomb, followed by the Soviet Union in August 1953.

However, Britain was inextricably committed to nuclear weapons. The programme for a new round of tests was announced with a fanfare in Britain and Australia, and because an even more ambitious programme of experiments was demanded by the three services, the next round of tests was to be held on land. What is more, because scientists and servicemen were agreed that the long sea voyage to Monte Bello and the logistical difficulties they encountered while there had made the islands an unhappy testing area, the new tests were to be held on the Australian mainland.

Chapter Six

'IS THERE NO REAL DANGER, Mr MENZIES?'

On his way to the Monte Bello Islands in 1952 Dr William Penney was taken by an Australian outback explorer, Len Beadell, to look for test sites on the Australian mainland. The British Government was preparing for further tests, but wanted a more permanent site. Penney's detour suggested that permission for second bomb detonation had been given by the Australians even before Hurricane and before the British had shown whether their assurances about safety could be believed. Beadell, a surveyor and an outback explorer, took the scientist to Emu Field, a claypan in the Great Victoria Desert, about 150 miles from the nearest town and apparently uninhabited apart from nomadic Aborigines. To Penney, the site looked ideal for the next round of bomb tests.

Beadell remembers the assignment well. The mission was considered to be of such secrecy that only an Air Commodore from among the RAAF personnel at the Woomera rocket range could be entrusted with the job of piloting Beadell on his preliminary reconnoitre. 'He was a good pilot in 1916!', Beadell recalls. 'After several fruitless detours, he managed to bounce down a make-do airstrip, going into sandhills at the end. He asked me how the landing was. I didn't know which one he was talking about'. Penney was then invited to look at the site, and Beadell jokes that 'he was considered too valuable for the Air Commodore. He was piloted there by a flight sergeant!' An oddly matched pair on the surface, Beadell and Penney were to become close friends and Beadell later found the major Maralinga site for Penney and in the 1960s, he supervised the building of a 3750-mile road across the vast desert areas of South-Western Australia for survey teams to gain access to the Woomera, Emu and Maralinga sites.

The Hurricane test on the Monte Bello Islands had confirmed the efficacy of the implosion method of creating an atomic explosion, based on plutonium 239. Operationally, it was designed to prepare the military for a particular kind of Soviet sabotage – the smuggling of an atomic bomb on board a ship into a British port – but the principle objective had always been to provide the RAF with an operational nuclear weapon, as requested by the Chiefs of Staff as far back as 1946. Along with work on the atomic bomb, the Air Ministry had ordered priority to be given to building a new four-engine jet bomber, designed to accommodate the bomb. The Vickers-designed Valiant was given the go-ahead in 1949 and it would finally be ready to drop the first operational nuclear weapon on the Maralinga test range in 1956. In 1953, it was up to Penney to design a bomb of use to the RAF and the new Valiants. As Penney himself described the task in his evidence to the Royal Commission: 'At that time [after the Hurricane test and the Russian atomic explosion in 1949], the Cold War took on a nuclear dimension and it became necessary to equip our forces for the possibility of nuclear war. The knowledge I had about the effects of atomic weapons, and the strategy, tactics and hardware needed to accommodate this new dimension, led to a requirement for physically smaller weapons and lower yield designs.' The Totem series of tests at Emu and the later Buffalo tests at Maralinga, ranging in yield from 1.5 to 15 kilotons, gave Britain this capacity.

A special kind of bomb manufacturing experiment was to take place at Emu. The Chiefs of Staff had decided that they needed two hundred atom bombs by 1957, but Britain's nuclear power stations were not producing plutonium fast enough to meet this requirement. Even the relatively small amount of plutonium needed for Hurricane had only been ready weeks before the testing date. The Aldermaston scientists wanted to know whether the economic Magnox reactors, which were able to produce electricity as well as fissile material for the bomb-making programme, could produce enough quality plutonium for bombs. The Totem trials at Emu were to see whether bombs could be produced out of lower-grade plutonium or, as the official brief to the Minister of Defence put it, 'The purpose of the test is simple. It is to find out how much of the isotope 240 can be tolerated in plutonium used for military purposes and if the results of the test are satisfactory, it will lead to economies in the long run. The need for carrying out this trial . . . is primarily due to the Chiefs of Staff proposal for doubling the production of fissile material. There is, of course, a price to pay. This is a delay in the order of three months on commencing the bomb production programme. In view of the importance of acquiring the information the trial is designed to give, this price is considered acceptable.'

Work began on the site early in 1953 and it was due to be ready by the time the British scientific team arrived a month before the October firings. Accommodation for some two hundred servicemen was built on the claypans of Emu Field, and all the scientific equipment, prefabricated offices, a photographic dark room and even tin mugs were imported from the United Kingdom. Australian contractors were employed on a building programme of makeshift roads and airfields, while the Australian army took on engineering jobs such as building the foundations for the towers from which the two devices would be exploded.

The test reports held at Aldermaston speak of 'rushed arrangements', of a 'trial hurriedly prepared' and of tension between the British and Australian teams. Even with the restraint characteristic of government reports, the picture is of furious rows and conflicting personalities. There were clashes over 'transport, flies and baths' and 'it must be clear that full mutual understanding [between the Australian and British teams] was next to impossible'. Nothing was built to last. Very early on the test organizers realized that the inaccessibility of the range and the inhospitality of the region meant that if the British wanted a permanent mainland site, it would have to be found elsewhere. Len Beadell was sent off to survey other more likely areas, and even while the bombs were being blasted at Emu, work had begun on the Maralinga site.

Despite the problems on the Emu site, the tests themselves were a technical success. 'Standby' for the first test, code-named Totem 1, was announced on 7 October but because of unsatisfactory winds, the firing did not take place until 15 October. It was the world's fiftieth atomic bomb blast, and although at first the test organizers wanted to exclude the press from their plans, after an outcry from Australian journalists, a press stand was erected on a hill fifteen miles from the blast and the newsmen were provided with a running commentary by one of Penney's staff.

The British journalist James Cameron, veteran of the Bikini Atoll tests, was disappointed. 'The welders' goggles we wore changed the landscape to a bleak coppery green. The fireball turned it momentarily to gold and flung a brief wave of brilliance over the entire sky. There was a measure of disappointment. It did not after all blow a hole through Australia ... so Adelaide and Melbourne may well feel cheated that nobody had to duck ... It was a long way to come for a loud noise.'

Onlookers remember that the initial cloud looked more like a cauliflower than a mushroom. It rose to fifteen thousand feet, and a circle of ground around the firing tower, about seventy-five yards in radius, was pulverized. The weapon's yield was 10 kilotons, double the yield expected by the test planners. Nor, because of stable wind conditions, did the fallout disperse as rapidly as forecast in the test plans: plumes of intense radioactivity drifted across the mainland and out to sea.

As with Hurricane the forward area was littered with materials planted by the military services and civil defence planners as part of their field trials. There were wooden human figures wearing various types of clothing, ammunition, radar equipment, medical stores, a ship's funnel, landrovers, three Mustangs given by the RAAF and a Centurion tank left with its engine running at the time of detonation – the Army wanted to know whether it could be driven away under its own power afterwards.

Warrant Officer Bill Jones of the Australian Army was among the team told to retrieve the tank. He was issued with protective clothing sufficient to protect him against a short stay in the heavily contaminated ground zero area, but the tank, damaged by the blast, would not start and according to Jones the rest of the team returned to base while he stayed with the tank for two days until the necessary repair work had been done. Thirteen years later, he died of cancer.

In the sky, air-sampling missions were undertaken to practise methods of analysing fallout, in order to keep abreast of the current American and Russian nuclear tests. In addition, Lincolns of the RAAF were detailed to track the clouds as they passed over mainland Australia and to sample the fallout. Both air forces were involved in sorties of a purely scientific nature, to measure the weapon yield. And there was Operation 'Hotbox', which involved a Canberra flying through the atomic cloud only minutes after the explosion to test the effects on the aircraft *and the crew*. The flight had been triggered off by the pessimistic calculations made at Harwell in 1950 by the British atomic spy Klaus Fuchs, who had concluded that in the aftermath of an atomic explosion, any plane exposing itself to measurable amounts of fission products would become dangerously irradiated, and so any such exposure should be ruled out for operational purposes. By 1953, however, Fuchs was 'out of reach', as the expedition's leader tactfully put it in his account of the operation, and 'an urgent operational need arose to test this position' for themselves.

Operation Hotbox was undertaken by the kind of men whose assessment of risk is stictly determined by their dedication to duty and by their appreciation, as they saw it, of Britain's urgent need for an operational bomb. The task force leader was Group Captain Wilson and he was accompanied by Group Captains Anderson and Dehin. Recalling the event for the Royal Commission hearings thirty years later, their bravery, or foolhardiness, is awesome. Did they calculate before the operation what dose they were likely to receive? They tried, explained Wilson, 'But it was necessarily fairly ad hoc because we had no information at all. All the people who designed the weapon were not particularly anxious to give us the yield of it and we were left with a statement that was based largely on American data' (which, as it turned out, was totally irrelevant to the Totem 1 trial).

Although they set out wearing oxygen masks, they knew there was a risk that they might inhale or swallow radioactive dust. They also believed that they could be in danger of hitting something solid in the cloud or that the plane might be involved in a flameout caused by the dust. Because of the possibility of losing control of the plane, Dehin remembers that 'we arranged for an RAAF Lincoln, piloted by a personal friend of mine, to stand by fifty miles away to locate us and drop supplies if we should crash'!

'Most important of all was the timing of the explosion. Since we wanted to be in a position to enter the cloud early, we must not be too far away. On the other hand we must not risk exposing the aircraft to the actual explosion, nor must we be looking directly at it when it occurred. Apart from the normal danger of looking at atomic explosions, a blind pilot cannot regain control of an aircraft – and a Canberra once out of control hits the ground very fast indeed. We therefore planned our position in space very carefully; exactly three minutes before the explosion we should be ten miles from the site at a height of thirty thousand feet on a course of 300, which would take us towards a dried-up salt lake with the melodious name Lake Meramangye. .... The first run was no more than a "sniff" as we called it – we just immersed our wings for a couple of seconds so that the Group Captain could tell us whether we could reasonably go through the middle. As I turned he made his calculations and decided that we could. I therefore headed the aircraft straight at the centre and got ready for a rough ride. The cloud as we drew nearer, looked distinctly nasty. In colour it was a dark red-brown, very solid but boiling as it were. I turned on all the cockpit lighting, for it was certain that I should not be able to see my instruments without lights. As we entered, it was indeed dark but not as turbulent as I expected; until just before we emerged, the forces on the elevators increased to such an extent that I thought I might lose control. Then, as the cloud gave us the parting kick, the light began to appear as at the end of a railway tunnel. We emerged having hit nothing solid nor lost our engines or instruments. The rest was easy – a run through the base and the top, a quick beat-up of the scientists below, then back to Woomera to drop our wing-tip filter and leave the aircraft.'

The Canberra was sealed with tape to maintain the cabin pressure, and the crew wore tight-fitting oxygen masks throughout the flight. Nonetheless, because the gamma rays from the radioactive cloud were so penetrating, the recorded radiation doses of the crew ranged from 9.5 to 14.5R, though because the film badges that they wore were unable to record beta radiation, it is possible that their doses were higher. In any case they were certainly higher than the maximum allowed by Penney for operations of 'extreme urgency' and they were not allowed to repeat the exercise again: the original intention had been for them to fly again at the second Totem test, but this was vetoed at the highest level. It was thought that the task did not warrant the risks.

The 'Hotbox' story doesn't end, however, with Wilson, Anderson and Dehin clambering out of the cockpit. Another of the operation's objectives was to test the aircraft's contamination, 'the subsequent ease of decontamination and to assess the risk to those engaged on decontamination procedures'. There was an RAAF ground crew standing by ready for the decontamination procedure at Woomera but the three pilots did the 'hot spots' themselves, leaving the RAAF ground crew to do the less contaminated parts of the aircraft. The operation involved repeatedly hosing down the aircraft and for this purpose each man was issued with protective clothing but not respirators, though it was known at the time that fission products are carried by water and there would have been a risk of them being swallowed. Asked why, as the officer in charge, he did not instruct that respirators should be used, Wilson explained that it would have been 'unproductive' and have 'inhibited' the efficiency of the operation. Was that safe? 'How safe is safe?', replied Wilson, 'you can make things safe but I doubt very much whether it would have made any difference. There was nothing to protect them against.'

But Wilson's appreciation of safe was questioned by a member of the health physics team who arrived at Woomera two days after the controversial flight, when Wilson had already left. On arriving at the base, Dr. Stevenson was told that the Canberra had been cleaned but when he nonetheless carried out a smear test on the plane, he found that it registered more than two thousand counts a second, that is, 'it was still highly contaminated'. Wilson later explained that because he thought the Canberra was to fly another Hotbox mission a fortnight later, he saw that the plane was decontaminated only within 'operational requirements', which were also according to 'international requirements'. Not true, says Stevenson, the radiation expert. 'Certainly, as far as normal peacetime standards were concerned, the aircraft was not clean.' If Stevenson had not carried out the smear test, the Canberra would have been back in use without anyone realizing the extent of the contamination.

While the Hotbox mission was the most sensational air sortie of Totem 1, the missions carried out by the RAAF Lincolns were without doubt the most ill-planned and therefore the most risky of the airborne exercises. When Wilson and Dehin arrived at Woomera for the two-week planning phase prior to Hotbox, they had no idea that the RAAF was to do air-sampling missions. They were even more surprised to hear that Lincolns had been involved in the earlier tests at Monte Bello. But above all, the two men, who had been briefed in radiation risks before coming to Australia, were taken aback by the apparent ignorance about radiation dangers among the RAAF officers. During a conversation with Wing Commander Rose (the 'friend', mentioned earlier, who would bring supplies in the event of the Canberra crashing), Wilson said later, 'I formed the impression that he regarded the dangers of contamination with insufficient seriousness', and was astonished when Rose quipped that 'he'd done this kind of thing before, during the Hurricane test'. Wilson assumed that the ignorance was all to do with the secrecy that surrounded the air-sampling missions. After all, the main purpose was intelligence, to gain practice in estimating future Russian and American blasts. 'I think this is one of the problems you come up against when you are dealing with intelligence flights. They are all so secret that very few people are briefed on them.'

It was perhaps fortunate for Wing Commander Rose that he and Dehin were good friends (they had played golf together) since the well-briefed Britons were able to give the ill-briefed Australian some timely advice. As Wilson remembers the exchange that took place in the officers mess in Woomera, 'It quite literally never occurred to us that he would not have been properly briefed. We told him to be a bit more careful on this one. I told him, "I think it may be slightly different".' Wilson warned Rose that he and his crew should wear oxygen masks as soon as the plane's instruments showed that they had contacted fallout, and because of that chance conversation, Rose and his crew *did* wear oxygen masks and Rose had the foresight to drop a dosemeter in his pocket before taking off. The other crews in the six Lincolns involved in the air-sampling mission were not so fortunately forewarned and forearmed.

The planes, carrying sensors for penetrating radiation and filters for sampling, flew from Woomera ten hours after the detonation to intercept the cloud and collect the samples. According to the RAAF test report, 'Each of the aircraft returned with filters well charged with radioactive particles and each was found to be contaminated. Due to heavy contamination, two of the aircraft were unable to accurately measure the dimensions of the cloud. The other three were able to do so. Decontamination of the crew and isolation of the aircraft had not been envisaged at any previous stage.' In short, there were no preparations on the ground to cope with the emergency, and during the operation itself, the air crews were flying 'blind'.

Ex-RAAF signalman, William Turner, of Brisbane was ordered to operate the instruments that measured the level of radioactivity. He remembers flying through the cloud at a distance of about eight hundred miles from ground zero, and staying about forty-five minutes in the cloud, which was a 'light rusty-brown haze'. The needle 'went haywire' as they entered it and stayed at the maximum measuring level while they remained there. He remembers that the plane was not pressurized and the crew did not wear oxygen masks or protective clothing. They ate a sandwich lunch on their return to Woomera, too late to heed the wireless message that came through instructing them not to eat. Turner does not remember being checked after the flight for radiation or going through decontamination procedures.

Lance Edwards, ex-RAAF wireless operator now living on the Gold Coast, also remembers eating his packed lunch on the mission. Unlike Turner, who at least waited until he was on the return journey, he and his fellow crew members ate while flying through the cloud. Once again the plane was not pressurized. When we interviewed him in his home in 1984, he knew that the crew's captain, a 'chap called Onions', had since died of cancer. Edwards himself developed cancer of the thyroid in 1959 and is convinced that his cancer is due to his bomb test service and that he and the others were used as guinea pigs. 'We now know from what happened in Japan that the risk of cancer of the thyroid increases by a factor of eight, six or seven years after a person is exposed to radiation. That is exactly when my cancer developed. Okay, we were naïve, but we were also duped. We started suspecting something was amiss when we landed after the flight to find the plane met by British scientists wearing white protective clothing. Our senior officers started asking what the hell was going on. The boffins seemed to know about the dangers. Why didn't we? After the flight, all our flying gear, suits, parachutes and so on were confiscated and later destroyed.'

The most eventful flight was that taken by Lincoln A73.25, which is vividly remembered by RAF Wing Commander Richard Nettley who was on secondment to the RAAF at the time under an exchange scheme. His unit was at RAAF Richmond when they were told that they would be required to help out the British with their cloud-sampling programme. 'I felt that the RAAF were being called upon to do this as a consolation prize but it may have been specifically required by the Australian Government. I cannot remember details of the briefing but I am certain that we were not told that the operation might be in any sense dangerous. ... We seemed an inexperienced crew for such a specialized flight. The captain was a Pilot Officer, as was the other navigator, and I was a junior officer accustomed to a very different flying environment.'

They located the cloud as it was drifting north-east at about fifteen thousand feet. It was shaped as an ellipse, about twenty miles by thirty and with the appearance of a brown smoke ring. 'We were absolutely cock-a-hoop at having found it and flew straight into it. We flew up and down through it taking measurements for at least three hours. Those reading the sensors were reporting to the captain and, of course, we could all hear. As we entered the smoke ring they reported the indicators on the special instruments as being "off the clock" and it was at first thought that the instruments must be unserviceable. They told us that the indicators went down to zero when we left the cloud and up again when we went back in. There was no radio communication with base at this stage. We were carried away with the discovery and the readings being taken of the radiation, and became progressively less certain of our position. Eventually we managed to land at RAAF Williamstown in northern New South Wales with very little fuel left in our tanks. We were not expected there and they had no idea what to do with us.'

It was fortunate for Nettley and his crew that an American squadron of B29s had been invited to witness the test and to assist in the air-sampling programme. Like the Lincoln crews, they located patches of high activity in the cloud, and they recall that their sensitive equiment became so saturated by the radioactive exposure that it stopped working properly. Afterwards the air filters on the outside of the planes proved too contaminated for the equipment at the US base at Guam to take recordings from them. However, the USAF unlike the RAAF had the knowledge and resources to help combat contamination and when the Americans heard about the emergency landing at Williamstown, a B29 was flown from the temporary US base at Richmond with a decontamination team and equipment to help out. The US crew monitored the Lincoln and declared it heavily contaminated, though the Australian crew nevertheless flew it back to Richmond. When the plane was checked by the British health physics team ten days later, it was found to be the most contaminated of all the Lincolns.

Nettley was afterwards summoned to Perth for a medical examination and blood test and then to Brisbane for more tests. He remembers that all his fingernails grew brown and fell out in the year after the exercise. While in hospital in Brisbane, he heard that one of the ground crew who had worked on the plane's engines had died of bone cancer. 'In retrospect I suppose that we should have been instructed to locate the cloud and return to base after having made an initial assessment of radiological strengths. My impression now is that there was little real understanding of this down at the base-operating level.' The RAAF official report on the incident comes to a similar conclusion: 'It was only through seeking the assistance of the USAF specialists and equipment that it was at all possible to ascertain that the Lincoln aircraft and personnel had obtained any degree of contamination. The precaution to have the Lincoln aircraft which landed at Williamstown inspected proved the importance of this aspect, and how ignorance on the part of RAAF personnel on all matters of this nature could possibly have proved dangerous.'

By the time Lincoln A73.25 landed at Williamstown, the other contaminated Lincolns were arriving back at Woomera. One of the pilots told the control tower that he believed something was badly wrong. The two senior Britons on the base at the time were Group Captain Wilson, who was resting after his Hotbox mission, and Dr Gale, the AWRE scientist in charge of examining the air samples. Gale remembers that as the air filters from the planes were brought into the laboratory they were so irradiated that they interfered with the calibration gauge designed to measure background radiation. He had to order that the filters be taken out of the room and then brought in again one by one.

Wilson remembers the panic at Woomera as the Lincolns came in. One of the Australian officers asked him to take a look at the first contaminated aircraft to arrive, and although when Wilson measured the radiation levels in the cockpit, he concluded that the exposure experienced by the crew was not dangerously high, he nonetheless recalls: 'I was upset and cross because they were not carrying any proper instrumentation and I rang up the Australian Director General of Medical Services in

Melbourne and told him so. . . . I am a doctor and I don't like people being irradiated. I get very worried.' Wilson left instructions for the Lincons to be isolated for at least twelve hours, and left for Melbourne to make his protest known.

The RAAF at Woomera were left with five contaminated aircraft, without the equipment necessary for decontamination and with no one to offer advice. They left the aircraft for twelve hours as instructed, then on the day after the test the ground crews began maintenance and refuelling work. Aircrewman Hobdell, who spent three hours clambering over the wings of the highly radioactive aircraft, received according to the official records, the highest radiation dose of 0.5R – equivalent to today's annual radiation limit for a member of the public.

Former RAAF serviceman, Rex Naggs of Inglewood, says that Hobdell was not the only member of the ground crew to be contaminated. He remembers cleaning the engine pistons on the Lincolns on Day + 1 and using his overalls to wipe away the fine red dust when he ran out of clean rags. The cleaning and servicing went on for four days before he was told to stop by a British officer. 'He had apparently checked the planes and discovered they were much more radioactive than had been predicted.' Naggs' body and clothes were found to be badly contaminated, and his work overalls were taken away on the end of a six-foot-long stick. 'It started to worry me. They were scared of my overalls and I had worn them'. He was ordered to shower and readings were taken every fifteen minutes until after four hours the level of contamination on his body was considered safe. He was summoned for regular blood tests until 1960 but he was never given the results. He knew only that the tests were 'to do with what was referred to as an overdose at Woomera'. In January 1984, Rex Naggs was diagnosed as having leukaemia.

It was not until D1 + 5 that British health physicists arrived on the scene and set up a health control operation. Today members of that health team admit that the RAAF had been ill advised by Wilson and they themselves would have taken a stricter approach. As one of them said, there is a 'distinction between the man who thinks in terms of military operations and the scientist'. The Lincolns should have been isolated for longer and Hobdell and Naggs should not have touched the aircraft for at least five days.

The aircraft constituted a serious radiation hazard for several months. According to a previously restricted RAAF report, three of the Lincolns were still 'highly radioactive' in February 1954 and had to be isolated in an 'active area' at Amberley Air Base near Brisbane. There was also the problem of the contaminated material that had accumulated during the ill-fated exercise: the air crews' clothing, the overalls worn by the ground crews and the equipment and water used in decontamination. Because it was 'highly undesirable' to leave the waste at Amberley and removal by road might 'attract undesirable attention', it was decided to dump the material at sea. The report said that 'containers for liquids must burst on impact with the water', suggesting that this method would allow the radioactive waste to be dispersed by the sea. Veterans who claim to have taken part in the dumping operation say that the material was dumped from aircraft about 250 miles north of Brisbane.

There were some radical changes made to the air-sampling procedures before the firing of the second Totem device on 27 October. Fortunately the winds behaved as predicted on this occasion and so the fallout was dispersed more efficiently than at the first Totem blast. Nonetheless, only two Lincolns took part, the air crews wore oxygen masks and carried personal dosemeters and film badges, and especially trained officers supervised all decontamination operations. The crews received one tenth of the contamination dose noted for Totem 1.

The Totem 1 fiasco had shaken the confidence of the Australians. The RAAF had been assured by the British test planners that 'there would be no risk to the crew or the aircraft consequent on flying through the clouds'. When the true facts became known to the RAAF Director General of Medical

Services, Air Vice Marshal Daley, he wrote as a postscript to the official RAAF record, 'It would seem that, although I may be open to correction here, this service is not informed sufficiently of the hazard that its own personnel may undergo on account of the apparent "outer position" of this service in the matter.'

During the Monte Bello operation, the Australian public had been given the barest details and Australian scientists had been allowed to watch but not interfere. The Totem detonations at Emu Field in October 1953 raised doubts in the minds of the Australian public about the safety of the test programme. A newspaper headline asked, 'Is there no real danger, Mr Menzies?' There were demands from Australian scientists and politicians for closer involvement in the planning and the Totem bomb tests were to be the last in which the Australians had no say over the firing of the atomic weapons and no say in the safety arrangements affecting their servicemen and their people.

Chapter Seven

'WHAT THE BLOODY HELL IS GOING ON?'

The establishment of the Australian Weapons Test Safety Committee in July 1955 gave the Australian Government a formal veto over every nuclear bomb firing. It was up to the Committee to examine the safety procedures being taken by the British before each trial and to decide whether they were 'adequate for the prevention of injury to persons or damage to livestock and other property'. It was then the Committee's duty to advise the Prime Minister of its conclusions and to recommend any 'additional, alternative or more extensive safety measures which are considered necessary or desirable'. However, the Safety Committee was entirely dependent on 'information and other data supplied by the United Kingdom', and not only was this information severely restricted but the Committee appeared suitably 'packed' to give the British back-up support from the Australians that they wanted. Its role as a watchdog has thus been the object of the Australian Royal Commission's most searching enquiry.

The deliberate British policy of concealing important information from the Australians went back to the very beginning of the test series. A memorandum dated January 1952 from the Commonwealth Relations Office in London refers to an assurance given to Robert Menzies that the effects of the first Monte Bello test would be 'innocuous' and goes on to say, 'We hope that now the announcement is over, there will be no further pressure from the Australian side for fuller details or for information about the grounds on which the assurance was given'. Providing more information might cause considerable inconvenience: 'The Australians might disagree with the United Kingdom scientists' assessment of the risks, or they might suggest that in order to ensure that necessary precautions against contamination were in fact taken, Australians should be allowed closer to the scene of the test than we at present propose.' Eminent Australian scientists, Professors Titterton and Martin, and Dr Butement, chief scientific adviser at the Ministry of Supply, had attended the first test, on board the command vessel, HMS *Narvik*, along with Dr. Penney. Penney told the Royal Commission that before the countdown, 'I asked each one of them at a time, "Are you happy?", and they all said, "Yes".' But could they say anything else with the little information they had access to?

A major part of the problem was that the British were restricted by their agreements with the United States. Almost everything that British scientists knew about bomb manufacture had been learned at the Los Alamos school and the British were bound by treaty not to pass any of that know-how on to a third party. The 'need to know' principle was adhered to for all parties involved in the tests. The naval rating was thus told the minimum necessary about his part in the operation and was assured that his safety was being taken care of by the experts. And members of the Australian Weapons Test Safety Committee were told the likely maximum yield of the weapon and the likely fallout risks but nothing about the weapon design or make-up that would allow them to make their own calculations.

Perhaps the most eminent nuclear physicist in Australia at the time was Professor Mark Oliphant, then head of the nuclear physics department at the Australian National University and later to become Governor of South Australia, but the prominent position on the Safety Committee went to his deputy, Ernest Titterton, and Oliphant himself was not invited to become a member. Titterton had worked in America on the

Manhattan project and at Harwell and was considered a friend of the British. Penney had especially asked for him to be involved. His commitment to the development of nuclear weaponry had never been questioned and he was also considered 'safe', one of the 'home team'. Oliphant, on the other hand, had grave reservations about nuclear weaponry. Even Even worse, he was considered a security risk by the Americans.

In 1952, the British had warned the Australians that 'Professor Oliphant presents a difficulty ... the Americans, regarding him as a security risk, would react very unfavourably.' In his evidence to the Royal Commission, Penney agreed that the decision to keep the weapon-wary Professor Oliphant off the Safety Committee was because of the potential damage to Britain's relations with America: 'We were at that time striving hard to get back on terms with the Americans and we had this awful disaster within security [i.e. Fuchs].' While Oliphant was kept out of the way, Titterton became more and more involved with the British. When members of the Aldermaston team visited Australia at a time of particular concern about the forthcoming 'minor trials' at Maralinga due to take place in 1962, they were careful to call on Professor Titterton alone in his laboratory. One of them noted that Titterton made no major complaint about the amount of information on the weapons trials that he was getting from the British, but was concerned to 'forestall possible criticism of granting security clearance on inadequate data. Titterton gave us his usual reassurances that the political worries of the Department of Defence are not to be regarded too seriously and there is no doubt that he continues to press his views on the Minister that the Department's doubts are unjustified.'

It could be argued that the Australians themselves were to blame for allowing themselves to be ignorant about the safety of the tests. In his evidence to the Royal Commission hearings in Sydney in 1984, Dr Donald Stevens, another Safety Committee member, said that the Committee saw their job as helping

94

the British: they hoped the tests would succeed because of British loyalty. It was with this attitude that the Australians set out to 'monitor' the next round of test firings, code-named Mosaic G1 and Mosaic G2, the biggest in terms of weapons explosive of all the Australian detonations. For these firings the British were returning to the Monte Bello Islands, where they intended to use 'boosted' bombs designed to test whether British scientists could trigger thermonuclear fusion. The Americans and the Russians had already proved their thermo-nuclear capacity and Britain was in danger of falling behind.

As Penney recalls the scene in 1956: 'The top priority job was thermonuclear. We wanted to see if we could make a few fast neutrons; and we wanted to do it in yields of 40, 50, 60 kilotons [more than twice the size of the first Monte Bello test]. . . . Maralinga was not going to be possible – I think [the Australians] would have said no. . . . The other possibility was to ask the Americans. Well, we had been through that hoop. And therefore it was either Monte Bello or wait – not do it. The Admiralty had been collecting weather information and I think the way they looked at it was, "Well, it is the only place. If the weather is not suitable, then it will just have to wait."'

Climatic conditions at the Monte Bello Islands were almost *never* suitable for firing. In January 1956, a weather forecasting expert employed by the Royal Navy, Robert Fotheringham, was sent to Melbourne to carry out with the Australian Meteorological Bureau a statistical study to establish how often the required conditions for firing might occur. They concluded that within the three months of April, May and June when the British task force would be anchored off the Monte Bello Islands for the Mosaic trials, the chances of the right conditions prevail-ing were one in a hundred, that is, just one day in that period of time! When Fotheringham was asked whether he thought, in the light of his pessimistic findings, that the whole mission should have been called off, he told the Royal Commissioners, 'That was not a decision to which I was a party. I suppose it depends on the importance of the project, whether you call it off or not. But I did not think that was a possibility.' He also said that the prospect of measurable fallout drifting over mainland Australia as a result of the Mosaic tests was accepted as an 'inevitable consequence'. This information was relayed to the Safety Committee, who agreed to that inevitability.

The British had decided to return to Monte Bello because certain trials had to be performed quickly if they were to build an H bomb, and the Christmas Island test range was not yet ready. Monte Bello, despite its imperfections, was the only alternative. Penney and the British Government have strenuously denied that they were taking a calculated risk by returning to Monte Bello for these huge explosions, but it is worth remembering that some £4 million were invested in the Mosaic trials and once the task force was assembled, it would have taken a brave man to advise that the firings could not take place. As it turned out, both bombs were fired in conditions that ultimately did not fulfil the expected safety requirements.

By the middle of May 1956, the five-month build-up of warships, aircraft and special test equipment had been completed. More than two thousand British Navy and RAF men, civilian scientists and technicians were assembled on the islands and at Onslow air base. RAAF crews were preparing to mount air-sampling exercises again from Onslow and from Broome. Huge tower structures built to accommodate the bombs by Australian and British sappers were already in place on Trimouille and Alpha islands. The five members of the Australian Safety Committee were to be on board the control ship, HMS *Narvik*, along with the operation commander, Admiral Hugh Martell, and the test supervisor, Charles Adams. The Safety Committee members were Professor Titterton, Professor Martin, Dr Butement, Mr Dwyer of the Commonwealth Meteorological Bureau and Mr Eddy of the X-ray and Radium Laboratory in Melbourne.

On 15 May 1956, the task force was put on standby. At 3 am

the following morning, the 'tower party', made up of scientists and sappers, were ferried from HMS *Narvik* to Hermite Island where Ian Maddocks would again start the countdown and detonate the bomb. By 10 am the RAAF Neptunes reported that the sky was clear in the 150-mile danger area. At 11.30, the Canberras which were to carry out the air-sampling operation were approaching their checkpoint eighty miles south of the islands. At 11.46, the countdown began. Those who had been taken aback by the muddy column of water and distorted cloud at the Hurricane test were rewarded by the sight of a more conventional explosion. Because the bombs for both the G1 and G2 tests were mounted on towers, they did not carry so much water and mud up with them on detonation and quickly blossomed into the familiar mushroom-shaped clouds.

The reports sent back by the press, accommodated on board HMS *Alert*, were recorded by the wireless operator. 'The countdown on the press ship began at minus four minutes. Even the oldest ratings stood rigidly on deck, tension in every line of their bodies.' 'The necks of the Big Brass, the scientists and pressmen were all seared by the heat of the fireball at a distance of twelve miles.' 'The blast wave that followed after the flash was a shocking violation of this calm world of jade-green seas, wheeling gulls and lazy fish'. And, from one American correspondent: 'Go it alone Britain produced its own open shot atomic test off Western Australia coast today with typical casual indifference in contrast to tubthumping ballyhoo of Las Vegas tests.'

The firing of Mosaic G1 was, according to one eye-witness on HMS *Alert*, a 'penny squib' compared with the 'Brock's thunderflash' produced a couple of weeks later by the second test, G2. The differing yields of the two blasts deserve the comparison. G1 was a disappointment and produced only 15 kilotons, while G2 produced a blast yield of 98 kilotons, a figure that the British concealed from the Australian Government for thirty years. The British Prime Minister in 1956, Anthony Eden, had assured Menzies that the yield from the Mosaic trials would not be more than two and a half times the 25-kiloton yield from the Hurricane test, and the Australian official reports claim that the explosive yields of all the tests in Australia were in the 'low or kiloton range', a phrase usually associated with the 20-kiloton detonations over Hiroshima and Nagasaki. In Britain in 1984, after a parliamentary debate about the tests, the Ministry of Defence produced documents which suggested that the yield from G2 had been 60 kilotons but in April 1985, in response to repeated requests from the Australian Royal Commission, the British revealed documents showing that the blast yield from Mosaic G2 had been 98 kilotons, four times bigger than any of the other Australian blasts and very nearly in the 1 megaton range.

The Mosaic trials gave the Navy a chance to test their men in conditions of nuclear warfare, much as the RAF had been put on trial in operation Hotbox. They wanted to test the effectiveness of 'pre-wetting' as a decontamination measure, which involved constantly washing a ship down with sea sprays as it was exposed to radiation. According to the Admiralty operational records, 'It was planned that HMS *Diana* should be stationed so as to receive as much fallout as possible consistent with ensuring that no member of the ship's company received a biologically significant dose of radiation, allowing for uncertainty in the calculated intensity of fallout and for the possibility that the ship's pre-wetting system might fail.'

The ratings on board HMS *Diana* remember getting no warning of the operation or briefing until the day before the detonation itself when they were told to prepare for Special Sea Duty Stations. They were issued with special clothing, including anti-flash gloves, an anti-flash balaklava, oil-skin coats and boots. One remembers, 'We looked very much like deep-sea fishermen.' They collected film badges and personal dosemeters as they sailed into the fallout cloud and the sprays were turned on. 'I think we probably looked like a celebrating New York tug which had turned its fire hoses to the air,' commented one

Royal Navy veteran, Kenneth Stevens, now living in South Australia. He remembers that after the operation they showered in sea water, first wearing their protective clothing and then without it. 'People were exclaiming how high the readings on their dosemeters were, before handing them over to the authorities. I have personal experience of seeing some of these personal dose rate meters being thrown overboard. I do not know why or which ones these were.'

Keith Syder, now living in Merseyside, was a naval conscript on board the *Diana*. 'Almost immediately after the explosion we began sailing towards the cloud, which was very obvious and seemed to be descending towards the sea. It was thousands of feet high and climbed for probably an hour and a half before it began to descend. The cloud seemed to be made up of fine brown dust particles. It was browner than fog and not so thick. When we had sailed through the cloud to its far perimeter, we went about and came back through again.' Syder remembers that when they finally left the cloud, the sprinklers were turned off and the decks hosed down. Sea water that had been in contact with the radioactive fallout was used for both operations, and no attempt was made to clean the sumps, gun turrets, drainage sections or other cavities.

The official report shows that the *Diana* received about the 'intended fallout' in the first test. For the second test, the Operational Commander noted that the 'intended amount of fallout could be increased by a factor of 10 in favourable circumstances, but an increase by a factor of 100 does not seem justified.' For G2, *Diana* was positioned to receive fallout from a height one thousand feet below the centre of the cloud, a distance chosen to give a peak total gamma dose of 9R, more than the 5R first specified in the Admiralty plans. The new dose fell into the operations of 'extreme urgency' category specified by Penney at the beginning of the test programme. However, the use of pre-wetting on HMS *Diana* confirmed the Navy's opinion about its effectiveness, for, according to the test reports, it considerably reduced the contamination on board the ship. Built-in hosing systems and pressurized 'cockpits' were consequently installed in Britain's warships to enable the crew to operate in a nuclear war.

One of the most remarkable recollections of G2 comes from Radio Operator John Perkins on board the control ship, HMS *Narvik*. He remembers that there were three or four abortive countdowns before the second explosion. 'Everybody was getting very fed up and one or two sailors were taken off the ship to hospital since they had had breakdowns. There was great tension in the air. I remember talking to one scientist who was working on a timing device. He said that the long wait was because the weather had to be right but that they had to hurry up because of time and money. He said that the weather was about to close up and the winds change. He said that if the second explosion was going to take place it would have to happen soon and that if it did not it would be the most tremendous waste of time and money.'

Before the actual detonation of G2, Perkins says that HMS *Narvik* withdrew four to five miles. He remembers watching the fallout cloud move away from the Australian mainland and then change direction and drift back across the land. 'I was not on duty when the explosion took place and I watched it from the deck. I went on duty at 4 pm. This time I was sending press releases from the journalists who were on board. Suddenly a signal came in direct from Sydney. It was written down on a pad in manuscript by the operator who took it. It was from the Australian Prime Minister to the Prime Minister of Great Britain. It simply said, "What the bloody hell is going on, the cloud is drifting over the mainland?" It was a very short message and everybody stood there looking at it. The pad was on the table and we were all reading it. We were very quiet because the Captain and the scientist had been asked to look at it.'

It is difficult to confirm all of Perkins' story. Vice Admiral Sir Hugh Martell admitted to the Royal Commission that there was indeed a great deal of pressure to carry out G2 'because we were nearing the end of the season when the weather would be suitable'. Perkins' description of the winds carrying fallout across mainland Australia tallies with the official account, but the story of the cable has been denied by the senior officers on board *Narvik*. Furthermore, the Prime Minister, Robert Menzies, was not in Australia at the time. However, given the growing restlessness about the tests among the Australians and the fact that G2 did result in more fallout going over the mainland than intended, it would not be unlikely for such a message to emanate from the Acting Prime Minister's office, or perhaps that of the Minister of Supply.

Keith Syder, aboard HMS *Diana* which had sailed through the fallout cloud, recalls that the Australian authorities would not allow the ship to dock at Freemantle 'owing to the fallout over the ship and the fuss about the fallout which had contaminated the coast of Australia'. In the planning records for the Mosaic trials, there is a footnote: 'It was further agreed that in the unlikely event of the ship requiring decontamination beyond her own resources, she should proceed to Singapore and not an Australian port'. Clearly the Australians did not want anything to do with HMS *Diana*, and she sailed on to Singapore.

Australian involvement in the decision making at the Mosaic trials had been strictly limited. The trials were supervised by Penney's second-in-command at Aldermaston, ballistics expert Charles Adams. Penney, still taking an overall supervisory interest, sent a cable from Aldermaston to Adams; 'Strongly advise not showing Safety Committee any significant weapon data, but would not object to their seeing outside of cable to ball in centre section.' This would allow the Australians to see for themselves the size of the weapon but not what was inside – and without knowing the amount of fissile material in the bomb and the way it was packed, it was almost impossible to estimate the yield. Professors Martin and Titterton complained that they did not have enough relevant materials to be able to advise the Australian Government in the way expected of them.

The committee did, however, have the power of veto over the timing of the detonations, even if they were unsure what they were allowing to go off. The Operational Commander, Vice Admiral Sir Hugh Martell, remembers round-the-table discussions between himself, Charles Adams and the Safety Committee. 'They could say: "No, we are not happy. Stop." But at no time did this happen. To my certain knowledge there was no occasion on which they were not unanimous.' And yet considerable uncertainty existed in the weather situation.

British and Australian meteorologists working on weather predictions admit that they were hampered by the lack of data existing for the Monte Bello area, where the atmosphere is dynamic rather than static. Essentially, they were being asked to forecast a period of twenty-four hours when the very infrequent easterly winds would blow the fallout cloud away from mainland Australia, avoiding the generally westerly flow that prevails in the area. It was a well-nigh impossible task, and on both firings, the westerly winds returned sooner than had been forecast, spreading fallout over areas of north-western Australia. The clouds were visible from the ships and from the mainland, and the subsequent furore that developed from the misunderstandings over yield and fallout nearly cost Britain the co-operation of the Australian Government and put the future of the bomb test programme at risk.

The trouble began when someone failed to impress on the Australian Minister of Supply, Howard Beale, that the G2 explosion was to be bigger than the G1. After fallout from the first detonation was detected crossing mainland Australia, Mr Beale assured angry journalists assembled for a press conference that contamination had been negligible and that anyway the next detonation would be smaller! When the mistake was learned, Beale asked Charles Adams whether 'I could suggest a reconciliation of his statement with the facts. What he wanted was to be able to quote that, for example, "the radioactivity was smaller" or "the effects *in any sphere* could be argued to be less than those resulting from G1".' Adams refused. He was quite adamant that he had told the Australian Government that the likely yields for G1 and G2 were to be 20 and 80 kilotons respectively.

Adams did, however, change the safety arrangements for the second test to help disguise the Minister's blunder. In a letter to the Ministry of Supply in August 1956, recalling the incident, Adams says: 'So far as I know there was no reason for Beale's making the statement either at the time he did or on any other occasion. The fact that he did was a slight embarrassment to us because, if the statement had not been made, we should have increased the area of the declared danger area (to warn civil shipping and aviation). We did in fact place greater restrictions on aircraft movements and these were arranged through the Director of Civil Aviation before G2 was fired. The reason that we did not proclaim a larger danger area for shipping, although we searched a larger area, was *that we did not wish to embarrass Beale.*' [our italics]

Although the test organizers had done their best to avert a diplomatic crisis, a further row involving Beale ensued over G2. As the main body of the atomic cloud moved north-east towards Australia some twelve hours after the test explosion, there were fears on the mainland that it would start depositing dangerous levels of fallout over north-western Australia. Beale, 'on the spot' in Woomera, was pressed into making a statement by some fifteen journalists who were there to record the test's progress. Referring to an interim report by the Safety Committee, Beale eventually announced, 'An atomic cloud from the Monte Bello explosion has drifted inland over the coastal regions of West Australia but this information need cause no anxiety. The cloud was tending to drift back towards the coast.' Beale had done it again. The main body of the atomic cloud was indeed moving north-east but it did not, according to official reports, reach the coast. It was the fallout particles at eighteen to thirty thousand feet and not so potentially dangerous that were drifting over Australia. Beale, by confessing to the former, more alarming scenario, had made the situation sound worse than it really was.

Unfortunately for Beale, the journalists chose to ignore 'need cause no anxiety' and ran such banner headlines as: 'A cloud over West Australian coast', 'Radioactive rain reported in North', 'A-dust is danger here' and, more ominously, 'Misgivings over atomic tests'. The UK Ministry of Supply's man in Melbourne, William Wheeler, telegrammed home: 'Something of a panic developed in Australia about 7 pm yesterday when it was reported that an atomic cloud had drifted inland following G2. ... The Commonwealth authorities are now in some difficulty attempting to reconcile the actual situation with the statement released by Mr Beale.'

Clearly, something had to be done about the information reaching the Australian Government in order to avoid further embarrassment and a breakdown in the working relationship between the Commonwealth partners. Wheeler later wrote to a colleague back home: 'It is undoubtedly very difficult for people in the United Kingdom to appreciate how powerful public opinion in Australia is in connection with atomic trials, but it is a fact that on two occasions connected with the Monte Bello tests the pressure on the Government from the press and Opposition was so great that there was real danger they would be obliged to refuse any further tests in Australia. As you may have noticed, political opposition has made the discontinuation of atomic trials one of the main props of its policy.'

Tension in Australia over the test programme had been growing. There had been some anger in Australia when it was discovered that the British, anxious about running out of time, wanted to detonate G2 on 10 June which happened to be a Sunday, and the Australian Government warned Adams and his team that a firing on that day would be most 'unsuitable'. Protests had also been made by the Australian Seamen's Union, expressing concern about ships positioned as far as five hundred miles from the blast. Such were suspicions about the tests that seamen blamed radiation sickness for the death of seventy-five cattle on board a ship that docked at Freemantle in July, though it later transpired that they died of red-water fever transmitted by ticks. Banner-carrying crowds gathered in Perth claiming that the British were using the Australian people as guinea-pigs, and the Opposition Leader, Dr Evatt, demanded a full Government report on the movement of the atomic cloud after G2. Finally in August 1956, a Gallup poll showed sixty per cent of the Australian population against the atomic tests.

It had of course been forecast in the test plans that some radioactive material would fall over mainland Australia, and the Safety Committee had agreed to this. It was up to them to advise the Ministry of Supply and the Prime Minister. With the wisdom of hindsight the test organizers thought that it would have been better for the Australian public to be forewarned and assured that any fallout clouds looming on the horizon were quite 'safe'.

The highest radioactive doses recorded by the air-sampling systems set up by the Weapons Safety Committee for the Mosaic trials at Broome and Port Headland were insignificant. But no provisions had been made for a full radiological survey of the Australian mainland for the Mosaic tests. The sampling system that existed took no account of errant stems and plumes from the fallout clouds, which create the so-called radioactive 'hotspots'. It will thus never be known how much fallout was deposited on the Australian mainland as a result of G1 and G2.

The Weapons Safety Committee suggested a more comprehensive system of air sampling for the next round of bomb tests at Maralinga and the Australian Government accepted the British offer of an experienced press officer. With that, matters were allowed to rest. After all, mistakes had been made by both sides. When Adams and Commodore Martell went to call on the Acting Prime Minister to offer their explanations, he was too busy with the Loans Council to see them and the Acting Secretary Mr Bunting, who saw them instead was, according to the Britons, 'very reasonable and made no real complaint'.

What the Australian Government did not know was that neither G1 nor G2 should have been fired. In cross-examination at the Royal Commission hearings in London, the Royal Navy's predictions man at the time, Mr Matthewman, admitted that there were 'not enough pre-event investigations undertaken' to meet the safety requirements for either test. Furthermore, he agreed that 'it would not have taken much by way of failure of the predicted weather system for G2 to turn very nasty indeed'. The first attendance of the Australian Safety Committee at the tests appeared not to have been a reassurance to Australians that their interests were being looked after.

Chapter Eight

BLACK MIST

In April 1984, leaders of the Pitjantjatjara and Yankunytjatjara Aborigines used the primitive radio station in a van in the back yard of the Pitjantjatjara Council's headquarters in Alice Springs to broadcast news of an important meeting. It was to be a serious gathering in the presence of a white judge, not the get-together of old friends usually announced over the bush radio. The Royal Commission was 'going bush' and would meet them at Wallantinna, about twenty-five miles from Alice Springs in the heart of the Australian desert. Groups of Aborigines started making plans to travel hundreds of miles for the meeting and to make their camp around the Wallantinna homestead for a few days. On the appointed day and with due formality, the judge, Mr Justice James McClelland, his two fellow commissioners, a dozen barristers and a 'press bench' sat in a makeshift open courtroom under an awning at Wallantinna station, with the Aborigines sitting cross-legged before them. When a lizard dodged past the Judge and on to the 'Witness stand', he remarked, 'That's a case for contempt, isn't it?'

Speaking through an interpreter, a Yankunytjatjara elder began telling the Commission his version of events of thirty years ago. 'We heard the bang early in the morning. Before the sun had set we saw a cloud coming. It was different from other clouds. This was in one spot and it was black. Towards late evening it was above us, there was like a sprinkling of rain, it was running down the trunks.' Another witness thought the bang had been made by a water-serpent, a mythical snake which makes noises while it creates waterholes. When the cloud drew near, one old man thought it was an evil spirit, a 'mamu', so he told everyone to shake their woomeras at the cloud to make it change direction. It didn't. Lilly Wallatninna told the Commissioners that she remembered feeling cold as the cloud came over: 'The cloud made the flour, water and tea taste sweet. People got bad eyes. They were vomiting and had diarrhoea. I was sick too. I tried to eat some food but vomited.' Her father was a 'ngangakari', a healer, and she remembers that he made some of the people better but then died himself. Others remembered dogs following the camp to eat the dead.

The legend of the 'Black Mist' goes back a long way. That a black oily cloud passed over them at the time of the first test at Emu has been part of Aboriginal oral history for nearly three decades, but the confusion between the black mist of 1953 and other terrors of Aboriginal folklore, including evil spirits and fatal epidemics, made it easy for the authorities to dismiss. Australian officials took great pains to show that black mist was a product of the imagination of an over-apprehensive people who had been warned of tests in their area and so dreamed up an unnatural phenomenon to explain away their fears. Nonetheless, the myth prevailed and in 1980 white Australian lawyers and doctors began taking an interest in it. They interviewed surviving eye-witnesses and decided that there could be some truth to it. So anxious were the British to clear the matter up that in 1983 the Atomic Weapons Research Establishment commissioned two scientists to examine whether black mist could have happened. Authorities in Australia and Britain were no doubt taken aback when the two scientists reported that it was indeed possible.

During the Royal Commission hearings in London it emerged that the central plume of the fallout cloud from the Totem 1 detonation at Emu could have passed over an Aboriginal community. Furthermore, by adding together a number of 'worst case' possibilities, it was possible that the Aborigines could have been subjected to a radiation dose as high as 80 rems, 160 times the recommended annual dose for members of the public under current standards.

The Commission heard from a white woman who had been camped at a place called Never Never at the time of the test. 'We saw a cloud roughly south-west of us, a very unusual looking cloud. ... It was darkish. It didn't have the compact, rolling look that a rain cloud can have ... the top was most unusual, like a banner that stretched right across the sky.' Dust fell from the cloud and into the family's cooking pots. Ellen Giles, a former station owner in the area now in her seventies, remembers 'a big, coiling, cloud-like thing, like a dust storm'. She and her husband shut up the house, 'but the trees were coated in this oily dust. They withered and died', as did two Aborigine employees on the station and her husband, Philip. All three died of cancer.

Yami Lestor, now Director of the Institute for Aboriginal Development at Alice Springs, was ten years' old at the time Totem 1 was fired. He blames his blindness on the day that he and his family had been engulfed by the cloud. 'I can't say how many died. All I can remember is that we moved camp many, many times after the black mist came. In our culture, we always move camp when someone dies. I know of people who lost parents, husbands, wives, brothers and sisters after the cloud passed over them. Many others have been sick, or have skin or other internal ailments.' By Lestor's own admission, the legend of the black mist has been given extra credibility by the recent publicity given to the test series as a whole: 'Thirty years ago, there was no one to listen to us. We didn't know much about the bomb and no one cared to tell us. People at Wallantina thought it was a water-snake. But now that many Australian and British servicemen are speaking out, we feel that the effects on our people should be made public.'

Lestor's particular disability adds to the confusion as to whether the tests are being used to explain away a personal tragedy or whether Totem 1 did have terrible effects on the Aboriginal people. Blindness and partial blindness are common among them and eye diseases such as trachoma and glaucoma are traditionally blamed as the cause. A survey is now under way to establish whether eye disabilities among Central Australian Aborigines might have been caused by radiation.

That black mist as a phenomenon did happen is now, generally agreed. The descriptions from Aborigines and white eye-witnesses tally with the official reports. One of the meteorologists with the job of checking out the black mist story, Bill Roach, has said that the mist would have been seen as 'a rolling or billowing cloud', its density caused by the action of the blast sucking up debris from the desert and by the heavy radioactive particles contained in the fallout. The cloud 'would have been seen settling on top of the boundary layer and would have stretched from horizon to horizon. ... It would have been a strange and awesome sight. ... A fine drizzle of black particles would also have been noticed.'

It is much harder to establish whether anyone suffered as a result of black mist. Even with what is known today about the possible drift of the cloud and taking the most pessimistic predictions, British scientists argue that the risk of cancer death would only have been in the order of one in three hundred among those affected. In 1980, Dr Tom Cutter of the Alice Springs Aboriginal Health Service claimed that at least thirty and possibly fifty aboriginals have died as a result of contamination, with a further one thousand seriously affected. A year later, a South Australian Health Commission survey into diseases among Aboriginal tribes that might be related to radiation concluded that apart from one small settlement, no higher than an average cancer rate had been detected. Nonetheless, the survey emphasized the difficulty in collecting data and called for a wider investigation.

At the Royal Commission hearings in the bush, the counsel for the Aborigines had to admit that lack of dating methods, medical records and the confusion of various epidemics that hit the Aboriginal communities in the 1950s made it impossible to ask the Commission to link any specific illness with the mist. Instead, the Aborigines asked for an open verdict, and they reminded the Commissioners that the South Australian Government are now carrying out a comprehensive epidemiological survey among Aboriginal tribes. Once its results are known and once specific cases can be studied in civil proceedings, they hope that black mist and its horrific results will be established without doubt. For the time being, the question remains open.

Whether or not Totem 1 caused civilian casualties, it should not have been fired. This much has been admitted by the chief British meteorological forecaster at the site, Edward Siddons, and the test supervisor, Lord Penney. With hindsight, the two men admit that the calculations on fallout were faulty, the weather was unsuitable and the yield was underestimated. In the planning document prepared by the high explosives research team before Totem, the estimated yield was 5 kilotons, whereas in fact it was 10 kilotons. This underestimate undermined the safety margin built into the fallout calculations. Why was their estimate so modest? Siddons explained to the Royal Commission: 'The weapon designers are always rather conservative with respect to what yield they declare for an event beforehand, because very obviously they do not want to be stuck with explaining a failure.'

In attempting to assess the fallout risks, the planners devised two levels: 'A', the 'zero risk' level, at which the quantity of fission products was unlikely to produce any measurable effect on the body; and 'B', the 'slight risk' level, 'which may cause some slight temporary sickness in a small number of people who have a low threshold sensitivity to radiation'. That 'small number of people' referred specifically to Aborigines whose nomadic lifestyle and scant clothing made them particularly vulnerable to fallout. Taking a 'worst case scenario' in which the winds remained constant and the fallout cloud was not dispersed, the estimate was that the 'slight risk' level would extend along a narrow path between fifty and one hundred miles from ground zero. The 'zero risk' level would extend from there out. Since the nearest population centre, that is the fifty or so Aborigines at Wallantina, was reported to be a little over a hundred miles away there was, 'on the face of it, no risk to any civilian settlement'.

The basis on which levels A and B were calculated would not now be tolerated by radiation protection standards. Level A was defined as the degree of contamination that would lead to a maximum dose of 3 rems over ten weeks, which compares with the current limit for a member of the public of 0.5 rems a year. And 3 rems was considered the 'zero risk' dose. For level B, the 'slight risk' area, the radiation dose was defined as 25 rems. It is now generally agreed that a person runs a risk of suffering long-term damage from the effects of radiation after exposure to 5 rems.

Penney arrived at his figures by drawing on what he knew of the American experience but since the Americans were not supposed to be telling the British about their tests, he had to make assumptions. Penney explains that he used a 'large-scale map of Nevada', the area where the Americans were currently testing their bombs, and noted that the nearest 'fairly big town was seventy miles away'. He then compared the American geography with the Australian, and noted that at Emu, the 'nearest sheep farm or little community was well over one hundred miles away'. Assuming that the Americans were abiding by the international safety regulations, he surmised that a 'slight risk' area that began at a hundred miles was safe.

Penney was asked at the Royal Commission hearings whether he took any steps to satisfy himself that the Americans had got it right? He replied: 'All I could do was to look for reports of trouble, people making rush visits. There was no such sugges-tion anywhere and they let off – again guessing – twenty or thirty atom bombs a year or so in that site. So, they must have been putting a lot of contamination down quite close.'

There may have been no fuss in America at the time but there has been a great deal since. In May 1984, a federal judge held the United States Government liable for the deaths of nine people who were exposed to fallout from the Nevada bomb tests. All the victims had lived in towns in Utah, Nevada and Arizona, up to two hundred miles from the test site. The judge awarded the victims $2.6 million. Over a thousand more plaintiffs, suing on behalf of 375 cancer victims, are awaiting a decision on their claims. The judgment made legal history as the first time civilians have won compensation over the effects of low-level radiation.

Whatever the American experience was supposed to prove in 1953, scientists today admit that the plans for the Totem trials underestimated the effects of fallout by a factor of three. Their calculations, as it turned out, were based on inadequate data. Siddons explained: 'The Totem explosions were the first occasion from which the Atomic Weapons Research Establishment obtained any real data on fallout; very little was obtained from Hurricane, for example. Of course the immediate reaction of the scientists given that data was to check it out with what was predicted and to attempt to improve the methods of prediction. That was done during the two years or so after Totem and before the next Australian trials.' But not in time for those unfortunate enough to stray into the fallout area from Totem.

Furthermore, that 'worst case scenario' did prevail at the Totem 1 firing. There was practically no wind shear and the fallout drifted in a narrow, cohesive, cigar-shaped plume. Scientists today concede that the 'slight risk' zone should have been extended to one hundred and seventy miles, sixty miles beyond Wallantina station.

How did those in charge at the Totem firings evaluate the risks? The counsel at the Royal Commission hearings. Peter

McClellan, put it to Lord Penney: 'You should not have been firing any weapon until you were absolutely sure no-one was in danger. Is that not right?' Penney replied, 'Well, if you take that argument in terms of what we know are risks, no atomic weapon should ever have been fired.' Siddons, however, was prepared to admit to negligence among the test team. In the light of the assumptions and calculations made by the test's planners, he said, 'I believe that it was unduly risky to proceed with Totem 1 at the time it was fired. ... If I had been asked at the time, my advice would have been not to run the risk. That is not to say that the outcome, I believe, caused any harm to anyone.'

The Royal Commission tried to establish whether the test organizers had been under pressure: in the minutes of a meeting between Penney and Butement of the Australian Department of Supply in 1953, the former mentioned 'rushing the Totem trials.' When asked if he had 'any recollection of the Emu trials being rushed?', Penney replied: 'This is semantics. We were in the Cold War situation and the pressure was on us to do the job. Is that being rushed or not? You can be safe and rushed. I did not say we were so rushed that we were not safe.'

After the Totem trials, the Atomic Test Safety Committee, made up of British and Australian experts, reassessed the sensitivity of the Aboriginal people to fallout. In a minute of a meeting in 1956, the Committee records the results of a study of the possible effects of fallout on Aborigines 'living in their tribal state, i.e. virtually naked and with bare feet'. The study concluded 'that the permissible levels of contamination are reduced by a factor of about five in the case of the tribal native, which means that for a nominal burst (maximum 20 kilotons) the acceptable level would occur at a distance of about 240 miles from ground zero'. That it twice the distance the 'no risk' area extended for the Totem tests at Emu. Questioned at the Royal Commission hearings, Penney claimed that he was never told of this revision of risk assessment and for the remainder of the test series the rule that the 'no risk' zone should begin at about a hundred miles prevailed.

The 'Aboriginal problem' existed for the rest of the test programme, particularly after the permanent testing site at Maralinga became operational in 1956. Quite reasonably, Penney believed that the problem was an Australian responsibility. He was there to specify 'safe' and 'risk' zones and it must be up to the Australian patrol officers, who knew the area, to enforce them. The problem was a huge one, involving surveying thousands of miles of outback for people who had perfected the techniques of blending with the landscape and avoiding patrol officers. The test areas bordered and in some cases crossed tribal reserve areas and straddled the main Aboriginal tracks from central Australia down to the coast.

The Chief Patrol Officer, Walter McDougall, almost went to pieces under the strain. He reported to his superiors at the Ministry of Supply that Aborigines were deliberately avoiding any contact with his officers. He told them that he was worried about the possible effect of fallout on the native people and that the Government's treatment of them was a 'first-class scandal. We might as well declare war on them.' The chief scientist at the Department of Supply, William Butement, who played a key liaison role between the British test organizers and the Australian back-up teams, claimed in a memo to a colleague that McDougall was 'placing the affairs of a handful of natives above those of the British Commonwealth of nations. The joint project has been agreed between the two Governments. These decisions having been taken at a very high level, it behoves all of us to implement them.' McDougall's opinions were 'out of step with those of the times and the sooner he realised his loyalty the sooner his state of mind will be clarified'.

The patrolling problems included staffing and equipment. For example, in September 1956, the records show that a man was detailed to co-ordinate the control of natives in the Maralinga area, but according to one official 'he informs me that he has no experience of dealing with Aborigines, that he has no knowledge of the roads, tracks or country'. In a subsequent exchange of messages, it turned out that the appointment was made because the South Australian Aborigine Protection Board needed to have an officer of the department in the area, whether or not appropriately qualified.

Extra patrol officers were drafted into the test areas when it was known that a corroboree was planned, in order to prevent Aborigines from crossing into the test area on their way to or from the gathering, but according to the range reports, one officer, Robert Macauley, was sent on such a mission without transport or a radio and so 'no guarantee can be given that the natives have not moved, or are not moving, out of the area for which he is responsible'. Macauley told the Royal Commission hearings in Melbourne that while he was patrolling before one test firing he spent at least four days sitting on a rock because of flooding, and when asked whether he had been able to do any effective patrolling, he replied, 'To my recollection, none whatsoever.'

In addition to the patrols carried out, or perhaps not, by range officers, there was a back-up survey service by the RAF and RAAF. Air Vice Marshal 'Paddy' Menaul, who was Air Task Force Commander at Maralinga, has become something of a celebrity for his remarks on Aboriginal people, which seem to Australians to summarize the attitudes of the British imperialist. He first made his mark during an ABC radio current affairs programme in 1980 when he was asked whether any Aborigine could have strayed into the test area. 'This is of course nonsense. We rounded up the Aborigines and took them to a safe place ... and when the tests were over, and the radiation levels had subsided, they were allowed back into their own particular areas, and they went walk-about again.'

Menaul was questioned in greater depth at the Royal Commission hearings. Asked why he only carried out air surveys every three or four days, he said: 'They were not necessary to carry out every day. Aborigines do not travel a hundred miles a day, I am afraid. They sleep most afternoons. If you had searched the area on Wednesday, you would not really expect to search it on Thursday.' This proved too much for Justice McClelland, who recited to the Air Vice Marshal the rhyme, 'I saw a man upon the stairs, a little man who was not there; he was not there again today, I wish to God he'd go away.' The judge then asked him whether he might have had any difficulty seeing Aborigines in the bush. 'Oh no', replied Menaul, 'for example, I went out looking for dingoes and it was easy to see them. I even saw emus." The judge: 'There is a difference, you know, between a dingo and an Aborigine.' 'Very much so', said the Air Vice Marshal, 'but since they [Aborigines] wear very little clothing, they might look exactly the same. But we never saw any.'

There is no reference in the official records to the likely social upheaval caused to the Aboriginal people by the 'rounding-up' operation described by the Air Vice Marshal. One can only speculate on the distress of enforced eviction from traditional Aboriginal tribal lands and relocation in missions and settlements. One graphic description of the events was given in Wallantinna by Mrs Darlene Stevens, who was twelve years old when she and five members of her family were found by two patrol officers in 1953. She said they were told to walk to an Aboriginal mission in Cundeelee in West Australia, over a hundred miles away. They were not offered transport or food or water for the journey and she told the Commission that they had to leave her mother to die in the desert.

It comes as no surprise that there were many sightings of Aborigines in the test area, some officially documented, some not. The official reports tell of four sightings of Aboriginal groups, all before 1957. The veterans tell of about ten occasions when they spotted Aborigines on the range, five of them after 1957, and Clifford Tomlinson tells of seeing three groups of Aborigines during the month of August 1957 alone. On his first day in the RAF catering corps at Maralinga, Tomlinson was taken on a tour of the bomb sites by an Australian captain who told him not to go near the bomb craters because they were 'still very hot. We've got to keep an eye open. The Abos like camping in these craters.' A week later, Tomlinson claims he saw a family of Aborigines at the police post at Maralinga. 'They were in the company of a number of security personnel, who seemed quite busy with them.' Two weeks later, he saw three Aborigines at the Watson security post – 'They were with two security officers' – and about ten days later, Tomlinson claims he saw an Aboriginal man walking towards the Watson railway line. All these Aborigines were well within the prohibited zone.

The most sensational incident was in May 1957 when two hundred soldiers were allegedly threatened with court martial and the possibility of a firing squad if they told anyone about an Aboriginal family found camped in a highly radioactive bomb crater. The story was told to the Royal Commission in Melbourne by a former lance-corporal, John Hutton. He said he was in a caravan about to put on protective clothing for work in a 'dirty area' around the Marcoo test site where a bomb had been tested seven months earlier, when he saw a young Aboriginal man. He, his wife and two naked children had apparently been camping in the crater for two days. They had drunk water collected from the bottom of the crater which had tasted unpleasant and they were looking for water from the caravan.

According to Hutton's account, only four or five men witnessed the incident but two hundred men were assembled and addressed by a British officer. 'He said to us what had happened today we had not seen' and that 'the person who let this out to the papers, or press or Parliament, would be tried for treason.' He then reminded them that they had all signed the Official Secrets Act. Those who broke the rules could face thirty years' imprisonment or the firing squad. The account of the incident in the official records differs substantially. We are told that the family did not camp in the crater, but 'had walked across 1.6 km of contaminated ground' and that the boy showed a 'trivial' degree of contamination and was duly showered.

One member of the Aborigine family concerned, Mrs Eddie Milpuddle, gave evidence to the Royal Commission sitting at Wallantinna station. She said that the family had been walking the 250 miles from Mimili to Ooldea Mission, south of Maralinga, not knowing that the mission had been closed on account of the tests. They had been found in an area where they had camped, a place 'where there had been smoke', and she described how soldiers had run an instrument that 'clicked' over her body and gave her a shower and clothes. In a private meeting with Justice McClelland and commissioner Mrs Jill Fitch, Mrs Milpuddle told them that she had given birth to a still-born baby soon after the incident. Her next child died at the age of two with a brain tumour.

More tales of threats have come from Australian veteran Kevin Woodlands, who also came across a group of Aborigines in May 1957. An army sapper at the time, he and a group of Australian servicemen and British scientists were dressed in protective clothing when an Aborginal family approached them, the man holding out a billy-can for water. 'They were thick with dust and we realized they had to be radioactive. We ran a geiger counter over them. The readings were frightening. We radioed back to base and a group of scientists came out to help. We tried to explain that they needed showers, but it was difficult. The girl was wearing a potato sack, and when we tried to get it off her the bloke got angry. He thought we were trying to assault her or something.' Woodlands remembers that they put them through the special decontamination showers they had in their caravans about seven or eight times. 'No one said they were all right after that. They were put in a truck and they disappeared very quickly.'

Woodlands and the rest of the group were told not to talk

about the incident. When we interviewed him in Queensland, he told us that he had been so enraged by Air Vice Marshal Sir Stewart Menaul's claim on Australian radio that all the Aborigines had been 'rounded up' to safety and that none had been in the radioactive areas that he disobeyed the order to keep quiet and spoke out. He also told us that his wife had received threatening telephone messages telling him not to say any more about the Aborigines.

Several veterans claim that they found Aborigines close to the testing areas during the highly contaminating 'minor trials' testing period that lasted from 1957 until 1963. Fewer servicemen were required for these tests and so many of the routine patrols and air surveys were run down, although these trials spread dangerous particles of plutonium and cobalt over the South Australian desert. Patrick Connolly, a former RAAF corporal, claims that in 1961 he drove his commanding officer to a side in a radioactive area where four Aboriginal bodies had been found. 'I was told to stay in the jeep but from where I was I could see four black huddled shapes on the ground.' He remembers that the officer who found the bodies was extremely upset. He had previously complained about the easy access to the range. Connolly first told the story to the press in 1980 and he too, he claims, has been threatened. He told the Royal Commission hearings in Perth that two Australian security men told him that he would be deported if he went on telling his story.

Another veteran, John Burke, gave a deathbed interview to ABC televison telling how, as a former senior technician with the RAAF, he found the bodies of four Aborigines in a bomb crater after one of the 'minor trials' in 1963. He decided to speak out because he believed he was dying of stomach cancer as a result of his exposure to radiation in 1963. It was Burke's deathbed statement that first drew attention to the whole series of hitherto secret tests that were carried out in Maralinga after the last major test series in 1957.

There are several other reported sightings – of Aborigines

camped in craters, of bodies and of groups just wandering on to the range. As Clifford Tomlinson remembers, 'My impression was that it was very easy to get in and out of the range. In our introductory lecture to Maralinga we were told never to leave the roads or they would not find us. For the same reason I think it would have been very hard to find Aborigines.'

The official reports remain vague about specific incidents and have nothing to say on the more sensational sightings mentioned above. Nonetheless, the official records of the Australian Ionising Radiation Advisory Council leave the matter open, concluding in their report on 'Aboriginal Welfare': 'It is evident that strenuous attempts were made to prevent the entry of Aborigines into hazardous areas, and although it would clearly be impossible to affirm that such an intrusion never took place, it seems most unlikely that any Aborigines were present elsewhere than the fringes of the Prohibited Area at the firing times and in the period following them.'

Chapter Nine

FIELD OF THUNDER

The bomb test programme in the late 1950s proceeded at a great pace. During the summer of 1956, while building equipment was being delivered to Christmas Island to set up a thermonuclear test base there, the bulldozers and cement mixers were moving out of the new testing site in Australia at Maralinga. The name is Aboriginal, meaning 'Field of Thunder', but the Australian Government preferred to call it the 'Los Alamos of the Commonwealth'. The multi-million pound 'atomic city' in the heart of the south-western Australian desert was to serve as a testing base for the British for seven years.

The Australian public were carefully coaxed into accepting the idea of a permanent atomic bomb testing site on the mainland. The test planners recognized that the Mosaic trials on the Monte Bello islands in 1956 had been a public relations disaster and efforts were afterwards made to supply the Australian press with numerous articles on the safety and importance of the test programme. Professor Titterton wrote a series entitled 'Why A-test sites are in Australia', and even Howard Beale, was mustered to write his own explanation. He began with the declaration: 'Atomic weapons are absolutely essential to the survival of Great Britain and the Commonwealth.' Care was taken to present the permanent test site to the public as a joint venture by the two Governments, a fiction which the British Government was quite happy for Beale to promote in public, though since the British were footing the bill for the

One that went wrong: Mosaic G2. The largest of the Australian tests spread fallout over mainland Australia (*official photo*).

Montebello. *Top:* Admiral Torlesse and Dr Penney admire Britain's first atomic explosion from on board *HMS Narvik* (*Associated Press*). *Left:* Scientists go ashore after the explosion (*official photo*). *Bottom:* The view from the deck on board *HMS Campania*. Seconds afterwards, men are ordered to turn and face the blast (*Associated Press*).

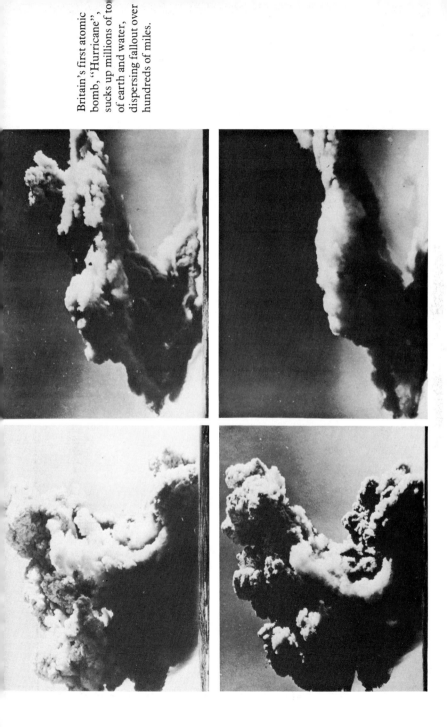

Britain's first atomic bomb, "Hurricane", sucks up millions of tons of earth and water, dispersing fallout over hundreds of miles.

Top: Black Mist. It would have been seen as a "rolling or billowing cloud" as it passed over Aboriginal settlements (*Associated Press*).
Bottom: Royal Commissioner, Justice James McClelland goes walkabout with Aboriginal witnesses, Wallantinna, April 1985 (*The Adelaide Advertiser*).

Top: "Sniffer" teams in action. Men of the Active Handling Unit remove radioactive samples brought from the nuclear cloud by Canberra jets.
Left: "Noddy" suit (*Colonel P. A. Lowe*).
Below: Vapour trails of Canberra sniffer planes entering the mushroom cloud (*Associated Press*).

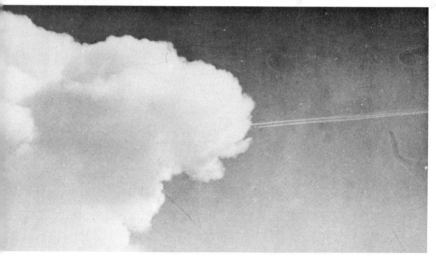

Tight security at the Maralinga range (*Ray Jones*).

Ground zero: The remains of a Land Rover and generator at Christmas Island (*taken illicitly*).

Christmas Island, a
Pacific Paradise.
Top: The good life
(*Wally Rainbow*).
Middle: Christmas at
Christmas Island
(*Wally Rainbow*).
Bottom: "Tent
City", Main Camp
(*Wally Rainbow*).

Left: Britain joins the Megaton club. The first successful Thermonuclear test in 1958 *(official photo)*.
Top Right: The moment of detonation.

An "H" bomb airburst off Christmas Island *(official photo)*.
Below Right: A low-yield "trigger" on Christmas Island.
Although an "airburst", it has sucked up large quantities of
d bris from the surr nd *(offici l h to)*.

enterprise there was no doubt in their minds who would retain control.

Australian servicemen and civilian back-up teams were, however, to be more involved at Maralinga than at any of the previous trials. The Australian Government was keen for her servicemen to have the experience and she had her own programme of 'field trials' to be carried out at each detonation. It is estimated that about ten thousand Australian servicemen and civilians passed through Maralinga. At the planning stage, the legal situation arising out of possible claims from Australians caught in the fallout area was looked at for the first time. It was agreed that the Australian government would take responsibility for any Australians who were on the test site at their request, that is, 'distinguished visitors, scientific observers, troops, civil defence trainees or others present for indoctrination purposes'. Claims from Australians who were in the test area at the request of Britain or who were caught in the fallout zone inadvertently should be the responsibility of the British Government. The latter group would include Aborigines.

After the mishaps over the firings at Emu and Monte Bello, the Australian Atomic Weapons Test Safety Committee was careful to be seen flexing its muscles over the forthcoming series at Maralinga. In their submission to the Australian Government, the members admitted that it would be impossible to prevent radioactivity from falling on the mainland: radioactive fallout from all the detonations would cross half the Australian continent before drifting out to sea. They warned the Government of the 'political difficulties that can arise from the detection of small quantities of fallout in the outback or elsewhere even when this does not involve a health hazard'. Their job, they said, was to ensure that none of this activity should cause any harm. They noted that for the previous tests no firm agreement on dosage levels had ever existed between the two Governments and for Maralinga, they asked that the low, Level A, fallout criteria should be strictly adhered to in any area that might include Aborigines, to ensure that no Australian national should be affected by radiation.

Whatever the Safety Committee's precautionary advice, the Australian Government was not losing its appetite for the tests. Menzies was said to be most put out when he learned that the Canadians had asked the British to build their permanent test site in Canada and that negotiations had opened between the Commonwealth Office and the Canadian Government. The Australian Government quickly assured the British that any local difficulties that had arisen over the Mosaic and Emu trials would not be repeated. And, if anyone should be in any doubt about the Australian Government's enthusiasm, Beale issued a statement designed to silence the doubters once and for all: the Maralinga set-up 'is a challenge to Australian men to show that the pioneering spirit of their forefathers who developed our country is still the driving force of achievement. The whole project is a striking example of inter-Commonwealth co-operation on the grand scale. England has the bomb and the know-how; we have the open spaces, much technical skill and a great willingness to help the Motherland. Between us, we shall build the defence of the free world, and make historic advances in harnessing the forces of nature.'

Work began on the Maralinga range during the summer of 1956. The site lies on the southern edge of the Great Australian Desert, three hundred miles west of Woomera and five hundred miles from Adelaide, flat limestone country interspersed with sparse desert vegetation. Its major advantage over Emu was its nearness to a small railway station, Watson, fifty miles to the south on the main transcontinental Perth to Adelaide railway. Prefabricated buildings to house hundreds of scientists and servicemen, and scientific equipment had to be imported from Britain. Building materials had to be transported there for offices, laboratories, cook-houses, a mess, a cinema and even an Olympic-size swimming pool. Sewerage, electricity and refrigeration amenities were laid on. Water bores were sunk.

The British Government paid the Kwinana Construction Company, a British firm, over £5 million for the job.

Miraculously, the site was ready by its August 1956 target date. Kwinana had had no difficulty in persuading one thousand men to work a six-day week for between $30 and $35 plus keep. A large proportion of them were new to Australia and the inhospitable country around Maralinga was their first sight of their new home. They complained about the climate and the lack of fresh water and fresh food, complaints that were to be echoed by the task force which arrived the following year and led to a former Royal Navy surgeon being brought out from the UK as range doctor. The men suffered from extreme changes in temperature, ranging from below 40 degrees on winter nights to anything up to 130 degrees in the midday sun. Above all, there was the dust. Contract workers and servicemen alike remember the Maralinga dust that got into food, clothes, bed-linen, everywhere.

The tests at Maralinga were to continue the development of the 'Blue Danube' nuclear warhead that the ballistics experts at Aldermaston had been working on since the first Hurricane test at Monte Bello. It was being modified and tested for intended attachment to an air-launched cruise missile, 'Blue Steel', and to a ballistic missile, 'Blue Streak'. The first, 'Buffalo', tests at Maralinga involved two tower-bursts, one groundburst and one air-drop, and the series was again supervised by Sir William Penney. For each test, the devices were modified to explore the varying power of the warhead and to test its operational efficiency as a small-yield weapon. The most significant test was without doubt the air-drop, from a Valiant aircraft, the first time Blue Danube would be tried in a tactical context. With that test, on 11 October 1956, Britain was able to prove that she could use her atomic weapon know-how in an operational context. Britain was armed for nuclear war.

The airburst was small in terms of yield, just 1.5 kilotons, and because the explosion was high in the atmosphere it caused no local fallout. The tower-bursts for the first and third trials were much larger, 15 and 10 kilotons respectively, and because they were at ground level, the risks from fallout were greater. Penney was determined to proceed with great caution in order to prove to the Australian public that safety was uppermost in everyone's minds. The long-term future of Maralinga as a permanent testing site was at stake. After an angry debate in the Australian Parliament over the Mosaïc fiasco, the Labor Opposition had stated that their aim was to suspend all atom bomb tests. Also prompted by the stand taken by the seamen earlier in the year, Australia's biggest union, the Australian Workers' Union, had called for an immediate ban on atomic bomb testing in Australia.

Standby for the first test, code-named One Tree, began on 11 September 1956 although the firing did not take place until more than two weeks later. Meteorologists found the job of predicting winds at Maralinga just as difficult as it had been at Monte Bello. There were violent fluctuations in the wind patterns over the test range but it was necessary to predict winds that would carry the cloud in an easterly, northerly or westerly direction for at least twenty-four hours to avoid contaminating the Maralinga village and Watson station that lay to the south. Penney was extremely wary of firing the first test if there was the remotest possibility of trouble. In a telegram marked 'top secret' sent by Penney back to Aldermaston after the sixth aborted test firing, he asked, 'Grateful advise if my number one priority not to prejudice future of Maralinga is correct'. He explained that they had missed a firing opportunity the previous evening when the Australian Safety Committee had advised against it because there was a chance that fallout being carried east over Australia might have been brought down by the rainfalls forecast over Adelaide and Melbourne. Penney believed that the amount of radioactive contamination in such an incident would be negligible and the decision to call off the firing was for political and not safety reasons. 'Am asking Safety

Committee to get Beale and Menzies approached to accept political disturbance due to counts in rainwater magnified by troublemakers'.

Clearly Penney was frustrated by what he saw as purely cosmetic delays. And so were the fifteen thousand servicemen and scientists assembled for the test. Chapman Pincher, at the range for the *Daily Express*, wrote that the strain of being on constant standby was telling on everyone. All were suffering from a complaint called the 'Maralinga miseries'. According to Pincher, the 'browned-off' soldiers and airmen had composed a new theme song, entitled 'Pining for the Mushroom Cloud':

In the Maralinga scrub, where there aint a decent pub
We're just sitting waiting for a weather change.
For Bill Penney to decree that the wind is southerly
And will keep the fall-out well north of the range.
Each night as our hopes fade remote from Adelaide,
Where the life seems really lush and really loud,
We all know to our sorrow we'll be more browned off tomorrow,
Oh, we're pining for the mushroom cloud.
We'll qualify for pensions by the time they've settled dissensions,
For the safety men are asking for perfection.
The scientists will prattle if their geiger counters rattle
And the Socialists might win the next election.

After eleven aborted countdowns, One Tree was finally fired in the evening of 27 September. Seven minutes after the detonation and as the mushroom cloud could be seen billowing over the desert, two Canberras flew in to collect samples. Only minutes later, seventy-five scientists, wearing all-white protective suits and respirators, could be seen making their way towards the crater to recover their recording equipment. They in turn gave the 'safe' signal to 250 British, Australian and

Canadian officers of the 'indoctrination force' who had watched the blast from trenches just five miles from ground zero. The officers went forward to examine the vast collection of tanks, planes, guns, radar sets and general paraphernalia of modern warfare that had been deliberately strewn about in the blast area. Scientists from the Medical Research Council then joined them to collect the goats who had been tethered inside air-raid shelters. Further out, sheep, rabbits and mice were awaiting inspection.

Technically, the firing had been a success but, despite all the precautions, it took place in unsafe weather conditions. As with the Mosaic trials, the decision to fire was only taken after consultation with British and Australian meteorologists and with the agreement of the Australian Safety Committee. According to the weather forecast one hour before detonation, the fallout would extend what the test planners called the 'slight risk' dose, that is, level B, over Coober Pedy, an opal mining town 170 miles away. The radiation dose corresponding to level B was 25R, very high by today's standards. During the Royal Commission hearings it was put to Lord Penney: 'Coober Pedy, of course, as you knew at the time, was a centre of Australian population . . . it is a town, in other words.' 'Yes', said Penney, 'not many people though were there.'

In fact, wind sheer after the detonation dispersed the worst of the fallout and the recorded fallout dose for Coober Pedy in the six months after One Tree was calculated as .087R for someone spending most of their time in the open. This was one of the highest recorded doses for early fallout on the mainland during the entire test period, although it is not in excess of today's dose limits for the public. The test projections had, however, allowed for higher doses and Lord Penney was asked at the Royal Commission hearings whether he and his advisers had taken a calculated gamble on the possibility of spreading measurable fallout over the town of 'not many people'. In cross-examination, Penney fell back on a frequent riposte during the

Commission hearings, 'I don't remember'. On paper, he agreed that it looked as if One Tree should not have been fired but he didn't remember whether wind sheer and sudden changes in weather had also entered their calculations. He denied that the decision to fire had been influenced by the pressures of the eleven aborted firings and the danger of falling behind in the test programme.

On the test range itself, elaborate precautions were taken against accidental exposure. Two prohibited areas, stretching 140 miles to the north and to the east and west of Maralinga village, were designated by the Australian Government, and no firing was made without a 'head count'. This was quite easily done as nearly every individual on the range was 'invited' to watch each detonation, enabling the health and safety officers to check the lists as the men stood with their backs to the direction of the blast. After the detonations, there was a control procedure to ensure against unauthorized entry to the forward test areas. The 'danger areas' were cordoned off with yellow tape and entry was monitored by a health control point. As at all the tests, anyone who was likely to be exposed to radiation from one of the tests or who had a job within a radioactive area was issued with a film badge or personal dosemeter. Responsibility for personal dosemetry lay with the British health physics teams from High Explosive Research, later the Atomic Weapons Research Establishment. Overall responsibility for range safety and security lay with the British during the test periods, and between tests the Australian Range Commandant took over control.

Despite the apparent infallibility of the procedure on paper, most veterans remember the atmosphere on the range as being very relaxed. With more than two thousand servicemen and civilians present at any one time, there were bound to be exceptions to the rules. As with the armada that set out for the Monte Bello Islands four years previously, few of the conscript task force remember getting a proper briefing on the tests or the hazards. 'It was a great adventure that nobody took very seriously', one veteran told the Royal Commission. 'Amongst the servicemen it was considered funny rather than serious if somebody became contaminated', said another. One remembers being told he was being sent to Australia on 'general duties'. 'By the time of the first test everyone knew what was the purpose of our being there but there had been no official announcement. There were still no lectures about safety or about the mechanics of the bomb or the after-effects of radiation. I did not know at the time that radiation could be dangerous. There was no attempt made to explain any details of what was going on.'

Out of ignorance or sheer boredom, servicemen went sightseeing and collected 'souvenirs'. A veteran remembers going into the forward area, without protective clothing, to clear up and recover the dummies that had been placed in battledress near ground zero. He and several others kept the battledress and a pair of boots 'and wore them because they were very good working gear'. Several veterans' accounts tell of borrowing Land Rovers for tourist expeditions to view the bomb craters at ground zero. After watching one detonation from the 'forward area' five miles from ground zero, an RAF flight commander and three men challenged a group of Australians to race back to camp. The Australians rushed off in cars, while the British took a helicopter and played at 'buzzing' the Australians until the helicopter's hydraulics failed and they crash-landed in the bush. An officer arriving on the scene warned them to get out quickly because 'it was a bloody hot area', and there was the usual joking, 'That is ten years off your sex life, lad.'

As with all the tests, there are stories of film badges not being issued or not being read and of dosemeters not working properly. The most startling allegation of deliberate negligence has come from Australian Doug Rickard who in 1983 told the press that he and his colleagues deliberately faked personal radiation readings. He was a member of the health physics team supplied by the Australian Department of Supply at Maralinga and he claimed that the dosemeters issued to hundreds of servicemen did not work because the batteries were flat. 'We faked the results', said Rickard. They estimated the amount of radiation that they thought an individual had been subjected to and recorded an appropriate figure. 'I shudder now when I think what went on. We were all so naive.' Senior members of the British health physics team who supervised Rickard at Maralinga have denied the allegations.

The detonations themselves were the highlights for the servicemen in the boring routine of range life. There were always more than the required number of volunteers ready to go to the 'forward area', generally between four and ten miles from ground zero. Men at base camp remember the volunteers returning proudly displaying their red necks, scorched by their closeness to the blast. The night-time detonation during the second 'Antler' test series at Maralinga in 1957 proved the most spectacular and frightening. 'The brightness of the flash was incredible. It gave the impression of a giant cinemascope screen narrowing in towards the middle.' For one group, the experience was more alarming than for most. The assembled men had been told by their officer that when the countdown reached ten they should turn round, close their eyes and cover them with their hands. 'We were all standing facing the blast and when the officer got to seventeen the explosion happened. There was an absolutely blinding flash. I placed my hands over my eyes and turned away. I thought, "Bloody hell, am I blinded?"'

At the second test in the Buffalo series, one RAAF sergeant remembers standing with British personnel less than two miles from ground zero. They pushed their fists into their eyes to avoid being blinded by the blast and when they opened their eyes they saw dozens of blinded rabbits around them. 'Half of my team were so terrified they turned and ran. The rest of us didn't move, but only because we were petrified.' Another veteran described the panic that followed the last detonation, a balloon-suspended blast, in the Antler series. According to his

account, the wind suddenly changed direction after the detonation and the order was given over the tannoy system to
evacuate north base, the forward observation post about three
miles from ground zero. 'Fortunately, the wind resumed its
original direction and everyone relaxed, although the civilians
had been taken back to the village rather quickly.'

The second test at Maralinga, code-named Marcoo, is famous
for the introduction of the 'Commonwealth Indoctrination
Force', the group of Australian, British and Canadian officers
who stood just over one mile from the blast to get real
experience of nuclear war. They were all middle-ranking officers
with good career prospects who could be sent back to their
regiments as visible proof that there was life for the conventional soldier after a nuclear attack. They were under cover,
wearing protective clothing, and after the detonation they
moved forward to ground zero to inspect the weapon debris.
They were positioned upwind of the fallout and were exposed
only to residual ionising radiation as they walked into the
ground zero area. It was nonetheless a risky exercise which the
army considered worthwhile for the valuable experience gained.
According to the Army Research Group's report, 'The value of
live indoctrination at a nuclear weapon test was considerable',
and the exercise should be repeated wherever possible. The 'indoctrinees' had assured their senior officers that there was 'no
substitute for the real thing' and as a result of their experience,
they were more likely to choose an atomic missile as the weapon
'for a blitz on the enemy four miles behind their front lines'
than they had been before.

One mile back from the 'frontline' Indoctrination Force,
there was another group dressed variously in 'battledress serge',
'gaberdine combat suits' and 'cotton khaki drill'. (All three
groups were wearing, the official records assure us, Atomic
Weapons Research Establishment combination underwear.) The
operation was designed to test whether conventional battledress
was adequate for nuclear war. After the detonation, the group

of men wearing cotton khaki drill were, for example, instructed to 'crawl in the accepted military manner for a total distance of thirty yards and carry out the rest of their march in bushy areas to ensure that as much contamination as possible gets on their clothes'.

A former RAAF Air-Commodore indoctrinee, Keith Therkelsen, has claimed that he and his colleagues learned nothing significant by being so close to the blast. He and about forty others were part of the second indoctrination force who stood in the open and without protective clothing just under two miles from the explosion. He said he was not so worried about being close to the explosion as about the cloud and fallout coming in the group's direction. He watched with alarm the random way in which equipment was carried from ground zero to the checkpoint and only then 'someone decided whether it was too hot or not to take away. There was this time pressure to get things done in a hurry'.

A further experiment was carried out to test the battle-worthiness of a tank and its crew after being exposed to an atomic explosion within two miles of them. Four officers, one of them Lieutenant Colonel John Willett Reid, climbed into the Centurion with strict instructions not to open any of the hatches until well after the blast. 'Sitting in the gunner's seat, I put both my hands over the gunsight and my major recollection of the explosion was that the flash was so bright that I saw the bones of my hands as if in an X-ray. After the flash I watched the mushroom cloud expand through the gunsight until the maximum elevation of the gun was achieved. We then (contrary to instructions) opened the hatches and after a short time a large lump of rock landed a hundred yards from us and four people very quickly closed their hatches again.'

Proximity to the blast of a different kind was experienced by the crew of the Valiant who carried out the first air-drop of an atomic bomb at the third test at Maralinga. Unlike many of the other tests, the drop took place on the scheduled day, 10

October, though because the upper winds began to veer, it was necessary to bring the schedule forward by one hour. The airfield was almost deserted as the crew left and there was a tense silence in the cockpit until the countdown and the bomb aimer reported calmly, 'Bombs away'. The Group Captain, Air Vice Marshal 'Paddy' Menaul, remembers, 'There was a slight bump as the weapon left the aircraft, but otherwise nothing unusual. But immediately the bomb was released, the crew had to carry out a pre-planned manoeuvre to take the aircraft clear of the weapon at the instant of detonation, at the same time counting down the seconds for the time of the fall, hoping that on the last one a blinding flash would signal a successful explosion. It did.'

For the RAF, the air-drop at Maralinga was the climax of the Australian trials. Most of the RAF men moved on to Christmas Island for the final test series, but the tests on the Maralinga range continued for another six years. After the four detonations of the Buffalo series, came the three Antler tests, two of them tower-bursts and the third suspended from a balloon. The object of these three was to improve the yield to weight ratio of the nuclear explosions and so develop a trigger for the thermonuclear warhead, 'Red Beard', a weapon which could be carried by the new V-bombers and which was to be tested at Christmas Island.

The test organizers and the Australian Safety Committee were particularly enthusiastic about the use of the balloon. The weapon was the biggest of the three in the Antler series, with a yield of 24 kilotons, but by suspending it from a system of three balloons held at a thousand feet over the desert, there was a considerable reduction in both the 'close-in' and 'long-range' fallout and the method was used for the two trigger tests at Christmas Island. In their report to the Australian Government on the Antler series, the Safety Committee said that the 'balloon experiment can be regarded as fulfilling our expectations, and we have pressed our British colleagues to use this firing technique wherever it is possible to do so'. However, the British had devised a method of fulfilling the Safety Committee's expectations too late. The balloon-burst was to be the last of the major tests on the Australian mainland.

According to the test organizers 'close-in' fallout, that is within a hundred miles of ground zero, was always a manageable problem. Dangerous exposure levels could be avoided by excluding people from the area, by using protective clothing and by positioning servicemen upwind of the explosions. 'Intermediate' and 'long-range' fallout were always less predictable and therefore less manageable hazards. The official records tell us that long-range fallout due to the tests had no observable effects on the Australian population. The effects of intermediate, early fallout from the tests in communities up to four hundred miles from the test sites are more difficult to quantify. According to the official records, from the Australian Ionising Radiation Council, during the entire test period only two locations received doses of radioactivity above those now recommended by the international radiation protection authorities, 'but not greatly so, and would not be expected to produce any evident effect'. The communities, at Wallantina and Welbourn Hill, received estimated upper limit doses in the six months after the Totem 1 test at Emu of 1.1R and 0.67R respectively. The former dose is double today's limit for members of the public.

The reliability of the assessment depends on the accuracy of the measuring equipment and the records available. Eighty-six fallout monitoring stations were set up for the mainland tests; they were scattered over the continent but were more closely spaced in populated areas downwind of the expected fallout. However, they had a poor track record. Donald Stevens, a former member of the Weapons Safety Committee, told the Royal Commission that ground air-pumps designed to monitor radioactivity often became clogged and so underestimated the airborne contamination. He remembered that the 'sticky paper' method of 'catching' radiation in order to measure fallout was unreliable because it lost its stickiness after rainfall. And radioactive cloud tracking methods often failed to provide adequate back-up. For one of the Buffalo tests, the official report states that 'unfortunately, the aerial survey made after this test provided no results, owing to the breakdown of the radio-altimeter'.

Often the sampling stations were simply in the wrong position. The contamination caused by a wayward 'plume' from the fallout cloud, for example, might remain undetected because the test planners never expected the cloud to go in that particular direction. The volatile wind patterns at Maralinga made forecasting there an inexact science, and there were particular problems in anticipating wind direction over twenty thousand feet. Meteorological balloons sent to the upper levels of the atmosphere tended to burst or get lost. The trajectories for the fallout after the third and fourth Buffalo tests were expected to travel north and north-east but instead they travelled north-east and then north-west. Independent sampling points set up by curious scientists showed that a secondary cloud from the third Maralinga test passed over Adelaide. It is impossible today to test the accuracy of the monitoring devices used, but these 'pirate samplers' recorded that the background radiation levels in Adelaide increased by between one hundred and one thousand times the normal background level

An attempt at a more sophisticated method of analysing fallout over mainland Australia ended in a public relations disaster. The task was given to Dr Hedley Marston, a chief scientist at the Commonwealth Scientific and Industrial Research Organization in Adelaide, who by examining the iodine-131 content in the thyroids of animals killed after the Mosaic trials in 1956, discovered that measurable amounts of radioactive fallout had passed over a relatively large area of northern Australia. Marston passed his findings on to the Australian Safety Committee and was surprised when he heard the

Committee report to the public that 'the whole operation at Monte Bello was carried out without risk to life and property and absolutely no danger to the mainland'. Marston was one of the people who monitored for themselves the background radiation over Adelaide during the Maralinga tests, and when a twenty-four hour sample taken the day of the third test showed dramatic results – several hundred times the background radiation on a normal day – he tried to publish his findings in a scientific journal.

Marston did not take into account the nervousness of the authorities at this stage of the test series. In fact, scientists today believe that Marston may have exaggerated the significance of his findings. But *any* reference to mainland contamination in 1956, in particular over a centre of population the size of Adelaide, was considered political suicide and Marston had to be silenced. It was decided by the Safety Committee that because of Marston's 'present state of health', they, rather than Marston, would arrange the collection and analysis of animal thyroids. Penney instructed Marston to rewrite his article and to delete the references to Adelaide. In cross-examination at the Royal Commission, Penney admitted that the future test programme could have been jeopardized if Marston's scientific case had been allowed to prevail. 'If a man of Dr Marston's scientific reputation was saying these things were terrible, the tests are awful, look at these results ... of course there would be an almighty row.'

Although the main trials ended with the balloon-burst in 1957, weapons work continued on the range with the so-called 'Maralinga Experimental Programme' until 1963. The 'experimental programme', or 'minor trials' as they are more usually called, were shrouded in mystery until the 1980s when veterans in Australia began talking to the press about the 'secret tests' and 'hidden nuclear burial sites' of the 1960s. Until then the British Ministry of Defence always maintained that the Australian test series came to an end in 1957 and, in Australia, the official test records published by AIRAC bear no reference to the minor trials. Officials are understandably reluctant to talk about the Maralinga Experimental Programme. Although 'minor', these trials brought more long-lasting contamination to the Australian mainland than all the nuclear debris left by the 'major' trials. Furthermore, the programme appears to have broken the spirit if not the law of the Nuclear Test Ban Treaty being negotiated at the time.

The minor trials had a string of eccentric code-names: Kittens, Rats, Vixens and Tims. Kittens examined various forms of 'triggers' or 'initiators' required by an atomic weapon to start the nuclear chain reaction; Rats and Tims were concerned with measuring the compressibility of materials used in the make-up of a nuclear device; and Vixens examined the variety of accidents that might befall a nuclear weapon such as a fire in a weapons store or the crash of a plane carrying a nuclear device. It was Vixens that led to the spread of plutonium, one of the most toxic materials known to man.

Fewer men were needed for the experiments and only a few hundred British and Australian servicemen and scientists were involved. Members of the Australian Safety Committee were not required to be on hand to give their approval to indvidual firings. The British were simply required to issue a 'Safety Statement' giving details of the site required to the Australian authorities in advance of the test. Responsibility for the safety on the range during the trials lay with the British Trials Superintendent. According to the agreement between the two Governments, after each test the Superintendent handed the details of contaminated areas to the Australian Range Commander, who was responsible for range security between trials.

According to veteran Barrie Roberts who arrived in Maralinga in 1961, life on the range was very relaxed during the experimental programme. He says that the Australian police officers who manned the access gate to the forward area would let people pass through without checking. In one incident, two army men were found in the forward area doing routine maintenance work, ignorant that a test was about to be fired. New film badges were issued regularly by the health physics team but according to Roberts few people bothered to use them. He says he remembers seeing the crater left by the Marcoo test in 1956 glow green in the evening like a 'luminous watch hand in the dark'. He was told that the Marcoo crater where the Aboriginal family were found camped in 1957 would 'be hot for a thousand years'.

It was at the minor trials that possibly one of the worst cases of accidental contamination occurred. It involved a civilian, Mr Dovey, who worked for the AWRE calibrating and maintaining radiation monitors on the test sites. He died, late in 1983, of multiple myeloma – a cancer known to be linked with low doses of radiation. According to Dovey's wife, Isabel, her husband became very agitated before his death about an incident at the minor trials when he believed he received a very high radiation dose in a few minutes. He had been operating remotely controlled calipers to manipulate fissionable materials (most likely plutonium) inside a 'hot-box' when apparently the remote instruments broke down, necessitating the rapid separation of the material to prevent it 'going critical' and a chain reaction taking place. Dovey had lent over the brick wall behind which he was working in order to do this. He told his wife that he believed he then received a very high dose which was not properly registered on his film badge because it was shielded by the wall over which he leant. After the incident Dovey remained on radiation duties, allthough he said it was known that he had been exposed to 'at least a year's dose in three minutes'.

Dovey became ill in 1969, but his illness was not diagnosed until 1978. Two years later, in recognition of the likelihood of his cancer being radiation-related, he received a small industrial disability pension from the DHSS. After his death Isabel Dovey instructed her late husband's solicitors to take action for damages, which will follow an inquest verdict. As her husband was not a serviceman, no legal impediment stands in Isabel Dovey's way to prevent her taking such action and if any legal case is likely to disprove the Government's contention that no one suffered as a result of their work during the tests, it is this one.

The contamination left by the minor trials has left sections of the Maralinga range 'hot' for 24,000 years, the estimated life of the plutonium scattered there after the Vixens tests, which involved burning small quantities of plutonium in 'controlled petrol fires' to release and then measure the effects of plutonium oxide in the atmosphere. The contamination is incalculable. Edwin Bailey, a former mechanical engineer with the AWRE and now an Australian citizen, told the Commission in Adelaide that he had been involved in assembling the bombs used in the Vixens tests and that 60 kilograms of plutonium had been flown out to Australia for the experiments. The British Government has admitted that 22.2 kilos of plutonium were used in the Maralinga tests.

Although now an Australian citizen, Bailey was clearly agitated at the Royal Commission hearings about whether he was still tied by the Official Secrets Act and how much he could therefore say. He had only come forward to give evidence because he had read that British officials were saying that Vixens did not involve nuclear explosions. 'Strictly speaking that is true, but it did involve nuclear weapons and the potential hazard is still there.' He told the Commission that he had been worried about the devices for a long time because they were being exploded when the atmospheric test ban treaty was being negotiated.

Lord Penney was similarly confused over whether the minor trials involved nuclear explosions when he was questioned by the Commission in London. Asked by Peter McClellan whether the Vixen trials involved very small nuclear explosions, he replied: 'Yes. No. Wait a minute. The difficulty was that no one could define what a nuclear explosion was. We discussed this with the Russians and we tried definition after definition and in the end everyone gave up.' Penney was Britain's representative at the test ban negotiations and was naturally anxious not to give the impression that he was supervising sizeable nuclear detonations in the Australian desert while pleading for test bans in Geneva. His formula of 'when a nuclear explosion is not a nuclear explosion' was where the fission yield is less than 10 tonnes – which happens to be the limit beyond which the Americans and Russians could detect that there had been a nuclear explosion somewhere in the world. Penney admitted to the Commission that once this technical limit was observed by the weapons makers at Aldermaston, Britain could carry on developing her bomb.

Whether Britain did fire nuclear devices after 1958 is still a subject of debate but whatever was fired in the Australian desert between 1957 and 1963 has sparked off more controversy than almost any other test issue. Australians feel affronted by the degree of permanent contamination that has been left in their midst. An idea of this anger was given by a member of the Australian Ionising Radiation Advisory Council who was cross-examined by the Commission in Melbourne in October 1984. On virtually every other count, the Council have supported the British test organizers in their handling of the operation. However, when Keith Lokan, a member of the Council and director of the Australian Radiation Laboratory, was asked about the Maralinga Experimental Programme, the minor trials, he said: 'My view is that they should not have been conducted.'

Chapter Ten

A DAMP SQUIB

Christmas Island was a Pacific paradise to some of the men who took part in Britain's thermonuclear tests. Work for those only involved with the detonations was limited to short bursts of intense activity; for the rest of the time it was possible to take advantage of the surroundings. The sniffer pilots in 76 Squadron, for instance, had plenty of spare time because of the nature of their flying duties. When they were not carrying out trials and practice runs, the men were able to go big game fishing, water-skiing, sailing and scuba diving. The less energetic sunbathed on the beach and drank in the bar in the evenings. Between the danger of the bombs, they had 'a very pleasant relaxed time'. Members of the units who hoisted low-yield weapons under barrage balloons devised their own way of breaking the tedium between the explosions by developing a technique for catching the many sharks which lurked off the island's treacherous coral reef. In the best Heath-Robinson spirit they used six-inch nails bent into hooks, and the wires and ropes from their balloon equipment as improvised fishing-line. After some trial and error they managed to catch quite a few of their prey, and proudly photographed themselves standing next to the dead fish.

However, many of the conscripted men found that the coral atoll meant enforced idleness in an uncomfortable and barren place made worse by the primitive living conditions. Tony Crossland went to Christmas Island as a military policeman: 'You lived in tents which were rotting away from the ground

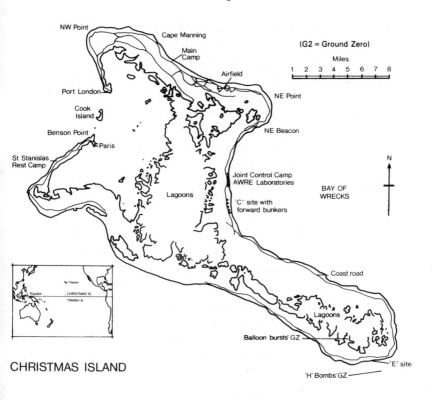

CHRISTMAS ISLAND

upwards; you were plagued with land crabs which stank terribly if you ran over them because they lived on stagnant water; and there was nothing to do outside any organized facilities. There was an open-air cinema – you took your groundsheet with you in case it rained – and whilst I was there it did. And it rained. Blue RAF uniforms turned green overnight, the fine coral dust turned into inches of thick coral mud and of course the mud walked into the tents.'

Christmas Island's isolation, which made it so pleasant to some and so dull to others, was precisely the quality the planners were seeking when they chose the atoll as the headquarters for Britain's H-bomb tests. The testing agreement with the

Australians had specifically excluded hydrogen weapon trials on their continent 'for safety reasons'. A new location was sought, therefore, immediately the go-ahead was given by Cabinet in 1954 for the development of a thermonuclear (hydrogen) bomb. Testing of the H-bomb's trigger – a low-yield fission device – was meanwhile to be carried out at Monte Bello and the Maralinga range.

The decision that Britain should manufacture its own H bomb was made secretly by a small Cabinet Defence Committee on 16 June 1954 and the question was put to the Cabinet itself in July. Minutes of the Cabinet meetings which discussed the decision, released under the thirty year rule, show three main arguments put forward in justifying the decision: the first, put by Churchill on 7 July was that 'We could not expect to maintain our influence as a world power unless we possessed the most up-to-date nuclear weapons'; secondly, that the 'thermo-nuclear bomb would be more economical than the atomic bomb'; and thirdly, that, in moral terms, 'no greater wrong' was involved in manufacturing the weapons than in accepting the protection already offered by the US hydrogen bombs.

The public announcement of Britain's go-ahead for H-bomb manufacture and testing was made in the following year's February Defence Statement. In retrospect the decision seems to have been inevitable. Even while the first atomic bomb was being constructed at Los Alamos in New Mexico, a group of scientists, including British representatives, was working on the theoretical principles of a fusion weapon. British scientists, with the traitor Klaus Fuchs, continued their research after returning to England. Despite some initial pessimism about the feasibility of a British project, the work had carried on with tacit Government assistance and when the Cabinet decision came Britain was only three years away from the successful completion of the project – a time-scale far shorter than that of either the United States or the Soviet Union.

The speed with which the H-bomb was built and then tested at Christmas Island was only partly due to the years of quiet preparation that had preceded the political action. The urgency of the project was also a direct result of the double-edged policy pursued by the Conservative Government at the time: on one side going all-out for the development and testing of the 'super' and on the other seeking an international treaty to end all atmospheric nuclear testing, in deference to the growing public opposition both at home and abroad. These parallel, yet contradictory, policies were neatly summed up by the Minister responsible for the the tests, Aubrey Jones: 'In the absence of international agreement on methods of regulating and limiting nuclear test explosions – and Her Majesty's Government will not cease to pursue every opportunity of seeking such an agreement – the tests which are to take place shortly in the Pacific are, in the opinion of the Government, essential to the defence of the country and the prevention of global war'.

Both the USA and USSR had, by this time, developed and tested their own hydrogen weapons and were working towards an international 'moratorium' on atmospheric testing. The British Government could not opt out of the super powers' diplomacy, but at the same time they saw the testing of an H bomb as an international demonstration of power that would restore lost prestige. British scientists, therefore, had to work faster and with fewer resources than their American and Soviet counterparts. It is a sign of their tremendous commitment that they succeeded; but the speed with which they worked, both at Christmas Island and in Australia, led to decisions which today are regarded as having been dangerous and even foolhardy. No Royal Commission has explored the safety, or lack of it, of the H bomb tests: yet the same – if not greater – fears exist about these tests. With no Commission there has been no release of documents about the hydrogen bomb trials but the available evidence points to a continuation of the questionable procedures that had been adopted in the Australian tests.

At the beginning of August 1955 the planning began of a series of thermonuclear tests. The H bomb series was given the code-name Grapple, meaning a four-pointed grapnel iron, symbolizing inter-service cooperation. The tests involved close-knit work not only between the three armed services, but also with a fourth party: the recently created Atomic Weapons Research Establishment (AWRE) under the directorship of Sir William Penney. The Ministry of Supply remained in overall authority, issuing the contracts for the manufacture of the weapons and providing the cash to pay for them. The first detonation was planned to take place early in 1957.

The immediate task for the planners was the choice of a test site. This job was given to a cell within the Air Ministry called 'Ops AWT' or 'Operations Atomic Weapons Trials'. Squadron Leader Roland Duck, ordered to find a location, looked for the largest area of sea with the least number of adjacent land masses and least number of people: 'We put our finger down and said: "Well this is where we are going", and that happened to be a place called Christmas Island, with another little island called Malden which we actually used as a target island for the first series.'

The Grapple planning committee, under the command of Air Vice Marshal W. E. Oulton, accepted the choice in November 1955, subject to clarification of its legal status, after the New Zealand Navy and Royal Air Force had carried out hydrographic and aerial reconnaissances. The committee agreed that in their isolation the two islands, Christmas and Malden, were ideal. Christmas Island, part of the Northern Line Island group, is situated just south of the equator in the middle of the Pacific Ocean. The nearest inhabited land, Hawaii, is a thousand miles way to the north, and the island of Fiji lies a thousand and a half miles to the south-west. It is the Pacific's largest coral atoll, thirty-five miles by twenty-four miles at its widest points. The Official Tests' Handbook, issued to all servicemen arriving at the island, described it as shaped like 'a large lobster claw, the jaws of which, opening to the north-west, contain a spacious and almost semi-circular lagoon'. The lagoon formed a natural harbour, which was named Port London. A channel had been dredged through it during the Second World War by the US Navy, but it was still too shallow for large ocean-going ships. This did not prevent the scientists' floating quarters, the technical command and control ship *Narvik*, coming in close: being a tank-landing ship she had a shallow draught and was ideal for the lagoon.

Although Christmas Island was 'discovered' by Captain Cook on Christmas Eve, 1777, it had been visited previously and was to be visited again many times by castaways. Because of the island's uniform flatness, the highest point being only twenty-five feet above sea level, several ships had sailed straight into the reef. The shipwrecked sailors did not find the desert island of their dreams: the atoll had little fresh water for them (for the tests, large distillation plants had to be installed) and the near-constant trade wind blew a cloud of fine coral dust in the air. This could penetrate everything and cause infection in the smallest cut or graze. The test servicemen had an extra unpleasantness to contend with: a plague of flies and mosquitoes attracted by the insanitary conditions. During the trials a daily flight by a light plane coated Christmas Island with DDT in an effort to keep the pests at bay.

Britain had taken formal possession of Christmas Island in 1888 but the island was not inhabited until 1902, when the Lever Brothers company started a coconut plantation using migrant labour from the Gilbert and Ellice islands to harvest the copra. Lever's pulled out of the operation soon after the First World War, but their workers remained. Three hundred of them and their descendants stayed on the island during the H-bomb tests under the management of the British District Officer Roberts. While the actual detonations took place, they were herded aboard one of the tank-landing ships and shown cartoon films below deck. Many of them remain to this day on

Christmas Island – no longer subjects of the British Crown but citizens of the independent Republic of Kiribati.

During the Second World War the United States Government, who considered Christmas Island to be American under an arcane Act of Congress involving guano (bird droppings), used the island as a transit base for supplies going to the Pacific theatre. A runway was built and the lagoon dredged; the island, however, remained under British administration.

Malden island, the target site for the first Operation Grapple, lies four hundred miles to the south of Christmas Island. It was formally occupied and claimed for Britain by a British subject from Australia, Benjamin B. Nicholson, in 1864. From that time until 1927 the flat and bleak little atoll was dug for guano (a very good fertilizer) and at one stage was producing 12–14,000 tons annually. The guano business ceased after the First World War and all the inhabitants of the island left. When the British arrived once more in the 1950s they found a colony of three wild pigs and a settlement of boobie birds.

At first very tight security was applied to the choice of location which for some of the junior planners was frustrating: the operation was to be so large that secrecy about it hampered their work. This problem was solved for them by the *Daily Express* journalist Chapman Pincher: 'When I needed to check a lead that Christmas Island was to be the base for Britain's H-bomb tests, I telephoned a most senior Defence Ministry friend [the Government's Chief Defence Scientist, Sir Frederick Brundrett] at home to ask, 'If I were to wish you a happy Christmas instead of a Happy Easter would it make sense to you?" His reply – "It would indeed!" – was enough.'

The formal announcement of Britain's hydrogen bomb test programme in the Pacific, required by international law, was made on 7 July 1956. It aroused some hostility in the Pacific and the Japanese, already fundamentally opposed to nuclear testing after their experience of Hiroshima and Nagasaki, were especially angered by Britain's plans in the light of the accidental contamination of some of their fisherman by the US hydrogen bomb test at Bikini in 1954. The Japanese Ambassador delivered a note of strong protest to the British Foreign Office and demonstrations against the proposed tests took place in Tokyo. They had little effect. A note in reply from the Foreign Office explained that Britain's tests were designed to cause the minimum fallout and that, as a result, 'There is no question of Japan's being in the slightest danger'. Official Japanese protests against each of the H-bomb tests continued until the detonations took place; on every occasion they were met with polite rebuffs from the British Government.

On 19 June 1956 the first part of the Grapple task force landed on Christmas Island in an RAF Shackleton from Coastal Command. The immensity of the job ahead of them was immediately clear: although the Shackleton had been able to land on the island's old US airstrip, the strip was clearly not suitable for the Valiant bombers and Canberra 'sniffer' planes that were to take part in the tests. Quite apart from the need for a new airstrip, the island lacked any amenities whatsoever, and even the most basic facilities necessary for the six thousand men who were to live on the island during the tests would have to be transported.

Straight away the operation to set up the testing base and target site began. By November 1956 Royal Fleet Auxiliary ships had landed over twenty thousand tons of cargo, which included six hundred vehicles. A completely new concrete airstrip was built, a tented city put up, water distillation units constructed, bulk oil-tanks put in place, field kitchens erected, and scientific laboratories built. It was a massive operation – the RAF alone moved ten thousand tons worth of spare parts and kit in the first year to the atoll to keep their planes flying. It was nine thousand miles to Britain and every single piece of equipment down to the last tent peg was brought out from home. Thirty years ago, however, Britain was still an imperial power with garrisons all over the world and the addition of the Christmas Island base did not involve the logistical difficulties which the Falklands garrison does today.

The authorities, mindful of the low morale during the first Monte Bello tests, tried to make sure that there was no shortage of organized recreation available to the men, who were mainly Royal Engineers and RAF ground crews required for the maintenance of the base. The island's two camps, the small Port London and the large Main Camp, each had a NAAFI. The Main Camp's was the more popular. It had a bar where the men could, to quote the official Handbook, 'drink a nice cold beer or squash in the beer garden pleasantly situated on the edge of the beach and listen to the pounding of the surf'. The hydrogen bomb test servicemen had their own specially brewed beer, each can stamped 'Operation Grapple, Christmas Island'. There were also photography and birdwatching clubs – the birdlife on the atoll was magnificent but many thousands of the birds were destined to be burnt and blinded by later tests; two cinemas operated by the Army Kinema Corporation with regular programmes; cricket, hockey and football pitches with regular games: and, of course, swimming in the lagoon. Special nets were laid to prevent the entry of sharks and the exit of servicemen, though despite repeated warnings many men slipped out to the reef. The RAF Westland helicopters had often to leave their test duties to perform search and rescue operations, and some men were killed swimming off the reef. In one incident five men drowned who had taken a boat out on the surf.

For those who wanted less excitement but perhaps more stimulation the Official Handbook had the answer: 'The Misses Billie and Mary Burgess of the Women's Voluntary Services have brought a touch of home to the camp. They are to be found in the main camp NAAFI organizing games, dancing, Highland dancing and concerts, and generally helping to make off-duty hours in the recreation room pleasant and free from boredom.' Since the first tests were held four hundred miles to the south of Christmas Island, there was no fear of radiation exposure for the Misses Burgess and for the later Grapple 'X' and 'Y' series off Christmas Island the two women joined the Gilbertese on board HMS *Messina* (where they were issued with protective clothing, unlike the Gilbertese).

For all the authorities' attempts to make life off-duty during the test bearable there were many complaints from the servicemen about their conditions. No overseas allowances or hardship money were paid to them in the early days of the trials. The tents in which they lived were notoriously cramped, and when it rained conditions inside them became atrocious. The lavatories were disgusting – so much so that the men preferred to dig holes in the coral dust rather than use the official facilities. Low morale and disorganization at the NAAFI in the New Year of 1959 led to a battle of beer tins and a mini-riot. The riot and the low standard of living conditions were made public after a letter of twenty-two-year-old Corporal Glenn Beckerton to his family was read out in the House of Commons. Questions were asked about the insanitary conditions and low-quality tentage which Corporal Beckerton had described, and the *Daily Mirror* ran a series of reports on bad conditions for the men on the island. As a result conditions were improved: more permanent accommodation was built for the second and final series of tests in the summer of 1958, and after an outbreak of dysentery sanitary arrangements were upgraded.

Men travelled the nine thousand miles to Christmas Island by troopship or, if lucky, across the United States and on to Honolulu by air, where they picked up the RAF's scheduled service of Hastings aircraft to Christmas Island. For most of the conscripted servicemen it was an extraordinary adventure: very few had ever travelled in an aeroplane before, let alone to such foreign parts. Co-operation with the United States had increased to the extent that transport and medical facilities were made available at Hickman air base in Honolulu. British servicemen were able to take advantage of the stop-over for rest and recovery, and a small RAF contingent was posted there for the duration of the Grapple operation. The American facilities were welcomed as a sign of greater Anglo-US co-operation and readily made use of, although the RAF continued a scheduled service to Edinburgh field in Australia.

Malden Island, the target for the first series, was established at the beginning of 1957 as a sub-base. The AWRE maintained instrumentation in and outside bunkers on the island to measure the effects of the bombs. The RAF also had radar beacons and batteries on the atoll to guide the bomber and its bomb to ground zero. In the period leading up to each of the trials, about seventy men camped on Malden preparing for the tests and a small landing-strip was constructed on the tiny atoll for them. Shortly before an explosion, all personnel were evacuated by air and as quickly as possible afterwards they returned to check their monitoring devices.

As the date of the first British H-bomb test in May 1957 approached, international opposition grew. The Japanese in particular, aroused by the failure of their diplomatic approaches, threatened to stop the test by sending a 'suicide fleet' into the 'danger zone', which was to be cleared of all shipping. In order to prevent any such embarrassments the British Government entered into an elaborate subterfuge with the journalist who had been so useful to the Air Ministry in the matter of the location of the H-bomb experiments: Chapman Pincher. He agreed to fake a story in the *Daily Express* and on 29 April 1957 he wrote a story which implied that the tests had been delayed because of technical problems, and that Penney himself was booked to fly out to Christmas Island to sort out matters personally. The story was, of course, rubbish and whether it had any effect on the Japanese is not known. There were, however, no 'suicide' protesters during any of the Malden island tests – the Japanese Council for the Prohibition of Nuclear Weapons decided that the protest fleet should merely sail as close to the danger zone as possible, and broadcast appeals for world peace.

The opposition to the H-bomb tests in Britain was confined to the Liberal Party, the Free Churches, individual members of the Labour Party, and trades unions, and groups of peace campaigners. The Labour Party, which might have provided the focus of any opposition, was split on the issue. The Shadow Cabinet, led by Hugh Gaitskell, was pressed by a group of nearly a hundred Labour MPs to call upon the Government to abandon the tests one month before they took place, but instead a compromise formula was worked out and accepted unanimously: it called for a 'postponement' of nuclear testing until the response of foreign nations could be considered.

The components of the first British H bomb were flown to Christmas Island in February 1957 and the bomb itself was assembled in two parts in special AWRE laboratories located at a camp on the island. Final preparation before detonation was performed on board the bomb-drop aircraft by a member of the plane's crew, who armed the weapon's fissile core, its 'trigger'. Code-named Red Beard, the bomb weighed 10,000 lb, was 5 ft in diameter and over 15 ft long. The fissile core which triggered the thermonuclear explosion was made of plutonium produced from uranium in British reactors. Relatively small quantities of radioactive materials of this sort did not take up much room on RAF transport planes but international and domestic law required that the countries over which such materials were flown be informed. However, owing to pressure of work and the necessity of achieving the test deadline, these permissions were not always sought and it was fortunate that for the early Grapple tests none of the aeroplanes carrying plutonium crashed in Canada or the United States.

Britain's first H bomb was detonated on 15 May 1957. It was dropped from a Valiant bomber, covered in white barrier paint to avoid radioactive contamination, flying at thirteen thousand feet. The bomber was flown by Wing Commander K. G. Hubbard: the bomb itself was dropped 'blind' by use of radar and detonated with barometric fuses at fifteen thousand feet. Two more hydrogen bombs were detonated over Malden Island in June 1957. No press representatives were allowed to witness the first explosion, perhaps because of fear of its possible failure. The official reports, however, were jubilant. The task force's own newspaper, the *Mid-Pacific News*, produced a special souvenir edition. Jingoistically headlined 'Bomb gone! H bomb puts Britain on level terms', it described the detonation: 'A flash, stark and blinding, high in the Pacific sky, signalled to the world today Britain's emergence as a top-ranking power in this nuclear age. . . . No one saw it! No human eye could survive the hellish glare of white hot-air brought to incandescence by the fantastic heat. . . . Ten seconds after the burst, spectators turned to see the dying explosion still threshing with the mighty powers that had been unleashed'.

The operation was carried out by a combined task force of ships stationed off Malden and aircraft from Christmas Island. Long before the explosion RAF Shackletons had patrolled hundreds of miles of ocean to ensure that no unauthorized shipping was in the area. The fleet, under the command of a Naval Commodore in HMS *Warrior*, a light aircraft carrier, moved into position twenty-four hours in advance of 'zero hour'. Two New Zealand frigates *Pukaki* and *Rotoiti* had the role of gathering meteorological material. HMS *Narvik* was positioned closest to Malden island and it was her radar which controlled the detonation of the weapon released from the Valiant bomber. More scientists and senior officers were present on HMS *Messina*, another tank-landing ship modified for the tests. Other ships in the task force were HMS *Cook*, a survey frigate in which scientific measurements were taken, and HMS *Alert*, 'the observer frigate'.

Nick Wilson was an able seaman serving in HMS *Warrior* and he kept a diary of the events which gives a truer account of what it was like to witness an H bomb for a young serviceman than the *Mid-Pacific News*: 'We were seated and all dressed correctly for anti-flash on the flight deck. Amusing but uncalled for jokes were cracked about failure. It was not until five seconds before the burst that I was concerned: then I became nervous. "Fire!" At the same time I felt my back warming up and experienced the flash, though I had my hands over my face and dark goggles on. Five seconds after the flash we turned round and faced the flash, but it was still bright so I replaced them. . . . There in the sky was a brightly glowing seething ball of fire. This rapidly increased and became more cloudy. Soon it was looking like a very dark ripe apple with a snow-white sauce being poured over it. . . . On the horizon at sea level a cloud appeared that must have been dust and spray from the island. . . . The whole sight was most beautiful and I was completely filled with emotions'.

Minutes after the mushroom cloud had formed Nick Wilson was able to see the Canberra aircraft flying through it to gather samples. Barely three hours later scientists and technicians were flown by helicopter to the target island to take readings of any residual radiation. Most reports at the time stressed their jubilation at the 'cleanness' of the air-bursts and the complete lack of fallout. Few details were released to the public about the first test other than that the fallout had been 'negligible'. The *Daily Telegraph*'s science correspondent, Leonard Bertin, detected that the bomb might not have been quite as large as expected: 'The device exploded, while not apparently of the same energy category as some of those exploded by the United States and Russia was, nevertheless, in the megaton range'. The phrase 'in the megaton range' neatly disguised the authorities' concern that the first bombs were not quite as powerful as their calculations had suggested. The two tests which followed in June 1957 were also described as being in the megaton range, and the authorities once again stressed that local fallout from these weapons was 'negligible'.

The question of radiation exposure for those aboard the ships of the task force did not arise in the public reports. Each of the H bombs was a so called 'clean' air-burst, and on each occasion the ships were thirty or forty miles from ground zero – well beyond the range of any 'initial' or 'prompt' radiation. The seamen responsible for routine radiation monitoring on board ship found no levels above the normal background count. 'Pre-wetting' operations did take place, however, after the detonations, as after the later Monte Bello tests but there are no records available, nor any reports, of any contamination of ships' companies occurring during such exercises.

For the scientists and technicians on Malden island the risks were greater. For all their jubilation at the low levels of radio-activity from the bombs, some residual radiation did occur. Ernest Cox, a member of the AWRE team, was responsible for gamma measurement instruments and before lift-off from HMS *Warrior* for the return to Malden after the second test he asked if clearance had come from health physicists. He was reassured that the island had been monitored and had been found safe, and proceeded to carry out his duties without a film badge or geiger counter. 'After a while my helper and myself took off up the island to retrieve some of my instruments. Before I did this I asked a principal scientific officer if he had seen any of the health physics team about, and he said it was rather strange, but no he hadn't.'

Cox set to work on his first set of gamma ray monitors and slowly progressed across ground zero towards the RAF's bomb radar marker. He had an uncanny sense that something was not quite right about the place: 'I said to my army helper "What the hell is wrong and what the hell are we doing here?" We both had a strange feeling; we noticed no flies, no movement of lizards and no booby birds. We found several burnt and dead birds and in the distance we heard one of the three wild pigs but we didn't dare approach too close to it. It was badly burnt and was going around in circles, blind. I said "This bloody place is contaminated, and what the hell are we doing here?" We went back to the camp area and by late evening two decon-tamination showers had been erected and so I went and had a good shower. Next day, back up the island again and in the evening I went for another shower which was very welcome. I had just taken off my shorts etc. when a chap came in with a monitor. He ran it over me and to my amazement I had a reading of 3.80R and another chap with me had a reading of 4.20R. The health physics chaps said: "What the hell could it have been yesterday? We would like to have known." This was a contaminated area and we should have been issued with protective clothing.'

After ten days small blisters appeared all over Ken Cox's body. He was repatriated to Britain from Christmas Island voluntarily on medical grounds. Today traces of those blisters remain, but he claims there are no details of a skin complaint in his medical records from the AWRE.

Terence Dale served on HMS *Narvik* as a Chief Shipwright and during the tests he was seconded to the scientists on Malden. He was one of the first to return after each detonation and remembers that this was some six to eight hours after the explosion. He was given no protective clothing. Today Dale is convinced that radiation exposure on Malden has since caused him a catalogue of illnesses, in particular the development of bilateral cataracts, at the age of forty-five. Cataracts have been associated with high doses of radiation at Nagasaki and Hiroshima, and normally they do not occur in a man of that age.

The British press were invited to observe and report on the second Grapple test off Malden island. To the dismay of the reporters from the dailies on arrival at Christmas Island, the test was to be held on a Friday which, because of international time differences and difficulties in communicating the stories back to London, meant that none of their reports could appear until the following Monday. They would be scooped by an agency man representing the Sunday papers. In order to get round this impasse the newshounds, led by Chapman Pincher, devised a scheme with an RAF officer: 'The Brigadier in charge of the press visit, who would join us on the sloop [the observation ship, HMS *Alert*] would tell us in advance exactly what the explosion would be like. He could do this with absolute accuracy because this second test would be almost identical with the first, from which the press had been excluded in case it should fail. We journalists would then be able to write our reports in advance and they could be held on Christmas Island. Then, once the bomb had been exploded, a fast plane would fly them to Honolulu where they would be transmitted at least in time for the late editions of Saturday's papers.' The deception worked. All the representatives of the daily papers took part except the late Sir William Connor – Cassandra of the *Daily Mirror* – who considered subterfuge immoral. The thrilling eye-witness descriptions of the 'super-bomb' which duly appeared the British press were thus quite false.

The first Grapple series off Malden was something of a damp squib. Britain had demonstrated the ability to air-drop a very large weapon, but the size of the first bombs were, according to senior members of the task force, only half a megaton. With this failure a second Grapple Series had to be planned. As the major powers moved to a moratorium on atmospheric testing, the pressure from the Conservative Government on the services and scientists to produce and test a true megaton weapon became intense. Air Vice Marshal Oulton remembers today that he had enormous obligations put on him: 'It was a question of time; the whole point was that we had to get another unexpected series of tests done before the moratorium'.

In order to save time the elaborate organization of a task force of two thousand men at sea off Malden was dispensed with: in future the tests were to take place off Christmas Island itself. The AWRE scientists had demonstrated their ability to detonate a 'megaton range' weapon in the atmosphere with little local fallout, and safety considerations would no longer prevent the testing of weapons close to Christmas Island. Much time and money was saved by the move from Malden to the main base but in the haste to complete the tests they become, in the words of a senior member of the Grapple task force, 'a matter of string and chewing gum'.

By dispensing with a naval task force as the focus of each test, many of the tricky problems of inter-service co-ordination and rivalry were removed. The first series, like all nuclear tests, had required the most exacting and carefully timed preparations, much in the same way that the launch of a space shuttle does today but the first Malden tests had the added problem of taking place four hundred miles away from the main base. The complex timing problems that this caused inevitably led to accusations of incompetence by one service against another, the worst occasion being when a naval ship was very nearly caught in the drop zone. It was a miracle that no accidents occurred.

The servicemen on board the ships of the task force can, however, rest assured that they were not exposed to dangerous radiation. Even those involved in decontamination duties on HMS *Warrior* do not appear to have been at risk. The inquest into the death of Kenneth Measures, who took part in decontamination drills on the aircraft-carrier, was preceded by a year long autopsy in which sections of his liver, subjected to the most exacting scrutiny, showed not even the minutest traces of plutonium or other long-lasting fission products. It seems that only those few men, like Ken Cox or Terence Dale, who ventured on to the target island after each test were in any danger.

By moving ground zero to Christmas Island itself, however, many more men were immediately put at risk. The decision was bred from the same scientific confidence and political expediency which produced the idea that tests should take place over mainland Britain. It was a confidence, indeed arrogance, which may have been badly misplaced.

Chapter Eleven

'A MATTER OF STRING
AND CHEWING GUM'

The last test over Malden was held on 19 June 1957. While the scientists returned to their drawing boards to redesign the Red Beard weapon, and to the Maralinga test range in Australia to detonate a few more fission 'trigger' devices, urgent preparations were made for the first hydrogen bomb test close to Christmas Island. It was scheduled to take place in the late autumn of 1957, just off the south-east tip of the atoll, only twenty-five miles from the main base. The Malden tests had been a political success for the Government of the day, demonstrating to the world Britain's new thermonuclear power, even if the scientific side had not worked out as planned. It was essential now to develop a really high-yield weapon, out of the glare of publicity, which could be carried and dropped on target by a V-bomber.

The haste with which the bomb test site had to be prepared left little time for improvements to the second-rate living quarters on the island. The Royal Engineers considered that they had enough to do without wasting time on the installation of pre-fabs to replace the tents, or proper sewage disposal to substitute for the stinking chemical lavatories used by the servicemen. Air-conditioned and blast-proof laboratories had to be constructed for the AWRE; the scientists and military required H-bomb resistant shelters from which to observe the tests at their forward control post; a 'balloon weapons construction area' was needed for the low-yield devices that were to be tested in the following year; the Vulcan, soon to enter service in place of the Valiant as Britain's main nuclear bomber, could not land on Christmas Island's runway, and plans had to be made to harden the landing-strip for it. All this work was of the highest priority, and the jobs which it involved were christened 'bomb stoppers'.

The procedure for the tests did not vary considerably from trial to trial. When a detonation took place the non-naval men – mostly servicemen in the Royal Engineers and the RAF – were assembled in units to view it from different points of the island. Many of them were mustered on the beaches twenty-five miles from the blasts. Those engaged in essential services, such as manning the airfield in case of an emergency, were closer – about twenty miles away. Closest of all were the senior scientists and officers, assisted by some sappers. They were given a grand-stand view of events from the specially constructed bunker at 'C' site, only ten to fifteen miles from the various explosions. At the same time the ships steamed a few miles offshore, in preparation for their 'pre-wetting exercises'. All the crew members who were not essential to the running of their ships gathered on the decks, while the Gilbertese copra workers – if aboard – were entertained below with film shows.

Despite the fact that the men were so close to the explosions, the scientists and military responsible for the six tests at Christmas Island – four H bombs and two A bombs, the latter low-yield devices hung under balloons – remain confident to this day that they were quite safe. Sir John Grandy, the task force commander for the second Grapple series, is adamant that the precautions taken to avoid exposure 'were of the very highest standard'. His view is shared by Sir William Cook, the AWRE Chief Scientist at the tests. The safety precautions were similar to those taken in Australia: meteorological conditions were taken into account before the command for a test to take place was given, and the movement of men was controlled before and after each explosion. Moreover, the Christmas Island tests, like those at Malden, were thought to have had a considerable safety advantage over their Australian counterparts: they were all air-bursts, and the weapons tested which were in 'the megaton range' were detonated at fifteen thousand feet. This should have prevented any danger from fallout.

William Jones was a scientist with AWRE on Christmas Island and is convinced that the safety margins were more than adequate: 'The yields of the various weapons were known pretty exactly so we knew what the size of the fireball was going to be. In addition to that we added a safety factor, so that when we fired the balloon shots for example, instead of them being fired at the height to which the fireball would expand, something like – in the case of a twenty-kiloton shot – around five to six hundred feet in radius, we more or less doubled that up and added a safety factor on top of that. So instead of the balloon shots being fired at something like six hundred feet, where the fireball would have touched the ground, we fired them at around one and a half thousand feet on a three balloon system.' The principle was the same for the H bombs, detonated ten times higher at fifteen thousand feet.

Jones, as an AWRE planner and 'controller', was responsible for the movement of all men and materials into the areas where the detonation occured. He was based at the AWRE control centre, 'C site', which was close to the Joint Operation Control camp about ten miles from ground zero, and it was not until he had said that he knew where every person was and that each had been accounted for, that the safety key was inserted into the firing desk, or the aircraft notified and the tests allowed to take place.

Although there was meant to be no fallout on Christmas Island because of the nature of the bursts, there was some residual radiation, caused by neutron bombardment, in the areas close to ground zero. For this reason no one was allowed into ground zero to collect their monitoring instruments or take part in exercises until the health physics decontamination team from the AWRE had set up its 'circus' in the area. Entry into the area, according to Jones, was only through a health physics centre, and those who came out of the area with their instruments were monitored. If a person had any contamination on him, he went to a decontamination centre and it was cleaned off. Thus anybody who picked up radiation as a result of going into the test area would have to report through the health physics people.

All those who worked in the forward area should have been issued with film badges. They were also ordered to wear protective clothing: thick rubber gloves to prevent the hands being exposed to alpha and beta radiation, and pressurized suits to protect against the ingestion of any airborne particles. The exercise to regain instruments and the subsequent decontamination were treated as rehearsals for nuclear warfare, though the hotter areas were cordoned off by advance parties who entered ground zero with portable radiation monitors.

Both the AWRE and the military monitored the rest of Christmas Island for possible contamination. According to senior officials at the Ministry of Defence, nothing above the background natural radiation count was recorded. For this reason, and because of their confidence in the safety of the tests, the authorities did not consider it necessary to take any special precautions with the men who witnessed the detonations from the beaches some twenty miles away. They were not issued with film badges as it was thought that there would be no fallout danger. The white cotton 'zoot' suits which they were given for the last three H-bomb tests were not worn to prevent radiation exposure but as a precaution against burns from the heat of the weapons.

The H bombs, when viewed from so close, presented a terrifying spectacle. Many of the men could not believe such incomprehensible releases of energy could be intentional, and would not harm them. Quite a few of them accepted a persistent rumour that the atoll was shaped like a mushroom, with the island a cap delicately resting on its coral stem, and they feared that a particularly strong blast would cause the stem to snap, plunging Christmas Island and all on it into the depths of the ocean.

The size of the first bomb off Christmas Island on 8 November 1957 seems to have taken everybody there by surprise. Clive Atkins, an RAF radar operator, recalls: 'When the bomb went off the flash dried out our clothing, which was full of perspiration, and I could actually see the bones of my hands over my eyes, the flash was so brilliant. Then we heard the sound of the bomb going off. After that we all turned round and we saw the blast hit the palm trees and bend them over. We were informed later by the AWRE that the bomb had been dropped slightly lower than they anticipated and it was far bigger than they had imagined.'

All the sizes of the Christmas Island test remain classified but today Ministry of Defence officials and the AWRE deny that any of the tests took the authorities by surprise. Other reports, however, suggest that events were not quite as expected. Sapper Brian Marks served with the Royal Engineers on Christmas Island and in December 1960 he died of a rare form of blood cancer which his parents were convinced was caused by his presence at the tests. They were most disturbed by his stories of the incredible power of the blast: how a ten-ton diesel generator was blown upside down and three-inch tent poles broken. When called to comment on the strength of the blast by his MP, the Under-Secretary of State for War, James Ramsden, commented: 'It is perfectly true that the blast was such as to cause a large diesel generator to be blown over in a controlled area and knowledge of this incident was quite widespread. That Sapper Marks knew of and commented on the blast effect does not, however, indicate that he was exposed to radiation'.

Many of the servicemen who witnessed the same blast were also astonished and terrified by its power. William Oates was a storeman on the island: 'Probably the thing that scared me most was not the ball of flame in the sky, nor the searing heat, but the blast and shockwave which followed later. . . . On that occasion I saw grown men at their wits end trying to run away from the blast.' It damaged many of the buildings on the island, tents and heavy machinery were knocked over, glass was blown out of windows, coconuts thrown from palm trees and vehicles smashed. It took Arthur Thomas, a sapper, quite by surprise: 'Then it happened, the blast, a lightning speed of wind and whistle of trees – a bang – it hit us all unexpectedly, lifting us off our feet and depositing us three to four yards away landing on each other in a pile of bodies. We were not told to expect anything of this nature.' Les Dawson was also unprepared: 'We had been expecting a storm-like strong wind but the sound and blast wave was nothing like that. Suddenly I was aware of being flat on my back and hearing a loud bang that made my ears pop. There was also the sound of shattering glass as the windows of the Joint Operations building shattered. This all seemed to happen at the same time. We were surprised, bewildered and slightly dazed'.

When the next hydrogen bomb tests took place in the summer of 1958 more precautions were taken. Doors and windows were left open 'to let the blast pass through' and more protective clothing was issued to the men to prevent flash burns. The move to Christmas Island had brought many men closer than ever before to weapons of up to 10 megatons – some of the largest ever detonated in the atmosphere – but despite being so near to the weapons there was no danger to the men from prompt radiation, and the stronger than anticipated blast effects did not present a great physical danger. However the authorities' confidence in the safety of the Christmas Island tests does not take into account the fact that, as in Australia, a number of the safety precautions concerning radiation were either inadequate or ill-observed. There is also a possibility that a number of men thought to have been in no danger were inadvertently put at risk.

There is no question that a radiation hazard was created by the 'sniffer' aeroplanes which flew through the H-bomb clouds minutes after detonation. As in the Australian tests these planes, modified B6 Canberras, were sent through the clouds in order to gain samples for the AWRE scientists who could then measure the various yields as accurately as possible. Many of the RAF pilots who had taken part in the Buffalo tests in Australia volunteered to continue their dangerous work at the Malden and Christmas Island tests, though if they had already received the maximum permissible dose of 25R, they were refused. Some of their Canberras had also become, according to Air Vice Marshal 'Paddy' Menaul, one of the RAF senior officers in charge of cloud-sampling, 'too hot to handle' and were left in Australia, where it was hoped they could be decontaminated. In the event most could not be properly cleaned and were buried.

The hydrogen bomb tests posed problems even more formidable than those of the Australian tests for the sniffer teams of 76 Squadron. The clouds of the thermonuclear weapons were much larger than those of the atomic bombs tested in Australia and rose higher in the atmosphere. It meant that cloud sampling was necessary at heights of fifty thousand feet or more, but no British jet at the time could fly safely at such high altitudes. Before the Grapple series took place the RAF did tests in the United Kingdom to see if they could find a way to cope with this problem: Scorpion rockes were placed underneath the Canberras in an attempt to give the planes greater power and stability in the rarified air of the upper atmosphere. The rockets failed, however, and the men suffered severe frostbite as a result of bailing out of their stalled aircraft. The experiment was abandoned and the pilots were instructed to fly as high as they could using their flying skills to prevent stalling. It was, in the words of one of them, 'like driving a car on a frozen lake at high speed in a thick pea-soup fog'.

The men who flew through the H-bomb clouds therefore did so in aircraft they understood to be unsuitable and exposed themselves knowingly to high doses of radiation. They were volunteers who undertook the work with willingness, bravery and dedication. Most of them have no complaints today about their experience with H bombs, which they consider to have been of national importance, justifying the risks they took. It was some of the men of 76 Squadron at Christmas Island who received the highest doses recorded in the tests: in two cases 30 rems, according to the Prime Minister, Margaret Thatcher.

Christopher Donne, a pilot with the 'sniffer' squadron at Christmas Island, has the dubious distinction of being the leader of the Canberra crew to have received in 1958 the highest recorded radiation dose referred to by Mrs Thatcher. Since the tests he has suffered no serious illness and is living proof that the effects of radiation may harm one man but leave another unscathed. Donne was selected to be the 'controller' or 'sniff boss' for Britain's last atmospheric hydrogen bomb test on 11 September 1958 and it was his duty to fly through the cloud as soon as possible after the explosion to assess how safe it was to send the other three sniffer planes through. The pilots selected the highest possible 'cut' in order to fly through the densest part of the cloud and gain the best possible samples for the scientists waiting expectantly on the ground.

The mushroom cloud on 11 September was much larger than Christopher Donne had anticipated as he carefully turned his aircraft towards it only ten minutes after detonation: 'I remember seeing this yellowy-brown thing ahead of me, stretching out almost as far as I could see, and I remember turning the aircraft and getting it straight and level and just scrambling up those last few feet and then approaching the cloud and hoping that I'd got a small part of it – we called it a 'cut' – from which, of course, we could work out when it was safe to send the other aircraft in. ... And then we hit it, and I can remember my navigator saying, "Bloody hell! Let's get out of here!" But, of course, we couldn't because there was no way I could turn the aircraft – the turbulence was causing me to concentrate very hard on flying it at all at that height. I can remember sort of glancing out of the side of my eyes to look at the instruments – the needles were pressed very firmly up against the stops ... showing the very high levels of radiation, which were very much higher than we'd anticipated. I can remember the health physicist muttering in his beard something about it being very much hotter than he'd thought.'

Once they landed Christopher Donne and his crew were immediately decontaminated. Their heads were shaved to minimize the risk of any fallout particles clinging to the scalp, their nails paired to the quick to remove any radioactive material lodging next to the skin, and they were thoroughly showered. Donne was told that he could receive no further doses and would have to return to Britain. On his return he was advised to have regular blood counts for a year. His mission was the only occasion when the radiation levels recorded were known to have exceeeded the higher 'integrated' dose level of 25 rems, though other members of 76 Squadron received high doses. Flight Lieutenant Hannam, the navigator of a Canberra 'sniffer' for the penultimate H-bomb test over Christmas Island, was exposed to 'about 28 rads' with his crew. The actual dose could not be recorded: 'The sampling would have been aborted at 10 rads but the dosemeter failed'. Like Christopher Donne, Hannam has suffered no ill effects from his high dose.

It was not only the sniffers in the RAF who were at risk. Other aircrews could, and did, accidentally come into contact with the mushroom cloud and its airborne fission products. Guy Templeman was the navigator in a Canberra on photographic and meteorological duties. Before each test, in common with the other aircraft at Christmas Island, his plane took off and flew race-track patterns. At the moment of detonation the aircraft were organized so that they were flying away from ground zero, and after the explosion they turned and flew back to base. On the 28th April 1958 test Templeman's Canberra returned, its duties finished, to the airfield but its approach flight path meant that the plane cut through part of the nuclear cloud. Templeman remembers that the Canberra was decontaminated after landing. The pilot, Tony Davis, was a young man in his early thirties. The two men lost contact after the tests but when Templeman tried to get in touch some years later he was shocked to find that Tony Davis had died from leukaemia in 1964. Ever since he learnt of his former comrade's death he has harboured suspicions about his accidental contact with the mushroom cloud. The Ministry of Defence deny that Davis ever came into contact with radiation on Christmas Island.

The men of the 'active handling flight' who decontaminated the 'hot' aircraft were also obviously at risk of exposure to radiation while at Christmas Island. Although procedures had been tightened up after the Australian tests, and the men wore respirators and white cotton protective clothing, their duties were difficult to carry out and potentially dangerous. A number of men who took part in the work at Christmas Island now believe it was as unsafe as in Australia. Bryan Young remembers: 'We were cleaning off barrier paint above me and water came off the back of the wing. I was only wearing cotton whites so, of course it went straight through, and bearing in mind that it was contaminated water coming off I wasn't a very happy person underneath. But we were all too busy at the time to do much about it. In the middle of decontamination you can't suddenly stop and say "Oh God, I've got to go and shower all this lot off!." Work has to carry on.' Even on the atoll Bryan Young began to suffer from skin problems and blinding headaches, and his health problems have persisted ever since.

Another small group of RAF servicemen who may have been at risk during the Christmas Island tests were the balloon crews. They were seconded to the AWRE and worked on the two low-yield tests held in August and September 1958 at the end of the Grapple series. The balloon unit was divided into two crews: one for each balloon test. The men were responsible for inflating the balloons with helium gas and, once the bomb had been placed in a cradle, for suspending the weapon under a configuration of four balloons. The balloons were the old barrage-type which had been used to protect towns and cities from German bombers in the Second World War.

The balloon crews were based about seven miles from ground zero. Before the tests they worked on the site above which the bombs were detonated, an area which may have been radioactive due to the neutron bombardment from earlier H-bomb tests. Thus as they were in an area with a known radioactive hazard, the members of the ballon crews were subject to the monitoring of the AWRE health physics team but John Lycett, a member of the unit which prepared the second balloon test, is not satisfied that the precautions were sufficient. When his unit was sent back to ground zero to prepare for the test, 'The area was covered with dead birds and debris from the first explosion; we even found bits of rigging that had supported the first bomb. When it was our turn to do guard and topping-up balloon duty we slept in a tent on the very site of an atomic explosion only a few weeks earlier. Yet at no time were we required to wear personal dose-monitoring devices.'

Members of the Royal Engineers also assisted the AWRE scientists in the forward areas. They were required to help with the protection of monitoring devices which were placed as close as possible to the explosions in order to gain the fullest radiation measurements. After each test the sappers were ordered to go to the forward area to remove the sandbags from the measuring instruments, and they were also required to kill as many of the maimed and blinded birds as possible. But ex-sapper Atwell remembers the strict precautions taken in the forward area: 'We always wore two film badges to monitor the amount of different types of radiation. And we always passed through the decontamination unit, where we left the white protective clothing and washed and scrubbed thoroughly before being checked by geiger counters.'

No details of the doses to which the men on Christmas Island were exposed have been published. One document (see p. 224), however, copied by a signals clerk who was on Christmas Island after the tests in 1959 and who has since died of cancer, may give some indication of the levels. The copy, made some four months after the last test in February 1959, is extremely difficult to read but it appears to be taken from a 'Master Check' of the different radiation levels at various points on Christmas Island. These include the forward 'C' and 'E' sites close to ground zero, and the main lagoon. The document shows that in the 'local area', which must have been close to ground zero, a dose of half to one rad would be expected in a normal working day. This is a relatively high dose considering the annual exposure limit at the time was five rads a year. If access to the area was properly controlled, however, there need have been no great danger from it.

The document also shows that stores brought in to Christmas Island from Honolulu appear to have been contaminated in five days, indicating quite high levels of radioactivity, but the most interesting and perplexing part is that which describes 'decontamination' and 'physical feelings'. For the decontamination process it lists: 'Shower, exercise, skipping, bare feet, hard met. plate surface.' For 'Phys Feelings' in 'Open Areas C, E' (sites at the eastern tip of the island), it lists 'Naus. Tingling sore joints. Vision. Clears PM after exercise.' According to scientists, this list indicates symptoms expected after a high dose in the range of 50 to 150 rads, or possibly even higher. That such high levels existed seems to be shown by the decontamination exercises: showering to wash off the radioactive particles and exercise to clear the total volume of the lungs in order to eject any fission products inhaled.

The copy of the document was found among the papers of the signals clerk on his death, written out in his handwriting. He had no scientific training and he presumably made it out of curiosity while transmitting the material to Britain. His family do not wish him to be named. According to the AWRE scientist who has read the paper the dose levels recorded show nothing particularly dangerous or unexpected. If the descriptions of radiation sickness are genuine, however, the document makes a mockery of claims that men were not subjected to high doses of radiation.

There is no evidence that the mass of servicemen at Christmas Island were deliberately exposed to radiation by the authorities, although as in Australia, the service chiefs were keen to observe the effects on morale of the men who experienced a nuclear bomb from close quarters. Exercises were arranged similar to the 'Indoctrination' that took place at the Buffalo test in 1956. Tony Crossland remembers: 'It was a rather arbitrary system. A number of us were selected to go from the main camp towards ground zero. I always thought that was a bit silly. We took no extra precautions, and no extra safety measures were offered to us. I understood that we were to be within seven to ten miles of ground zero.' Crossland was detailed to witness an atomic explosion, one of the low-yields which took place in the late summer of 1958, but he was given no explanation of the purpose of the operation, nor any reassurance that there was no radiation hazard. 'It was just one of those things: you did as you were told because you were in the armed forces.'

After each detonation men were ordered to take part in the clean-up operations. Thousands of birds were killed, maimed and blinded as a result of each explosion. Fish too were stunned by the blasts and rose in huge quantities to the surface of the sea where they floated before being washed ashore. The putrefying remains were collected in small amphibious transports and taken out to sea for dumping. Birds which had been blinded, or whose burnt feathers rendered them unable to fly, were put out of their misery by shooting. The dead remains aroused in the men fears of contamination for many believed that the birds and fish had been irradiated. Carol Wratten's husband Brian was a laboratory assistant and pathologist on Christmas Island. Having handled animals killed by a test, he became convinced that he had been in contact with radiation. He died twenty years later of a rare blood cancer. 'As soon as he was diagnosed he was aware that it was a radiation-connected disease, and he felt that he had received some degree of radiation on Christmas Island, and that undoubtedly he had contracted the disease because of it. He couldn't understand how they could have done these tests with the little protection they had and not received radiation.'

The dead birds and fish collected by the men on Christmas Island could not however, have been highly radioactive if the tests were successful airbursts. It is likely that because for many men the dead animals and fish were the only tangible contact they had with the after-effects of the tests, they became in retrospect a focus of their fears and anxieties.

Undoubtedly the main radiation hazard recognized at the time of the tests by the authorities was at the south-east tip of the atoll, closest to the H-bomb's ground zero, where the low-yield devices were exploded. William Jones, the AWRE officer responsible for movements in the area, is convinced that there could have been no accidental exposures in this area because entry and exit was so carefully controlled. He agrees, however, that it would have been possible for men to flout the rules and go into ground zero without proper authority: 'If people wanted to get into the test site without going through the normal controls, yes, they could have done it. After all, the place was full of lagoons, little tracks leading all over the place. It would be foolish to say that nobody could get into the test site if they wanted to. Anybody who wanted deliberately to get in there could do it.'

Of course a number of the men could not resist the temptation to go and take a look for themselves. Christopher Donne remembers that he managed to borrow a Land Rover and some protective clothing, and then drove into the ground zero area with some friends. The men did not go very close, but for Donne it had a strange sort of eeriness about it that meant he did not want to go very close: 'I can remember vividly seeing where ground zero had been, and it was rather like an enormous football pitch in very good condition: there was nothing there at all, everything had just disappeared. Totally flat, except one could see what looked like grass as far as the eye could see, green. And we discovered that of course it wasn't grass at all. It was where the heat, the colossal heat from the explosion, had actually fused the sand of Christmas Island into green glass.'

The areas of potential risk at Christmas Island were clearly delineated: the washdown pads, the contaminated aeroplanes, and ground zero. It was assumed that servicemen in other areas would be quite free from any radiation exposure above the natural background level, which happened to be extremely low at Christmas Island. This assumption was based on the fact that all the tests were airbursts and therefore produced no fallout. If, however, the meteorologists got their forecasts wrong it remained a possibility that Christmas Island could be contaminated by 'rainout': when the products of nuclear fission are brought to the ground by rain when it passes through the mushroom cloud. After the explosions at Hiroshima and Nagasaki, both airbursts, this phenomenon occurred. It is thought that nuclear explosions may themselves trigger changes in the weather.

Safety precautions for a change in the weather were taken on the island. Known as Pied Piper, they involved servicemen getting into vehicles and heading for assembly points from which they would be evacuated by boat and ship. During the second H-bomb test in April 1958, Grapple Y, many men remember that the weather changed causing Pied Piper to be put into effect. Arthur Thomas recalls: 'Suddenly over the loud-speaker system came the order to get under cover quickly and to clear the open ground. Apparently the wind had changed and the fallout cloud was heading back to Christmas Island. I dashed to my motor vehicle and sat in the cab compartment, closed the doors and windows and remained there for half an hour. Every one else seemed to find cover eventually.' Shortly afterwards, however, the wind direction reversed and the men were ordered back to their positions

There is evidence that 'rainout' did occur over some part of the island during the second April H-bomb test and if so the risk of exposure would have been extended to the six thousand servicemen whom the authorities believed to be in no danger at all. The late Bernard Geoghan was on board HMS *Narvik*, just off Christmas Island, during that test and remembered: 'That particular morning the cloud developed and developed and developed. It was absolutely enormous and eventually came right over the top of the ship. Then it started raining – it absolutely bucketed down – a real tropical drenching! We were all soaked to the skin and were very apprehensive. Here was this rain coming smack out of the nuclear cloud right over our heads, and inevitably everybody was pretty petrified about it.' The men with Bernard Geoghan were reassured that the rain had not contaminated them, but if it had come straight out of the nuclear cloud it must have brought some of the radioactive fission products with it. Many of these, the alpha and beta emitters, would not have been detected on their film badges.

Captain Glen Stewart was the co-pilot of a Shackleton on shipping patrol during the same test: 'The explosion set off a line of thunderstorms, below which we were forced to fly to Christmas Island. There was torrential rain which entered the unpressurized aircraft like a sieve. It turned the only available detector, a small rudimentary device on the captain's lapel, immediately to the wrong colour. On landing the aircraft was scrubbed down for days, if not weeks, to rid it of contamination.' Captain Stewart's experience has not affected his health. Today he flies Jumbo jets for British Airways.

That it did rain after the second April H-bomb test is confirmed by a meteorologist on the island (who has asked to remain anonymous as he still works for the Government). He remembers that after the blast there was some hot rain which mostly fell into the sea but some of which landed on Christmas

Island: men were ordered to lie under vehicles to keep out of it. After Grapple Y the men sat on huge tarpaulins placed on the beaches: should it rain, they were expected to crawl underneath. Fortunately for them the need did not arise.

If the rain which fell during the test carried the fission products of the nuclear explosion, a large number of men would have inadvertently been put at risk. Much of the island's life involved the use of sea water: men washed and swam in it; they drank water distilled from it, and they ate fish caught locally. After rainout all these activities could have exposed them to radioactivity, both externally and internally. When washing or swimming tiny radioactive particles may have entered the body without being monitored at the time, and fish may have ingested particles brought down by rainout which could have lodged in the bodies of those who ate them without being detected on monitors. Major James Carman has been with a party which had caught over 150 crayfish on a fishing expedition, and the crayfish were prepared for a dinner to celebrate the opening of a new officers' mess. As he relates it: 'Out came the crayfish on big dishes and everybody ate them. I was talking to the Nuclear Biological Chemical Division Officer. His job on the island was to take a background count to check the radioactivity – he'd been out there almost a year and he had never had a reaction on his geiger counter at all. This night half way through the party, he said, "Well I've got to do my background count", and he did it with great ceremony. He had to go out and leave the party. And I said, "Bring the damned thing in here!". So he did – and for the first time he got a reading on it.' The reading came from the remains of the crayfish.

The Ministry of Defence denies that men could have been affected in this manner, and points out that regular checks of local fish were made by AWRE scientists. This is indeed the case: men on board ships, in particular those on HMS *Narvik*, were ordered to catch the fish for the scientists. Although not meant for consumption, the fish – once checked – found their way into the fish-frying black market which thrived on the island and relieved the monotony of tinned bully-beef. The NAAFI also legitimately sold locally caught fish. The steaks were called 'Alloha' and judged the equal to any cod sold back home.

There is no indisputable evidence that large numbers of men at Christmas Island were unknowingly exposed to radiation. It remains a possiblity that can only be confirmed by statistical analysis. What seems more clear, however, is that the men who worked in areas known to involve radiation exposure may have been the victims of lax security and safety precautions. The hydrogen bomb tests were administered and carried out by the same authorities responsible for the Australian tests, and there is no reason to believe that the safety precautions changed for the better once the move had been made to the Central Pacific.

The British nuclear testing programme ceased after the last low-yield device was exploded under balloons in September 1958. Britain had developed her hydrogen bomb in the nick of time. In the following month she joined the USA and USSR in a moratorium on nuclear testing and although Britain was never to test in the open again, Christmas Island played host for H-bomb tests once more in 1962. After the collapse of the East-West moratorium, with the resumption of Soviet testing in 1961, Britain lent the base to the United States for a major H-bomb series of twenty-five tests called 'Operation Dominic'. A small British contingent of three hundred men attended these tests to keep up a show of sovereignty on the island.

Christmas Island was transformed by the Americans from a small British colonial outpost into a multi-million dollar testing base, called by its proud new occupants 'a giant outdoor nuclear laboratory': 60 warships, 110 planes and 11,800 men took part, and 15 special weather stations were set up on nearby islands. Balloons and rockets were used: test towers and computers were put to work. Britain's Operation Grapple paled by comparison.

For the United Kingdom the American invasion of the old testing base marked the end of a truly independent nuclear deterrent, for while Operation Dominic progressed, Britain's Prime Minister Harold Macmillan was negotiating a deal with President Kennedy to buy Polaris missiles. It was Polaris warheads which were being detonated high above Christmas Island in Operation Dominic. In return for the United States' use of the base, British scientists were at last granted the access to American test data that they needed so badly to improve their own warheads. Britain's short era of atmospheric nuclear testing had ended. Many of the difficult objectives had been achieved cheaply, quickly and efficiently, but the questions raised about the safety of the trials have left a bitter legacy to many of the men who took part.

Chapter Twelve

THE NUMBERS GAME

Two highly criticized statistical studies of test servicemen have been carried out in Britain and Australia. They have both demonstrated the difficulties which such studies present. Their figures have been disputed and their methods rejected. The British survey raised questions about the safety of the tests, and the Australian study claimed to show that no one had suffered as a result of them. Statisticians of disease, epidemiologists, are notorious for the varieties of conclusions they draw from their data. The British Government may hope that the controversy over the tests will be ended by the publication of the National Radiological Protection Board (NRPB) study of the health of test participants, but judging by the two previous surveys it seems more likely that the debate will grow still fiercer.

The British survey was carried out in 1983 by epidemiologists at the University of Birmingham, who had been commissioned to do the work by the now defunct BBC Nationwide television programme after it had received a flood of anecdotes about men suffering as a result of their role in the Christmas Island tests, and to a lesser extent the Australian tests. The Ministry of Defence's argument that the tests were quite safe could not be countered by anecdote alone. No scientists, let alone a court of law, would accept the allegations of servicemen as firm evidence of negligence during the tests.

The University of Birmingham was sent all the case histories which were received, in their hundreds, by the Nationwide programme. In turn the study team, led by Dr Alice Stewart, an authority on the effects of low doses of radiation, sent out a questionnaire which sought details of medical history and service at the tests. Documentary evidence, such as a death certificate, had to be produced for a death from cancer. The purpose was to establish whether the number of cancer deaths reported, when compared with the number expected among men of similar ages who had not been at the tests, was higher and showed anything suspicious. Epidemiologists use a mathematical technique to show whether an excess number of cancers in a group is a product of chance, or is 'significant', and has a cause, like radiation. If the Birmingham study showed any statistically 'significant' excess of cancers among test participants, a fuller, objective and independent study would be justified.

The study team was burdened from the beginning by the unreliability of the Government's estimates of the number of men who had participated in the nuclear tests. It was essential to have an accurate figure if any valid comparison of the rates of cancer deaths suffered by the test veterans and those who did not attend the tests could be made. Dr Stewart assumed that a total of 12,000 British servicemen took part in all the British nuclear tests in the 1950s and 1960s. This assumption was based on a figure given by the Prime Minister in the House of Commons early in 1983, when Mrs Thatcher stated that 12,000 servicemen took part in the entire test programme, with 1,500 civilians and 1,500 Australians. It later turned out that the Prime Minister's figures were wrong.

At first sight, however, the sheer number and coincidence of the illnesses and deaths seemed to justify the fears of ex-servicemen or their widows and families. To a non-scientist the numbers coming forward with anecdotes about the tests and tales of subsequent illnesses appeared to confirm the fears that the men had been exposed to radiation. There is an obvious tendency, however, for a response to a request for information to be inaccurate or unrepresentative of the larger group. A man suffering from a radiation-linked disease is more likely to report it than someone who is not; and those who believe that their illnesses are caused by the tests are keener to respond to a programme on the subject than those who do not.

By the spring of 1983 the University of Birmingham was able to present a study of 330 cases of men who had participated in the Christmas Island tests to the medical journal *The Lancet*. The findings seemed remarkable. On a provisional estimate of 8000 men at the Christmas Island tests, based on the Prime Minister's figures, there was evidence already of 'an abnormally high incidence of leukaemia and reticuloendothelial system (RES) neoplasms' (cancers of the blood often linked with radiation exposure). In the small sample of 330, there were 27 cases of death from blood cancers; ten more than might be expected in a normal group of 8000 men. The study also reported ten cases of cataract in men in their forties.

In spite of the inevitable bias, the fact that the number of blood cancers exceeded the number expected if the entire group had been surveyed seemed evidence that something had gone very wrong in the tests. Even if the figure of 8,000 men was wrong and many more men had been at Christmas Island, the fact that so many cases had been reported in such a small group was suspicious. Dr Stewart and her colleagues put forward several explanations for the apparent excess of blood cancers. They suggested that far more men may have been at risk than the 8,000 they allowed, or that the men had been exposed to very high doses of radiation. It was also possible that they had found new evidence that low doses of radiation are more damaging than had been supposed, or that there may have been other causes for the blood cancers which are not yet known.

There was little official response to the reported findings. A senior Defence Ministry spokesman said off the record that the University of Birmingham's report was 'unscientific' and 'biased'. Professor George Knox, who had supervised the study, dismissed the Ministry's comments as a 'blanket denigration'.

According to the Professor, the methods used were quite normal in epidemiology. The study only lacked a full response because dead men were unable, obviously, to respond to requests for information. It was possible that there were still more cases of blood cancer which had not been counted in the study.

Soon afterwards, the Ministry of Defence declared that it was uncertain about the number of men at the tests. The Ministry cast doubt on the Prime Minister's figures and, therefore, the result of the Birmingham study. A spokesman told the *New Scientist* that the number of men attending the Christmas Island tests was 'nearer 12,000'. David Alton MP asked the Prime Minister to clarify the position and in her written reply, referring to the Government-commissioned NRPB study, she stated: 'The survey will be higher than previously estimated, and could be around 20,000. These will include support personnel who worked in areas away from the test areas and others who were at the time not considered to be at risk from radiation exposure'.

Because proper records had only been kept of the men who took part in the tests whose radiation doses had been recorded, the Government was unable to make a firm statement about the total number who had participated. Many thousands were never monitored for radiation exposure at all because it was considered that they were not at risk. The Prime Minister's earlier declaration of the numbers of men at the tests had been mistakenly based on radiation records, which did not exist for many men and they had not therefore been counted. They had, however, been included in the University of Birmingham's study.

David Alton had his own suspicions about the Government's announcement of the new figure of 20,000. 'It increases the figures to lessen the impact of any illness statistics. It builds in a statistical bias. The Minister should tell the House who are these additional 5000 people. Have they been included so that the percentage of people appearing to have contracted cancer will be reduced?'

In the same debate of July 1983 the Minister for Defence Procurement, Geoffrey Pattie, put on the record that the Government-sponsored survey would cover 'about 20,000 men': 'There is plainly no change in the number of 4000 men who were radiation-monitored. They are well-recorded. The uncertainty lies with those who were assessed at the time not to be at any radiation risk and therefore did not figure in the lists maintained by the radiological protection authorities. For the Pacific tests our best estimate of the number to be considered is about 12,000. The remaining 8000 are associated with the Australian tests and other operations like the Maralinga experimental programme and the clean-up operations at Maralinga and Christmas Island.'

The high figure of blood cancer deaths among test participants in the Birmingham study could now be explained by the increase in the Government's estimate of the number of men at the tests. There was no longer a 'significant excess' of blood cancer mortality because as the Birmingham team had themselves suggested, there were many more men than they had allowed for at the Christmas Island tests. They now estimated the figure as 13,000, but their study still showed an excessive number of blood cancers suffered by a group of ex-servicemen under thirty years old at the time of the tests. Among the total of 594 cases which had been sent to the University for analysis, there were 42 cases of blood cancers reported by test servicemen under thirty years old when at Christmas Island, whereas only 30 cases would normally be expected in a similar population of men who had never been at the tests. Curiously, however, there were far fewer cases of blood cancer reported than normal in the older age group. To Dr Stewart and her team, the discrepancy between the older and younger age groups pointed to the conclusion that the survey, as might be expected, had not screened all the cases and that there were more in the pipeline, given the already worrying incidence of cases among the younger men.

Professor George Knox gave cautious support to this view. Although the figures were not 'statistically significant', it looked as though there might indeed be a higher incidence of blood cancers among the men who served on Christmas Island. Professor Joseph Rotblat, the acknowledged expert on the effects of radiation in warfare, was more categorical. His opinion of the study remains that 'it definitely indicates an effect of radiation. Already the reported numbers of blood cancers in the sample of 594 respondents is nearly equal to the total number one would expect from 13,000 servicemen. This sample comprises less than five per cent of the total number. Therefore can one assume that nearly all the blood cancers were contained among the 594 and hardly any among the 12,400 who have not replied? To me this is inconceivable.'

Soon after this last set of figures from the University of Birmingham was published, the National Radiological Protection Board announced its plans for the Government-sponsored health study of the test participants. The Board proposed a full survey of the number of deaths from cancer suffered by test servicemen. The objective of the Birmingham University study had been achieved.

In the same year, 1983, the Australian Government's Commonwealth Department of Health published a study of 15,364 men identified as having participated in the tests. The survey, which was carried out by Dr J. W. Donovan, came to the conclusion that the tests had caused no particular damage to Australian civilians and servicemen. The study had two parts: a survey of the number of cancers among living test participants who could be found; and a mortality study of those whose deaths had been traced. The Donovan Report, as the study came to be known, was widely criticized both for its methods, its impartiality and its conclusions.

The first part of the survey was based on Government records held in Australia which showed that 15,364 Australian men had some part in the test programme. This, the true figure, was widely at variance with Mrs Thatcher's estimate of 1500 earlier in the year, which was based on the known radiation records held by the AWRE. Postal questionnaires were sent out to all those whose addresses could be traced. Only 2440 fully or partially completed questionnaires were received in return and Dr Donovan based his study on these replies.

Like the Birmingham survey, the Australian report had a strong bias: the men who had contracted disease were much more likely to respond to the requests for information than those who had not, and those who had suffered some illnesses were more inclined to believe that they had been exposed to radiation, even if the records showed this to be highly unlikely, if not impossible.

Australia, unlike Britain, has no central cancer registry where the rate of the disease can be observed and it was not possible, therefore to compare the incidence of cancer among test veterans with that of a similar group who had not participated in the nuclear trials. Instead the 2440 replies were divided into groups according to the work the respondent claimed to have done. Each group was then compared with another of the same size which had taken part in the tests in order to establish whether any aspect of the test programme might have been dangerous. For example, those involved in decontamination were compared with a group with no known exposure, such as Maralinga construction workers. If many more cases of a particular illness were found in one group exposed to known radiation doses than in another not exposed, an effect of radiation would be established.

The survey did indeed find excesses of a variety of illnesses, but Dr Donovan refused to draw any conclusions from them. Those who had taken part in decontamination procedures were found to have 2.6 times the expected rate of melanoma – a skin cancer. This excess was not related to radiation for two reasons. First, according to the study the men with this skin cancer had a wide variety of jobs within the decontamination process and it was not therefore possible to find a common source of radiation exposure which could explain the higher than average incidence of cancers. Second, there was no record of doses considered high enough to cause skin cancer and without evidence of high doses, Dr Donovan concluded, it was not possible to attribute the skin cancers to radiation.

Dr Donovan also found 'statistically significant associations' between cataracts and the men who cleaned up radioactive areas or handled and transported radioactive materials. Again, because the radiation doses for the men reporting this condition were below the threshold assumed to cause cataracts, Donovan argued that radiation could not be the cause of the association.

Infertility among the men who had 'taken part in the construction of support facilities, cleaned up radioactive materials or had visited signposted areas' was 1.5 times higher than among those who had responded to the survey but had not carried out any of those tasks. Once more the report rejected radiation as a possible cause because 'there was no association between infertility and measured exposure to radiation'. The same conclusion was drawn about the higher prevalence of skin cancers among the men who flew through the atomic clouds, or the excess of cataracts among those who passed through the health physics check-points.

Dr Donovan also studied the causes of death of 1560 test participants and found a slightly higher proportion of cancer deaths among the test veterans than in a normal population. This was almost entirely explained by lung cancer. He concluded that there was no reason to believe that attendance at any of the tests raised the risks of dying from a radiation-related disease.

The report's conclusions were based on the assumption that the measured radiation doses were accurate enough to be relied upon. As they were so low Dr Donovan believed they could not explain the excesses which he found. Instead he put down the high frequency of certain conditions to chance. Today it is difficult to agree that all the recorded doses were accurate enough for any firm conclusions to be drawn about them. It is also quite possible that exposures occurred which were not recorded: the first Australians to fly through the atomic clouds, for example, were not monitored at all.

Dr Donovan's refusal to explain 'statistically significant' findings by radiation because there are no records of exposure to fit the cases reported brought howls of rage from the test veterans' associations. So many accounts of the tests in Australia point to inadequacy of monitoring that the excesses discovered may themselves be the best indication of radiation exposure, but like the British Black report (see Chapter 2) Dr Donovan shied away from this conclusion.

The fact that the report was produced by a government agency brought further criticisms. At the Royal Commission Dr Gun, a Senior Medical Officer with the South Australian Health Commission, said he could not accept its impartiality: 'Neither the findings nor the methods really mean much to the experienced reader unless one feels confident in the attitude of the investigators.' He felt the report did not justify that confidence because 'it should never have been given to a government agency for carrying out', Dr Gun suggested that the study be done again by an independent team, and he also proposed that a separate control group be found with which to compare the test participants. The method of comparing groups of servicemen with one another might have masked the effects of radiation exposure: 'The exposure data is acknowledged to be of poor quality. If too many presumed high exposure personnel were in fact not highly exposed and too many presumed low exposure personnel actually received appreciable exposure, group differences would tend not to be visible in the statistical sense'.

The accusation that the Australian health study was biased

because it was carried out by a government agency was immediately levelled at the National Radiological Protection Board in Britain when it announced the methods of its study of all British test participants. Even before the terms of the survey were proposed its impartiality was questioned in the House of Commons in July 1983 by David Alton: 'Surely the truth is that there will be little confidence in the NRPB, because it is not wholly independent. The Ministry of Defence, in whose interests it is to disprove the findings of the University of Birmingham, is to be paymaster for the survey. The Ministry already uses the services of the Board and will be open to the charge of being in the Ministry's pocket.'

His feelings were shared by Ken McGinley, Chairman of the British Nuclear Test Veterans Association: 'How can we rely on their results when we know that they're a government body, and the Goverment ordered the tests in the first place?' The self-appointed Joint Committee on the Medical Effects of Nuclear Weapons questioned the NRPB's competence to carry out the study: 'The National Radiological Protection Board's expertise is in monitoring radiation exposure, not in carrying out health surveys'.

The NRPB firmly rejected these criticisms. Dr John Dennis, the scientist in charge of the study, pointed out that the Board is a statutory body, and not therefore responsible to any government minister. He added that the NRPB was only partly financed by the Government, and that half its income comes from commercial work. Of the study itself, he said: 'The protocol has been looked at by the Medical Research Council and by the BMA Ethical Committee who have to be satisfied before we are allowed access to death certificates or morbidity data. We have Sir Richard Doll as an outside consultant, who was Regius Professor of Medicine in Oxford and a noted epidemiologist. As regards our competence to carry out the study, we have a highly qualified team who have demonstrated their ability to carry out this sort of analysis.'

The terms of the NRPB's health study were outlined in a document called 'Protocol for a Study of the Health of the UK Participants in the UK Atmospheric Nuclear Weapon Tests'. It confirmed that the Government did not at first have access to a comprehensive list of participants in the tests. At the time of the publication of the Protocol in October 1983, the Ministry of Defence had compiled a list of 12,000 names entitled 'the Blue Book', which was based mainly on the radiation exposure records. By the beginning of 1985 Ministry of Defence researchers had found more details of men who had attended the tests and the list had increased by 8000 names to 20,000.

The study intends to compare the 20,000 men with a control group approximately the same size and with similar characteristics apart, of course, from having witnessed or participated in nuclear tests. Those characteristics include some service in tropical or desert climates so that the long-term effects of different temperatures and exposure to sunlight can be accounted for. The first task of the NRPB study team is to compare the number of deaths within the control group, and within the study group of test veterans, with the number of deaths which might be expected on the basis of national death rates. The NRPB has recognized that both the control group and the test veterans – the study group – are likely to show a lower number of deaths than would be expected from national rates because men selected for the forces and for service overseas were fitter than men taken from an average cross-section of British society. The first comparison will show to what extent this so-called 'healthy worker effect' should be allowed for in working out the significance of the results. It will also indicate whether the control group is a reliable sample with which to compare the test veterans.

Once this has been established, the control group will be compared with the study group to see if the test participants have suffered a higher rate of cancer deaths. If they have, then it will be an indication that participation in the tests has damaged the test veterans. Should this be established, the study team would go on to see if there was any connection between the known radiation doses and the excess of cancers. Smaller groups of test veterans will also be studied for cancer rates where their records have been well kept: the companies of ships or RAF squadrons, for example.

The third part of the study will examine all those who wore film badges that recorded radiation exposure above the minimum detectable threshold. The NRPB will examine the death rate among this group to see if there is any link between the number of deaths and the strength of the dose. The study group will also be looking at the mortality rate for different age groups: the younger men are likely to have been more frequently exposed than their older counterparts.

The NRPB's Protocol also announced plans for a 'Morbidity Survey' which would seek to find out whether there are more cases of cancer among living test participants than among the control group. The Protocol did not announce the methods of the study and was rather lukewarm about its possibilities: 'Such data presents problems in interpretation and may not provide a reliable measure of differences between the Study and the Control Groups.'

The proposals in the Protocol were widely welcome as broad-ranging and effective. The NRPB was criticized, however, for having left out any study of cataracts or genetic problems suffered by the test veterans and the following year the British Nuclear Tests Veterans Association started a campaign for the recognition of birth defects caused by the tests. Ken McGinley, the Association's Chairman, said: 'We've had so many reports of children of veterans being born with defects in some way or other that we're convinced that these problems have been caused by our men being exposed to radiation at the tests.' Frank Cook, MP referred to evidence from his constituency in the House of Commons in December 1984: 'I heard of a man who during his first marriage had three deformed children. That is unusual, but not so unusual that one would justify it statistically by exposure to a nuclear test. However, he divorced, remarried and had a further two deformed offspring'. Dr Shirley Ratcliffe, a leading paediatrician and member of the Medical Research Council, also believes that a genetic study is essential. In her opinion so little is known about the genetic effects of radiation that the test participants merit a proper scientific study.

The NRPB sympathized with the demands for a genetic study but its members believed that such a survey would best be carried out only if an excess of cancers was first established among the test veterans. Although animal experiments have shown that there is a link between radiation and birth defects, no such link has yet been found in humans: the most sensitive evidence, from Hiroshima and Nagasaki, shows no increase in human birth defects after exposure to high doses. As so often the problem is a lack of knowledge: for this reason alone, the test participants may be considered by scientists a worthwhile case to study.

The test veterans' associations are not satisfied with providing evidence about the effects of low doses of radiation only to fuel scientific controversy. They want clear answers to their claims that they were unknowingly exposed to dangerous doses of radiation. These may never be forthcoming. Even if an excess of cancer deaths is found among the participants, it will not be accepted as proof that large groups of servicemen were exposed to damaging radiation because, according to the Ministry of Defence, only five hundred measurable radiation exposures were recorded by test participants. The same argument used by Dr Donovan will apply. The battle to show that men were exposed will remain to be fought.

The cruel fact is that the small number of appreciable radiation doses recorded at the time of the tests could not, even by the most radical interpretation, have caused a measurable excess of cancers among all the ex-servicemen. If an excess is found, it will be up to the participants to prove that it is not a chance result and that they were negligently exposed to doses of radiation without being monitored. For those who took part in the Australian tests the task has been made easier by the Royal Commission. Without any such British inquiry, the Christmas Island veterans in particular will be left to make their case relying only on their repeated anecdotes and fading memories.

Chapter Thirteen

THE CROWN'S DEFENCE

The British and Australian servicemen who witnessed nuclear tests in the 1950s were not the first Commonwealth troops to find themselves near atomic explosions. In August 1945 hundreds of Allied prisoners of war were in camps close to the first atomic bombs in Hiroshima and Nagasaki, and almost all of them survived the bombings. Today some of them and their families are claiming compensation for the long-term damage they claim was caused them by radiation in the Japanese cities. The British Government has rejected all their appeals. Any link between cancer and presence at a nuclear explosion or test is firmly denied.

If men who survived the nuclear devastation of Hiroshima and Nagasaki are refused state disability pensions, it seems unlikely that the nuclear test participants can hope for much from the British Government. In Australia the test ex-servicemen and their families at least have the right to seek compensation through the courts under common law. Several cases have already been brought against the Australian Government. But no similar right exists in Britain, and no damages have been paid.

In the autumn of 1984 the European Commission on Human Rights ruled that the British Act of Parliament which prevents servicemen from suing the Government for damages was legal under the European Convention on Human Rights. The ruling was a terrible blow for many ex-servicemen and widows of test veterans who had hoped it would enable them to take the British Government to court for the damage they believed had been done by the nuclear tests. The Commission's decision was especially unwelcome to the British Nuclear Test Veterans Association, whose avowed aim is to gain compensation for test servicemen. Their battle will now be a long and arduous one, made especially galling by the fact that Australian men, with whom they may have shared a trench in a test, are free to take their former employers to court.

The Act of Parliament which prevents a British serviceman suing his employers, the Crown, or a fellow-serviceman for negligence is called 'The Crown Proceedings Act 1947'. It effectively prevents any test veteran or any relative of a test veteran suing the Government for damages to compensate for injuries which they believe were caused by the tests. It is just one of the many barriers which exist to make any form of compensation extremely difficult, if not impossible, for British participants in nuclear tests. They face an impenetrable bureaucracy whose policy, it appears, is to deny at all costs any links between cancer and radiation.

The Crown Proceedings Act was passed by a Labour Government in 1947 and was meant to be a liberalizing Act which would allow the state to be sued by an individual. Coming so shortly after the Second World War, however, it was feared that former servicemen or their families would sue the Government for compensation from injuries they had sustained while in armed service. Service chiefs also feared that the right to sue for negligence would be 'bad for discipline' and lead to insubordination among the troops. Parliament agreed, therefore, to add a new immunity to the Bill, listed under 'Section 10' of the Act, which provided that if a member of the armed services should be killed or injured by another member of the armed services, or as a result of the condition of any premises belonging to the armed services, then that serviceman would not be able to sue in British courts to obtain damages for negligence or any other civil wrong. Section 10 met with considerable opposition in Parliament and even those who framed the legislation were clearly unhappy about it, as the Lord Chancellor made clear in the House of Lords: 'Let me be quite frank. This clause is one of the clauses I have been pressed and indeed compelled to insert by the service departments to overcome the misgivings, or if you like reluctance, which they feel about the introduction of the Bill. The short and the long of it is that I am under an obligation either to get this clause as it is or withdraw my Bill'. Some MPs pointed out that a fundamental common law right of soldiers to sue for negligence was being removed, but the Bill became law despite their concern. Sir Hartley Shawcross, then Attorney General, tried to give some reassurance by promising that pensions for servicemen and their widows would remain on a level with damages gained in court. The commitment was never maintained and pensions now are a tiny fraction of the damages which might be received in court.

The operation of Section 10 is typical of the labyrinthine complexity of Whitehall's bureaucracy, which effectively prevents compensation. Today if a serviceman, or his widow, declares an intention to sue the Government for damages, a 'Certificate of Attributability' is issued automatically by the Ministry responsible for claims, the Department of Health and Social Security, under Section 10. This certificate admits that the condition suffered could be considered due to service but blocks any action in the courts. The irony of the position is shown by the certificate issued in 1980 to a widow of an ex-serviceman who worked at a nuclear test site which, in order to avoid an action for damages, declares that the serviceman's death resulted from service on Christmas Island. Yet the Government's official policy is to deny that any serviceman suffered because of the tests.

That particular certificate was issued to the widow of George Pollard, a boilerman who had emigrated to New Zealand after service with the Royal Marines. He died in June 1978 of peritonitis, a condition which arose after he had suffered a thrombosis, which in turn came about because of his long-lasting illness, a refractory anaemia. Such an anaemia can be caused by radiation. In 1956 and 1957 George Pollard served on Christmas Island, taking part in the first Grapple series. On his return to Britain he complained of a general malaise and lack of energy. Tests were carried out at St Mary's Hospital, Paddington, where he was found to be suffering from secondary anaemia. He was discharged from the Royal Marines as medically unfit for service and was awarded a disability pension – a recognition that his illness arose as a result of service.

After George Pollard died in 1978 his wife, Amy, applied for a war widows pension. Such pensions are awarded to widows of servicemen when the Department of Health and Social Security (DHSS) accepts that the deaths resulted from service. If the DHSS does not accept that death occurred because of service to the Crown, it does not make the award. There is, however, an appeal process whereby the widow can seek to have the Department's decision reversed. In Amy Pollard's case, there was no need. The DHSS accepted that her husband's death had resulted from his service with the Royal Marines and although it did not specify exposure to radiation on Christmas Island in particular, this cause could not be ruled out. It is known that anaemia can be caused by radiation, and indeed George Pollard's surgeon himself did not rule this out as a possibility. The other known causes of anaemia are not of the sort that could arise during, or be attributed to, service in the armed forces and the DHSS, after examining Marine George Pollard's records, assumed that radiation exposure could have caused his death, and made the award of a war widows pension on that assumption. Amy Pollard was quick to realize this and instructed her solicitors to sue the Crown for negligence.

Immediately the Ministry of Defence were informed of the claim they told Mrs Pollard's solicitors that the Ministry would raise the defence of section 10 of the Crown Proceedings Act. At the same time the Ministry of Defence Claims Commission requested the DHSS to issue a 'Certificate of Attributability'.

Reg Prentice MP, then Minister for the Disabled at the Department of Health and Social Security, duly issued such a certificate. According to the DHSS, it was issued 'upon the advice of one of this Department's Senior Medical Officers that your late husband's death was substantially hastened by his service in the Royal Marines between 21 April 1947 and 10 February 1960'. It may be that the Senior Medical Officer was privy to records of radiation exposure on which he based his advice.

The Certificate of Attributability itself, phrased in the arcane language of bureaucracy, was much more specific about the circumstances in which George Pollard contracted his radiation-linked disease: 'Insofar as the death of Marine George Pollard, PO/X6499, Royal Marines, was due to anything suffered by him as a result of service with the Royal Marines at Christmas Island during atomic tests there in 1956 and 1957, I hereby certify his suffering that thing has been treated as attributable to service for the purposes of entitlement to an award under the Order in Council relating to the disablement or death of members of the force of which he was a member.' In other words, Pollard and his widow received their pensions because his illness was treated as having resulted from his service on Christmas Island. Mrs Pollard was now unable to proceed with any action.

After she wrote to the Prime Minister, she received a letter of explanation from the Ministry of Defence's claims department in November 1980: 'In the case of your husband he was a member of the armed forces of the Crown when the alleged act of negligence occurred and on duty. He was also put into that position by members of the armed forces of the Crown in the course of their duty. Further, the Department of Health and Social Security accepted his condition of secondary anaemia as attributable to service and awarded him a war disablement pension. His death from peritonitis was also accepted as attributable to his service in HM Forces from 1947 to 1960 and you were awarded a war widows pension. It is therefore clear that the conditions of section 10 of the Crown Proceedings Act 1947 at satisfied. . . .'

Amy Pollard was outraged by the denial of her freedom to sue: 'If I were the widow of a civilian in receipt of a pension I would be able to sue. Because my husband was a serviceman who suffered from the effects of radiation I am unable to sue – even though the Government, by awarding me the pension, believe his illness and death were caused by service on Christmas Island'. Were Amy a civilian, it is likely that she would by now be in receipt of a considerable sum in damages. The mystery remains how her husband's anaemia could have been caused by radiation at Christmas Island, and because the DHSS and the MoD have all the records in the case and have blocked any legal action, it is unlikely ever to be solved.

One other Certificate of Attributability has been issued to a former test participant who had intended to sue the British Government. Melvyn Pearce served on Christmas Island with the Royal Engineers. He was seconded to the AWRE and operated their refrigeration units at nuclear laboratories on the island. He now suffers from multiple myeloma, a rare bone cancer often linked with radiation exposure. Although Pearce receives no disability pension for his condition, he has received a Certificate of Attributability preventing him from suing the Government. In his case the Certificate states that if his condition can be proved to be caused by service on Christmas Island, he will be eligible for a forces disability pension. In effect the Government has prepared an absolute defence based only on the contingency that he may successfully prove his case and win a small pension. Mr. Pearce is challenging the certificate in the Courts.

Several British MPs have recognized the injustice of the Crown Proceedings Act, in particular when applied to actions concerning the nuclear tests. In the House of Commons in March 1984 David Alton called the Act 'an unacceptable and unnecessary deprivation of the rights of servicemen engaged in normal day-to-day activities', and Frank Cook in December 1984 spoke of the 'almost anachronistic failure of the legislation to cater for the future not only of those who have given good service to the Crown but of their offspring and future generations'. The Minister of Defence, Geoffrey Pattie, gave the Government's usual reply on the matter: 'Servicemen are called upon to risk injury and sometimes death not only in operations, but in training, and it would make the conduct of the armed forces impossible if a serviceman could bring an action against another serviceman, possibly his superior or subordinate in rank, or against the Crown, for alleged negligence during service activities'. Mr Pattie did make clear, however, that the legislation was under review.

The only recourse left for those ex-servicemen and their widows who believe that suffering or death has been caused by the tests is to apply to the Government for disability or war widows pensions. Here, as with the Crown Proceedings Act, extraordinary anomalies have occurred because of the Ministry of Defence's refusal to acknowledge the possibility that damage may have been caused to a single serviceman by his presence at any of the tests.

Warrant Officer Howard Stephens died on New Year's Day 1980 after a long battle against leukaemia and septicaemia. He had spent most of his working life with the RAF and during the Second World War he suffered three years' imprisonment at the hands of the Japanese. After the war he continued in the RAF and took part in 'Operation Repack', the clean-up of Christmas Island after the Grapple series. It was there that the may have come into contact with ionising radiation, though the details have never been made available to his widow, Marjorie Stephens. Like Amy Pollard, Mrs Stephens applied for a war widows pension. Her case was rejected by the Department of Health and Social Security but with the help of the Royal Air Forces Association she appealed against the decision, convinced that her husband's death had resulted from exposure to radiation at Christmas Island.

When a widow appeals against a DHSS decision on war

Catch ²²

widows pensions, the appeal is heard by an independent
tribunal consisting of service and ministry representatives, legal
advisers and medical officers. The tribunal is empowered to consult expert medical opinion in Britain and to call on evidence
from service records which would not normally be available to
the widow in question. Its decision is binding on the DHSS. The
pensions appeal tribunal found in favour of Marjorie Stephens
and issued a certificate in September 1981 which stated: 'The
Tribunal finds that the death of Howard Garfield Stephens
(deceased) was hastened by an injury, wound or disease namely
1a. septicaemia, b. blast transformation of Chronic Myeloid
Leukaemia which was attributable to service.' Marjorie
Stephens' representative at the tribunal, the Royal Air Forces
Association, was more specific about what exactly the tribunal
has established: 'Mr Stephens' death was through leukaemia,
caused or hastened through contact with ionising radiation
during his service on Christmas Isle in 1959.'

A widow who receives a war widow's pension normally also
qualifies for the Ministry of Defence's Attributable Forces
Family Pension, which is a small 'top-up' to the meagre DHSS
pension. However, when Marjorie Stephens applied for this
pension, to her surprise and consternation the Ministry of
Defence refused to pay it. She has been fighting for the extra
pension ever since, not because, as she says, 'I am keen to have
the money, but becaue I must establish the point and make the
Ministry of Defence accept the findings of the tribunal'. The
Ministry has refused to move and Mrs Stephens is in the curious
position of being paid a pension by one department of Government while another, which originally employed her husband,
refuses to recognize it. The Ministry's views were made clear in
a letter of 10 May 1983 from Jerry Wiggins MP: 'It was decided
that as there was no medical basis for believing that Warrant Officer Stephens' death was caused by his service – and this, of
course, accorded with the original decision reached by the
Department of Health and Social Security on the basis of advice

from their medical advisers – it was decided that the award of the Attributable Forces Family Pensions could not be made.'

The independent tribunal which found in Mrs Stephens' favour would have sought expert medical advice, but because that opinion did not agree with the DHSS's view, nor with that of the MoD, it was found convenient to ignore it. The irony is that if Mrs Stephens were to begin legal action (for which she has neither the inclination nor the finances), the Ministry of Defence would order the issue of a Certificate of Attributability declaring that Warrant Officer Stephens' death had been 'attributable to service'.

There are other cases of test veterans' widows who have received war pensions, and some who have also been given the extra Attributable Forces Family Pension. These women naturally tend to shun any publicity lest the bureaucracy of government turns on them and removes the small recognition which they have received for their husbands' service and subsequent death.

Hundreds of ex-servicemen have applied to the DHSS for the disability pensions which they believe ought to be paid to them as a result of service on Christmas Island and in Australia, but almost all of them have been rejected by the DHSS and its appeals tribunal. The Royal British Legion, which has represented more than 131 test servicemen of their relatives, knows of only one case, Michael Saffery, where an ex-serviceman has received a pension specifically related to service during the tests. Michael Saffery, who now lives in the United States, suffers from bilateral cataracts, a radiation-linked condition. He was not in fact on Christmas Island during the tests but with the meteorological team at Samoa in the Pacific, but he may have come into contact with radiation after the tests when he handled contaminated aircraft used during the nuclear explosions. In 1983 his application for a disability pension was refused by the DHSS, but on appeal it was accepted. The tribunal which heard the case argued that, because it could not be disproved that radiation was a possible cause of Saffery's cataracts, even though his records showed no high doses, he should be awarded the pension.

Michael Saffery was lucky. Most ex-servicemen, or relatives of ex-servicemen, who believe they have suffered as a result of radiation-related illnesses have an often insuperable obstruction in their path to compensation: the 'seven-year rule'. If a pension is claimed more than seven years after service, the burden of proof shifts from the Ministry of Defence to the claimant, who has to show that the injuries did result from service. Before the seven years are up and if the Ministry cannot disprove the claim that radiation caused a death or illness, the Government must pay a pension – as they did to Michael Saffery. It is much more difficult to prove that an illness or disability was caused by radiation than to prove beyond doubt that it could not have been attributable to it. The nature of radiation-related illnesses is that they are not specific, and it is almost impossible therefore to prove beyond doubt that a man's illness has resulted because of service at any of the British nuclear tests.

The seven-year rule affects most of those claiming a pension for what they believe to be radiation-linked illnesses or deaths. At low doses, radiation's effects do not begin to manifest themselves until many years after the exposure, perhaps even twenty years or more. Most cases concerning test veterans, as a result, would arise after the seven-year rule has elapsed. Few can succeed. Yet sadly the seven-year rule was introduced to benefit ex-servicemen who suffered as a result of gassing in the trenches in the First World War, the effects of which were not always immediately apparent. Before that time the burden of proof was always on the ex-service man from the moment he left the services.

Late in 1983 the Department of Health and Social Security surprised test veterans by awarding pensions and small compensation payments (around £2,000) to a number of servicemen who took part in the Australian and Christmas Island tests.

According to the British Legion, the payments and pensions were made to men suffering skin cancers. The awards came with a statement that they were made on grounds other than past exposure to radiation: 'You will see that on the advice of the Department's doctors your claim is admitted on the grounds that your rodent ulcer is due to exposure to strong sunlight. It is not accepted that your condition is related in any way to possible exposure to radiation from atom bomb tests as claimed by you.'

The DHSS seems determined that if awards are made to test ex-servicemen or their widows, the connection with the tests should be hidden. Any attempt to find out how many awards have been made by the DHSS since the nuclear tests is not possible because the Department claims it does not keep records of individual cases presented to it, nor does it isolate claims for pensions resulting from service at a specific place: 'When considering claims for a war widows pension, geographical location is not of itself of general significance. Each case is looked at separately. Our concern is whether in an individual case the particular conditions of service experienced in that case led to that person's death and we have not therefore kept records of the indvidual factors of service which led our doctors to advise on awards.'

This tortuous logic protects the Department from making any admissions about awards, such as Mrs Pollard's, which have already been made and which appear to be made on the basis of exposure to radiation. If any war widows pensions are granted to widows of test veterans in the future, a similar safety valve exists for the Government: 'When it is decided to award a war widows pension, the widow is simply told of the award. The widow may have put in her claim that her husband was in service at Christmas Island but this does not mean that the award was made for that reason – in fact it could well have been made for an entirely different reason.' Owing to official secrecy the widow, whom one would imagine would be entitled to know the official view of the cause of her husband's death, is deprived of a right which would be granted by any other court.

The British Government's desire to protect itself from any possible admission of liability has led to a cruel denial of the rights of test ex-servicemen and their widows. The men who participated in the nuclear tests gave loyal service to the Crown in uncomfortable and sometimes dangerous conditions. The Government has a duty to look after them and their families in return. In cases where pensions have been awarded, liability should be admitted and proper compensation paid.

No doubt the British Government fears that a single admission of negligence could lead to the payment of compensation to every test participant who has suffered from cancer, and to the families who have lost their husbands or fathers through cancer. Since it is not possible to distinguish between radiation-induced cancer and any other cancer this may seem a daunting possibility to Whitehall. Such payments to all test ex-servicemen suffering from cancer, or to their relatives, could cost hundreds of millions of pounds. It is unlikely, therefore that a British Government, whatever its political hue, will concede that the tests damaged the health of servicemen. If the Government-sponsored survey of British test participants shows an abnormally high number of cancer deaths, payments may be made to those with known radiation records. Should compensation ever be paid to those without a recorded dose, it will be small. It is most unlikely that there will ever be an admission of negligence.

The British Government is notorious among those who have ever sought redress from it. No evidence, however, strong, no arguments, however forceful, can make it move from its pre-ordained and carefully defended position. For those like Amy Pollard and Marjorie Stevens who have come up against the labyrinthine bureaucracy of claims and the serpentine arguments which seek to bypass them, the experience of government is a shocking one. Their lonely fights for recognition will continue, but the fact is that Ministry of Defence policy, tried and tested with the veterans of two world wars, is to block and prevaricate until no survivors remain to press their case.

Chapter Fourteen

RETURN TO MARALINGA

On 24 May 1984 a special VIP flight of the RAAF left Adelaide for Maralinga. On board were the Minister of Resources and Energy, Senator Walsh, and the South Australian Premier, John Bannon, accompanied by scientists of the Australian Radiation Laboratory. The tour of the bomb sites took no more than four hours and the politicians learned little more than they already knew from their briefings in Canberra and Adelaide. But the importance of the trip was symbolic. The representatives of the Federal and South Australian Governments were there jointly to express their regret that the atomic test series had ever been allowed to take place in Australia and to pledge their support for all investigations into the possible harm done to servicemen, Aborigines and the environment.

The Minister's office in Canberra had carefully allocated the few places on the plane to maximize media coverage, and journalists from the Australian television networks and the major newspapers were included in the ministerial party; the only British journalist on board was the author Sue Lloyd-Roberts. The return flight from the bomb range was timed to ensure that the minister's message would be broadcast across Australia on the television news that night.

As the plane circled the deserted and desolate test range before landing at Maralinga air-strip, the visitors were impressed by the sheer size of the Australian atomic ghost city. From the air, a web of concrete runways and roads could be seen sprawled across the desert as a reminder of the huge engineering and construction effort that the site had entailed. On the ground the huge 'Welcome to Maralinga' sign that was put up to encourage the nervous conscript as he was driven from the airstrip to the village remains, but the prefabricated dormitory huts and mess houses that would have been his 'home' have gone, carried off as scrap. The only buildings still standing were those built in concrete: the control tower, the central communications building, the cook-house, the officers mess and the swimming pool. Electricity pylons, telephone poles, water tanks, air-conditioning and refrigeration equipment lay rusted and abandoned.

The test site visitors were presented with an array of desert landmarks that bore witness to the nuclear events that took place at Maralinga only three decades before. They saw the debris of major tests, minor trials, clean-up operations and burial sites: the remains of which had been variously exhumed, relocated, auctioned and, in one case transported back to Britain. Where there once were craters, there were now concrete pyramids solemnly inscribed 'Test Site A British Atomic Weapon was exploded here on . . .'. Where there would have been trees and scrub before the explosions, there were now the burnt-out skeletal remains. Nuclear burial sites were surrounded by barbed-wire fences with radiation warning symbols and written warnings in English, Greek, Italian, Serbo-Croatian and Spanish. More ominously, teams from the Australian Radiation Laboratory guiding the ministerial team showed the presence of radioactive material on the surface of the range with their constantly clicking geiger counters.

The Maralinga site will be a no-go area for many hundreds of years. At the One Tree test site, the scene of the first atomic bomb exploded at Maralinga, scientists have recorded the highest residual radioactivity level of any of the blast sites. It will be unsafe for human occupation well into the next century. At Taranaki, scene of the balloon-burst, twenty-one burial pits contain over 800 tons of contaminated material, including plutonium. At the test sites code-named TM 100 and 101, the experiments carried out in the minor trials left some twenty kilos of plutonium scattered over the surrounding area, and evidence of minute particles of plutonium on the surface of the ground are still picked up on the detection devices used by survey teams. The Australian Radiation Laboratory has declared that the British attempts at cleaning up after the tests were inadequate.

The clean-up operation, code-named Brumby, was carried out by a team of Royal Engineers and scientists from AWRE in 1967. Before that date, the plutonium was left where it had been scattered. During Brumby it was ploughed back into the earth, under 10 centimetres of topsoil. Those who know the famous Maralinga winds and dust have argued that such a precaution was inadequate and the plutonium-contaminated soil was bound to get dispersed over the surrounding country. 'The storms were like whirlwinds', one veteran remembers, 'and very powerful'.

There was also the problem of Cobalt 60, a powerful gamma emitter. It was not until British records showed that Cobalt 60 pellets were found scattered at Maralinga that it became known that Cobalt had been tested as a bomb component. One of the British clean-up team at Brumby remembers 'hand-scavenging' the pellets, which involved locating the pellets and scooping them up on a trowel of sand and placing them in a lead tin under the supervision of AWRE scientists. 'Although we all started keenly enough and aware of some danger, after a while things started being rushed and our boffin friends seemed homesick! This is when to my mind things got skimped. I *know* we did not recover all the pellets before the site was taken as cleared. I hope no Aborigine ended up carrying a pellet of cobalt between his toes one day!' Another veteran remembers hand-picking the still radioactive material that had been fused into glass by the heat of the atom bomb at the One Tree site. They were given protective clothing for the job but because of the temperature in the 120s they wore just army shorts and boots and dispensed with their respirators.

The details of the 1967 clean-up operation were all carefully catalogued in a report by AWRE scientist, Noah Pearce. The Australian Weapons Safety Committee said they were happy with the operation and the 'Pearce Report' was subsequently classified by the British Government. Britain told Australia that she had no further use for the site, which remained under Federal control pending a survey and its 'return' to the South Australian Government. A permanent police presence was established at the site, located in the former cook-house, and a perimeter fence was built around the prohibited area. The authorities no doubt hoped that the story of Maralinga would remain safely behind barbed wire and in the vaults, hidden in British classified documents.

It was not so easy for the Federal Government to forget about the other 'remains' of Maralinga – the Australian veterans and their families who claimed that men had suffered as a result of the tests. In 1966, Melbourne widow Peggy Jones began her campaign for compensation for the death of her husand Bill. Warrant Officer William Jones was the serviceman who had stayed beside his tank in a forward area for two days after one of the 1953 detonations. He died of cancer thirteen years later. In 1974, she won a lump sum of $8600 under the Compensation (Australian Government Employees) Act. At the same time, Maralinga veteran Rick Johnstone successfully persuaded the authorities that his blood condition and nervous disorders had been caused by his experiences on the range. He was awarded a fortnightly payment of $220 by the Commonwealth Employees' Compensation Board. It was a breakthrough despite the small payments made. The authorities had admitted responsibility for injuries incurred because of the tests. The veterans' cause in Australia was launched.

The Australian Nuclear Veterans' Association (ANVA) was formally set up in 1979 by two Vietnam veterans, Pat Creevey and Harold Crosbie. Both men had had experience of fighting the Government on behalf of the victims of Agent Orange and they were armed with the necessary know-how to organize a medical questionnaire for their members. A year after its foundation, the Association had enlisted four hundred veterans, of whom ninety had cancer, seventy-seven of them terminal cases. Crosbie immediately challenged the Government to set up a proper epidemiological study to prove whether a disparity existed between their cancer victims and a control group. Other veteran organizations, such as the Maralinga and Monte Bello Atomic Ex-servicemen's Association, have been established in ANVA's wake.

In the face of anxious questions from the veterans, both the British and Australian Governments assured the Australian associations that safety precautions at the test were second to none. Sir Ernest Titterton made a public statement that 'no one suffered on account of the test programme in Australia'. Nonetheless, the 'Maralinga question' became a national issue and the veterans' associations have grown steadily since their formation. In 1980, when Adelaide's *Advertiser* ran a bomb test veterans' campaign, hundreds of veterans began to tell their stories. Some were incredible but others were genuinely alarming. The issue was frequently debated in Parliament, highlighting the differences between the Liberal Party, whose predecessors had invited the bomb tests to be held in Australia, and the Labor Party, more traditionally ambivalent about the Commonwealth and nuclear matters. The main anti-Government protagonist was the Labor MP, Tom Uren. He told the House of Representatives that the Maralinga story was one of 'negligence, dishonesty and secrecy on behalf of the Liberal-National Country Government. Public concern has been answered by a series of untruths and half-truths about what testing took place at Maralinga, and the hazards present.'

Senator Carrick's statement in 1980 that his Government

believed there was 'no case to answer' and that there was no need for a full medical or judicial inquiry served merely to incense the veterans' organizations and redouble their efforts to win compensation. After their first successes under the Commonwealth Employees' Compensation Act, ANVA pushed forward a claim from Lance Edwards, the RAAF squadron leader who had eaten the packed lunch on the flight through the cloud after the Totem 1 shot. He developed cancer of the thyroid and, after acknowledging that his illness was due to the atomic blast, the Compensation Board awarded him only $4000. Widows who applied for compensation fared rather better. Four widows were awarded the maximum allowable under the scheme, $36,000, about one year's salary for a squadron leader.

While the Government tried to shelve the veterans' issue, they were unable to ignore the publicity given to the stories of plutonium waste left at Maralinga. The secrets of the Pearce Report were revealed to the public by Australian veteran, Avon Hudson, whose television interview in 1976 caused a sensation. Hudson gave the first details of the 'minor trials', in which he had worked as a construction engineer on the bomb platforms. He revealed how the shots scattered plutonium, Cobalt 60, beryllium and natural uranium over the South Australian desert, and he alleged that 40 kilos of plutonium remained at Maralinga.

In reply, the South Australian Mines and Energy Minister, Hugh Hudson, confirmed that 800 tonnes of radioactive waste was buried in Maralinga and suggested that the area should be monitored. The following year, the Australian Ionising Radiation Advisory Council reported that plutonium was scattered over some of the test sites and that they were unsuitable for permanent settlement. Furthermore, in a report to the Prime Minister, Defence Minister Killen said that it was possible for a small, determined group of terrorists to remove the plutonium and use it against the population. The Australian Government had recently ratified the Nuclear Non-Proliferation Treaty and ministers believed it would be wiser to get rid of their nuclear inheritance.

In October 1978 the Australian Foreign Affairs Department sent a telegram to the British Foreign Office asking Britain to remove some of the plutonium. The British sent out a team to survey the possibilities and Britain agreed to clear up some of the nuclear rubbish. On 17 February 1979, three Hercules aircraft arrived at Maralinga containing supplies and equipment for the job. The clean-up 'task force' was made up of members of the Commonwealth police, AWRE scientists and members of the Australian Atomic Energy Commission. In appalling heat, the team started work at sunrise and after a midday break continued working under floodlights into the night in the so-called 'airport cemetery' where the bins containing the radioactive material lay buried. Because it was considered unwise to handle the bins, a crane had to be improvised to raise them to the surface. It took four days to remove the first bin to examine its contents. An area around the excavated site was cordoned off and access denied to all except scientists wearing protective clothing and respirators.

The burial records were imprecise and there was some confusion as to which bin contained the plutonium. Dr Symonds, chief scientist at the Australian Energy Commission, had to put his gloved hand into one of the containers. The first time he carried out this hazardous operation, plutonium contamination was detected on his glove and the men knew that they had located the bin containing the recoverable material. It took ten buckets of grout to reseal the container and the official records show that Dr Symonds lost three kilos in weight during the operation. Emergency oxygen supplies were on standby throughout and the medical team present forbade anyone to spend more than an hour at a time on the operation. After the grouting, tin drums sealed with concrete were used to transport the plutonium 'home' to Aldermaston.

With hindsight, scientists today agree that the operation was unnecessary and possibly foolish. The British only repatriated half a kilo of plutonium – all that was transportable. The rest was left churned up in the Maralinga soil, and at least nineteen and a half kilos of plutonium remain. Nonetheless, 'honour' on the part of the Australian Government was satisfied and the International Atomic Energy Authority noted with gratitude that no reportable nuclear material from the tests was left at Maralinga. The operation had been carried out on the understanding that Britain would never again be asked to remove waste from Australia.

In 1982, the Australian Government sought to regain the initiative by commissioning a study by the Australian Ionising Radiation Advisory Council into the safety measures during the tests and their possible after-effects. A second study was made by the Commonwealth Department of Health into the 'Health of Atomic Test Personnel'. The report from AIRAC, which came out in 1983 claimed that no Australian who worked on the test range was exposed to levels of radiation higher than those permitted by international recommendations. There was 'no evidence' that members of the RAAF or ground crews received excess doses of radiation. There was also 'no evidence' that any Aborigine was injured by the nuclear tests. AIRAC's only concession to human error was in admitting the possibility that unauthorized entry to a contaminated area could not be entirely ruled out, but here again 'no evidence has been found that such an incident occurred'. A year after the report's publication, a Radiation Council member told the authors that 'AIRAC 9', as the report is known, was 'written without wanting to offend the British'.

The special committee chaired by Professor Kerr, set up in 1984 by the Hawke Government to review all the literature concerned with the test series criticized AIRAC 9 for its obfuscation, especially in those parts dealing with matters of political and public sensitivity, and for significant omissions of highly relevant data. Most of all it disagreed with the philosophy behind it: 'the use of simplified assumptions which do not accurately reflect the complexities of what took place and the constant endeavour to present the best possible case, which results in a comfortable picture of the British nuclear tests'.

1983 brought a new government and a new attitude to the test debate. In March, Bob Hawke's Labor Party, the party which had promised a full inquiry in October 1980, was voted back into office after eight years in opposition. Labor Ministers used the historical association of the tests with the Liberal party and their own 'innocence' in the affair to full advantage. Never one to mince words, the Minister for Resources and Energy, Senator Walsh, told Parliament during one of his early debates on the tests that the real villain was Sir Robert Menzies, 'the lickspittle empire royalist who regarded Australia as a colonial vassal of the British Crown'. In his first ministerial visit to London, Foreign Minister Bill Hayden asked the Thatcher Government to 'open up the files' so that his Government could resolve once and for all whether sufficient safety measures had been taken during the test series. In a press conference held before Australian and British journalists at the Australian High Commision in London, Hayden said that the tests had taken place 'in an atmosphere of incompetence and ignorance'.

The new Goverment brought a rush of revelations about the test series. The premiers of South Australia and Victoria both protested when it was discovered that fallout over Adelaide and Melbourne had been higher than previously admitted. A former worker in the physics department at the Peter MacCallum Clinic in Melbourne told the *Melbourne Age* that a survey in 1957, after the Monte Bello and early Christmas Island tests, detected radiation levels up to 167 times the normal background radiation. Laboratory technicians in Adelaide claimed that one of their team, Keith Oliphant, brother of the nuclear physicist Sir Mark Oliphant, had admitted falsifying the records of radiation levels over Adelaide after the Maralinga tests by moving the decimal points 'one or two places'. In fact the fallout recorded by the now dead Oliphant should have shown radiation levels one thousand times those normally recorded.

There was renewed concern over the environmental hazards at Maralinga. In March the Maralinga Tjarutja Land Rights Act was passed, handing back to the Aborigines the land that had been 'requisitioned' by the Federal Government for the bomb tests in 1955. Two months later, however, the Pearce Report with its full revelations about contamination at Maralinga was tabled before the Federal Parliament. During his trip to London, Foreign Minister Hayden had asked the British to issue the full unexpurgated version. Before this, Parliament had had to rely on an edited version deposited in Canberra in 1979. The Aboriginal Legal Rights Movement wanted to know how safe the area surrounding the bomb site was. While it was agreed that the immediate test site area should remain cordoned off, there was concern about contaminated wildlife straying beyond the limits of the prohibited area. Aboriginal groups had been seen camped within thirty miles of the bomb craters and it was possible that they were eating contaminated rabbit flesh.

The deathbed confession of John Burke added to the furore. He claimed that he had found four dead Aborigines in a bomb crater in 1963. He also revealed details of the hitherto un-publicized minor trials and claimed that he knew that Aborigines had already taken advantage of their salvage rights in the area. They had, according to Burke, dug up con-taminated articles such as Land Rovers and heavy engineering equipment and had sold them in Coober Pedy. Within days of his death, South Australian senators were calling for a public inquiry. At its caucus meeting on 8 May, the Labor Party called for a full judicial inquiry into the tests. On the same day Adelaide's *Advertiser* said that with all the new allegations, Bri-tain should stop repeating its blanket assurances that no one suffered during the tests. 'It behoves Britain to give a much more detailed explanation than has been given so far.' In its leader, entitled 'Maralinga cover-up', the *Melbourne Age* claimed that 'what we are witnessing is a conspiracy of silence; a conspiracy to which the Australian Government is party, albeit a reluctant one'.

The Australian Government reacted with the establishment of the Kerr Committee. Senator Walsh, Minister for Resources and Energy, gave Professor Kerr and his team just sixteen days to review all the published scientific literature on the tests, to assess any dangers that the tests might have caused the Australian people and to recommend to the Government any appropriate action. The Government wanted to be seen to be treating the matter with the highest priority and urgency. A week after announcing the Kerr Committee, Senator Walsh accompanied Premier Bannon on the flight to Maralinga. In prepared statements to coincide with the trip, Walsh announced: 'Let me assure the Australian people that this Government has no interest or intention of keeping facts relating to the nuclear tests in Australia secret.' Premier Bannon said that the tests should never have taken place and 'it's now up to us to make amends'.

On 31 May 1984, Senator Walsh received the report from the Kerr Committee. Contrary to all the assurances on the safety given by the British and Australian Governments, the Committee had concluded that 'with such a large and prolonged endeavour it is unrealistic to assume that things did not go wrong and on occasions they did.' The report said that the task of unravelling the truth about the tests was impossible without full access to the documents and that, notwithstanding Britain's thirty-year rule laid down by the Public Records Act, the declassification process should begin right away. Above all, the Committee recommended that 'the Government hold a public inquiry to determine how the conduct and consequences of the British nuclear tests affected the health and well-being of Australians who served at the nuclear test sites and on those, mainly Aborigines, who lived in the region of the tests'.

Exactly twenty-one years after the British testing team fired their last shot, the Australian Government announced a Royal

Commission to look into Britain's conduct of the test series. The Commission was asked to examine the safety measures carried out during the tests and whether the health of people in Australia at the time, British servicemen included, had been adversely affected. They were also asked to look at the management of the test sites, both at the time of the tests and afterwards. The Commission was given the authority to recommend to the Australian Government that it should make provision for certain individuals or groups and, if necessary, recommend ways of making the test sites safe.

The decision to set up a Royal Commission created many political and legal problems. It was the first time that a Commonwealth country had summoned a Royal Commission to look into the behaviour of the 'mother country'. Hostility from Britain was only to be expected but, as the Kerr Committee had already pointed out, there was little a further inquiry could achieve without access to Britain's documents. The Australian Government took a gamble. Britain might snub the Australian request for documents, in which case the Commission was unlikely to achieve anything, though if Britain took that attitude she would lay herself open to accusations of a 'cover-up'. Or Britain might weigh the consequences of a diplomatic row against the indignity of having to 'come clean' and decide to cooperate.

In the early days of the Commission, relations between the two countries were acrimonious. When the Commission opened in September 1984, it was still not known whether the British Government would hand over all the documents required by the Commissioners or whether the British Government would be represented when the Commission moved to London. The Chief Commissioner, Mr Justice James McClelland, a former Labor Cabinet Minister under the Whitlam Government, made no secret of his dislike of the British and Australia's pro-British politicians. When after the first few weeks of the hearings, the British High Commissioner in Canberra complained that

Britain's name was being dragged through the mud, Justice McClelland asked whether the High Commissioner would prefer Australian history books to remove all reference to the nasty way Henry VIII treated his wives. 'If he wants the Royal Commission to be fully appraised of the British Government's view of the way the nuclear trials were conducted, he should advise his Government to do what it has repeatedly been invited to do but which it has not yet deigned to do: be represented before the Commission.' The Sydney *Morning Herald* paraphrased the Judge's challenge to the British with the headline, 'Show Up or Shut Up'. A few weeks later, the British Government announced that it would be present at the Commission's hearings.

When the Commission moved to London in January 1985, McClelland adopted the same technique to goad the British Government into handing over all the documents required by the Commissioners. Before a crowd of barristers, press, television and veterans assembled for the Commission's first day's hearings, the judge lambasted the British. He said that they had only agreed to be represented before the Commission because he had accused them of 'dragging their feet'. On Britain's reluctance to hand over documents that might involve military secrets, he said 'secrecy, in the national interest, has always been a convenient alibi for failure of disclosure. But today it is hard to believe that Britain is in possession of any atomic secrets unknown to the great powers', The British had 'told the Australian authorities almost nothing' about what they were doing in Australia during the tests and they were now morally obliged to make everything known.

McClelland was successful in his campaign to gain access to secret documents. When the Commissioners left London three months later they had few complaints about co-operation from the British. Except for extremely sensitive weapons data, the British Government had made available almost all the thirty-eight tons of material on the tests stored at Aldermaston, in the

Ministry of Defence and in the Public Records Office. Where necessary the thirty-year rule was broken.

The outspoken and brash behaviour before and after the Commission by Justice McClelland was an indication of the strong anti-British feeling aroused in the aftermath of the tests in some Australian quarters. However, his loud-mouthed *obiter dictum* about Margaret Thatcher and a divided British nation caused anger and embarrassment to many Australians. Critics of the Royal Commission accused the Labor Government of establishing it as a sop to anti-nuclear and anti-British feeling: while US bases remained and uranium mining continued in Australia attention could be turned to the proceedings of the politically unimportant and possibly biased Commission. That the comments of Justice McClelland caused little diplomatic ill-feeling between Britain and Australia was, perhaps, an indication of the importance with which he and his Commission was regarded.

Political leaders in Britain have shown little interest in the tests or the Royal Commission. Neither major party has been keen to condemn its predecessor's handling of the bomb test programme: both Conservative and Labour Prime Ministers ordered the construction and testing of nuclear weapons in the 1950s. Even the Liberal party, traditional champion of environmental causes, has steered clear of formally associating itself with the veterans' cause. Politicians on all sides are aware that the causes that appear attractive in opposition can prove expensive in Government. A single admission of negligence could open the floodgates to costly claims and stir up the simmering nuclear controversy in Britain.

The prospects of reaching a satisfactory conclusion to the veterans' campaigns in Australia and Britain look remote. The political will is lacking and the scientific uncertainty about the effects of low levels of radiation makes any attempt at proof almost impossible. In come cases, the veterans have been their own worst champions. The tendency to blame every death from cancer on the test programme is understandable but misguided. Similarly, the accusation that birth defects can be blamed on the tests needs proper examination before it is made.

Nevertheless, there is no doubt that the tests in Australia and on Christmas Island were undertaken in haste. The nuclear scientists responsible were under strong political pressure to build and test the atomic and hydrogen bombs at almost impossible speed. In this the men of Aldermaston were successful. They reaped both personal and political rewards. William Penney was elevated to the peerage, and other senior nuclear scientists received knighthoods for their endeavours. Britain's weapon design team was firmly established: in a far shorter time-scale than either of the super powers and with fewer resources, effective kiloton and megaton weapons had been built. It was, in its own terms, a great political and scientific achievement. Britain was enabled to exchange secrets with the United States and, for the next three decades, the atom scientists could draw on enormous financial resources without reference to Parliament.

The senior Aldermaston men questioned at the Royal Commission appeared bewildered and upset by the hostility of some of the questioning. They had served their country well and had worked in dangerous conditions far beyond the call of duty. They considered the risks for the majority of the test servicemen to have been negligible. Yet they were now indicted by a foreign government for actions faithfully undertaken on behalf of their Government many years ago. They will suffer no more than damaged reputations. The British Government has ensured their protection from any prosecution. The senior politicians responsible for the tests will not suffer either. They are either forgotten or have gone to the grave. The British Government has steered a difficult but successful course between revelation and self-protection.

However, the aftermath of the tests, at one time a symbol of Anglo-Australian co-operation, has been to drive another nail into the coffin of Anglo-Australian friendship. The long tradition of Australian resentment at the seemingly superior and knowing attitude of the British, leading simple and trusting Australian manhood into danger, has been reinforced. Just as Gallipoli and the Bodyline controversy built up a deep feeling of righteous anger against the pom, so the nuclear tests today appear the epitome of cynical and arrogant British botching. The feeling is not entirely justified. Australia willingly and eagerly co-operated in the nuclear trials, having fought with other Commonwealth countries for the honour of playing host-country. Her scientific and nuclear knowledge benefited enormously from the co-operation and her armed services were only too happy to be able to learn as much as possible about the nature and effects of nuclear warfare.

The real victims of the tests are often forgotten in the orgy of righteous indignation against the authorities responsible. They are the ex-servicemen and their widows, and the Australian Aborigines, who face years of complex legal and scientific argument before their cases are resolved. Deliberate exposure of many thousands of men to radiation may not be possible to prove, but there is no doubt that the men 'fortuitously' exposed to radiation were guinea pigs in an extensive and often mismanaged operation. No doubt history will refer to the tests as another footnote in the catalogue of grandiose attempts to restore Britain's declining post-imperial prestige. Unlike the victims of the Falklands war, however, there will be no memorials to the men who may have given their lives in the effort to put 'Britain on level terms again'.

APPENDIX 1

UK ATMOSPHERIC NUCLEAR TESTS IN AUSTRALIA AND AT CHRISTMAS ISLAND 1952–8

Code-name	Location	Date	Yield Range	Explosion Conditions
Hurricane	Monte Bello (off Trimouille Island)	3 Oct 1952	25 kt	Ocean surface burst (HMS *Plym*)
Totem 1	Emu	15 Oct 1953	10 kt	Tower-mounted
Totem 2	Emu	27 Oct 1953	8 kt	Tower-mounted
Mosaic G1	Monte Bello (Trimouille Island)	16 May 1956	15 kt	Tower-mounted
Mosaic G2	Monte Bello (Alpha Island)	19 Jun 1956	60 kt	Tower-mounted
Buffalo	Maralinga (One Tree)	27 Sep 1956	15 kt	Tower-mounted
Buffalo	Maralinga (Marcoo)	4 Oct 1956	1.5 kt	Groundburst
Buffalo	Maralinga (Kite)	11 Oct 1956	3 kt	Air-dropped – high airburst over land
Buffalo	Maralinga (Breakaway)	22 Oct 1956	10 kt	Tower-mounted
Grapple 1	Malden Island, Pacific	15 May 1957	megaton*	Air-dropped – high airburst over ocean
Grapple 2	Malden Island, Pacific	31 May 1957	megaton	Air-dropped – high airburst over ocean
Grapple 3	Malden Island, Pacific	19 Jun 1957	megaton	Air-dropped – high air burst over ocean

Antler	Maralinga (Tadje)	1 kt	14 Sep 1957	Tower-mounted
Antler	Maralinga (Biak)	6 kt	25 Sep 1957	Tower-mounted
Antler	Maralinga (Taranaki)	25 kt	9 Oct 1957	Balloon-suspended – high airburst over land
Grapple X	Christmas Island	megaton	8 Nov 1957	Air-dropped – high airburst over ocean
Grapple Y	Christmas Island	megaton	28 Apr 1958	Air-dropped – high airburst over ocean
Grapple Z	Christmas Island	kiloton†	22 Aug 1958	Balloon-suspended – airburst over land
Grapple Z	Christmas Island	megaton	2 Sep 1958	Air-dropped – high airburst over ocean
Grapple Z	Christmas Island	megaton	11 Sep 1958	Air-dropped – high airburst over ocean
Grapple Z	Christmas Island	kiloton	23 Sep 1958	Balloon-suspended – high airburst over land

*few hundred kiloton to several megaton
†1–1000 kiloton
(Information taken from Ministry of Defence, 20 March 1984)

APPENDIX 2

$\underline{\text{Nucl.}} = x.$ } *copy mas. ctk.*
$\underline{\text{Vol.}} = y.$ *Feb. 59.*

$\underline{\text{No. }7\times1(R)}$

Time	Loc.	Reading Scale RKN.
0730	Local area	$+4-5 = X$
1000	,	
1300	,	$+7-.9 = X+y.$
Noon	,	
AM	, Soil	$Low +1$
P.M.	, ,	High
P.m.	under soil	$High + 20 = X.y.$

Vol.

Time	Loc.	Reading Scale $\phi^c - \cdot 2$
noon	Local area	Bright $+7 - \cdot 2$ (y)
,	,	Hazy $+25 - \cdot 2$ (y) ?
,	,	Heavy $+9 - \cdot 2$ (y)
AM. P.m.	Store Dump 1st.	50 yds. $+ 30 = X = X = X$ ⌇⌇⌇⌇ !
Pm ,	Lagoon ,	open = Nil shelter sides $+5 - 9$ y.x. ?
/ ,	Fish , shell , 1st.	N.o. $7\times1(R)$ / $Lt_1 + 2 = X$ $+6 = X$ $+6 - 8 = X$
/ ,	Personal Body ,	feet $+ \cdot5$ Legs $+ \cdot4$ X.y. ? overall $+ \cdot 5$
/ ,		Clearance shower De-con. exercise, skipping, bar feet, Hard met plate surface. Result $+ \cdot 1$.

Time	Loc.	Phys. feeling
?oon	Open area "C' 'E"	naus. Tingling sore joints, vision, clears ½n. after Exercise
/	Trees Fruit C. nut. —juice	+ · 1 · × . + · 2 · × + · 3 · ×
/	Raw Stores Ex. H/Lu Lu.	= Nil after 5 days (shelter) = + 3 ××
/	Ins. Cons. ? 'C'	+ + + 60 ×××× continuous

Readings to meas. th. recorded accuracy
against main Rad. measuring Eq. 87%.
R.G. " 5 (1050)
Do. 7× / (R) To Med. Cen. Stock per attemp.

Document detailing radiation levels at Christmas Island 1959 (see page 171).

NOTES

Chapter Two
Counting the Risks

One of the clearest guides to ionising radiation is *Nuclear Power: Both Sides — The best arguments for and against the most controversial technology*, eds M. Kaku and J. Trainer (Norton, 1983). Other useful guides include: *Nuclear Radiation in Warfare*, Prof J. Rotblat (SIPRI, Taylor and Francis, 1981); *Living with Radiation*, (NRPB, 1981): *The Effects and Control of Radiation* P. A. H. Saunders (UKAEA, 1981, revised 1982); *Radiation*, Martin D. Ecker and Norton J. Bramesco (Random House, 1981); *From Hiroshima to Harrisburg*, Jim Garrison (SCM Press, 1980); *Health Implications of Nuclear Power Production* (WHO, 1978); *Nuclear War. The Facts*, Peter Goodwin (Papermac, 1981); *Working with Radiation* (BNFL). An excellent contemporary account of radiation hazards is *Fallout*, ed A. Pirie (MacGibbon and Kee, 1958). The MRC set out the Government's assessment of the dangers of radiation at the time of the tests in *The Hazards to Man of Nuclear and Allied Radiations* (HMSO, June 1956).

The possibility of testing bombs in the British Isles was put forward by Dr W. G. Marley in a paper for Harwell Atomic Research Centre in 1955. It was first made public at the Australian Royal Commission in London on 19 March 1985. The Ministry of Defence's response to the revelation and Gordon Wilson's comments were quoted in the *Daily Telegraph*. 20 March 1985.

The authors are grateful to Dr Philip Webber of Imperial College London for his guidance on the effects of radiation.

Cyto-genetic tests on servicemen have been carried out at the University of Manchester.

The National Radiological Protection Board's study is outlined in a 'Protocol for a Study of the Health of UK Participants in the UK

Atmospheric Nuclear Weapon Tests', ed J. A. Reissland (NRPB, September 1983).

Professor Edward Radford spoke of the risks of radiation exposure at the Royal Commission's proceedings in London on 29 January 1985.

The clearest guide for the layman to changing radiation standards was published in the British science journal *Nature*, vol 313, 17 January 1983, p. 175: 'Moving Standards in the 1950s'. A comprehensive contemporary account of changing philosophy and standards by Dr G. Failla was published in 1960 by the Joint Committee on Atomic Energy in its report on the 86th Congress, second session. The Australian Ionising Radiation Advisory Council's 'British Nuclear Tests in Australia — a review of operational safety measures and of possible after effects' (Report no. 9, January 1983) also gives a clear account of changing ICRP regulations. The most recent and most comprehensive guide to the changes from 1934 to 1977 by F. D. Sowby, the Scientific Secretary, ICRP, was published first in the *Radiological Protection Bulletin* no. 28, May 1979. The British interpretation of ICRP standards for the nuclear tests is given in AIRAC's ninth report and in evidence to the Royal Commission from Mr David Barnes on 28 January 1985. The authors are grateful to Mrs Lorna Arnold for her guidance on the subject.

In May 1953 confidence that a 'tolerance dose' existed was stated in the *High Explosives Research Report*, no. A32, p. 3: 'Airborne Contamination at Totem Trial'. Medical Research Council work in 1947 showing no threshold dose for genetic effects was detailed in a report by Dr D. G. Cathcheside, MRC Cttee on the Medical and Biological Application of Nuclear Physics, Protection Sub-Cttee, MRC 477/77, 6.2.47.

Official policy to keep the doses to a minimum was outlined in 'Hurricane Trial Orders, 1952'.

Adam Butler's summary of doses is listed in *Hansard*, House of Commons, 19 December 1984, col. 395.

The authors are grateful to Dr Alice Stewart for her comments on the Hanford Study.

The Hanford Study's methods have been critically assessed in Britain by J. A. Reissland and S. C. Darby of the NRPB in the *Journal of the Royal Statistical Society* (A, 1981, 144, part 3, pp. 298–331: 'Low Levels of Ionizing Radiation – Are We Underestimating the Risk?').

Recent evidence from the US Department of Energy on radiation studies was published in the *New Scientist*, 11 October 1984, p. 3: 'Higher Cancer Rates Found in Nuclear Plants'.

The findings of the 'Smoky' study have been published twice in the *Journal of the American Medical Association*: October 1980, vol. 244, p. 1575, and December 1984, vol. 252, p. 662.

Details of the revised dose estimates were published in the US scientific journal *Science*, vol. 212, 22 May 1981, p. 900: 'New A-Bomb Studies Alter Radiation Estimates'. The authors are grateful to Professor Edward Radford for his guidance on the subject.

Professor Lindop and M. W. Charles published in the *Journal of the Society for Radiological Protection*, vol. 1, no. 3, 1981, 'Risk Assessment without the Bombs'.

The 'Black Report' or 'Investigation of the Possible Increased Incidence of Cancer in West Cumbria' was published by HMSO in 1984.

Chapter Three
Calling the Shots

The most comprehensive guide to nuclear weapons is *The Effects of Nuclear Weapons* by Samuel Glasstone and Philip J. Dolan (Castle House Publications, 1980; First issued in USA 1957 and since revised). Other sources used by the authors were *The Effects of Nuclear War*, Office of Technology Assessment USA (Croom Helm, 1980); *Nuclear Weapons*, Home Office and Scottish Health Dept. (HMSO, 1975); *Nuclear War. The Facts*, Peter Goodwin (Papermac, 1981); *Crucible of Despair: the Effects of Nuclear War*, Anthony Tucker and John Gleisner (Menard Press, 1982); *Effects of Nuclear War on Health and Health Services* (WHO, Geneva, 1984); *Nuclear Radiation in Warfare*, Professor Joseph Rotblat (SIPRI, Taylor and Francis, 1981); 'British Nuclear Tests in Australia' (AIRAC, no. 9, January 1983); 'Report of the Expert Committee on the Review of Data on Atmospheric Fallout Arising from British Nuclear Tests in Australia' (Canberra, May 1984); and evidence to the Australian Royal Commission. The authors are grateful to Dr Philip Webber of Imperial College, London for his help with this chapter.

Mrs Thatcher's denial that servicemen were used as guinea pigs was given in a written answer, House of Commons, *Hansard*, 15 January 1985, col. 84. The British Government's position on the tests is fully outlined in a Ministry of Defence briefing paper for MPs: 'UK Atmospheric Nuclear Weapon Test Programme' (3 December 1984, D/D3/5/8/10).

Details of 'indoctrination' were set out in the minutes of the Atomic Weapons Trials Executive, 17 May 1955 (ref. DB/36/01, Buffalex 55/M.2).

AWRE submission to the Royal Commission in London shows the AIRAC report to be mistaken in the distance of the indoctrinee forces from the bombs.

The state of Christmas Island twenty-five years after the tests was detailed in a New Zealand report commissioned by the Government of the Republic of Kiribati: 'An Environmental Radiation Survey of Christmas Island, Kiribati' (NZ NRL Report, 1981/9).

Calculations of the effects of 'global' fallout are made in 'The Effects of Nuclear War' (US Office of Technology Assessment, Washington, 1980, p. 113).

Details of Dr Sikora's study were published in *General Practitioner* magazine, 5 October 1984.

The National Radiological Protection Board published a survey of all sources of radiation to which the people of Britain are exposed in 1979 and 1985.

The General Municipal Boilermakers and Allied Trades Union's 'Evidence to the Sizewell Inquiry' 1984 summarizes the study carried out by the University of Michigan.

Chapter Four
A Bomb for Britain

For this account of the history behind Britain's decision to build the bomb, the authors are indebted to Professor Margaret Gowing and Lorna Arnold's exhaustive treatment of the subject in *Independence and Deterrence*, vols 1 and 2 (Macmillan, 1974) and to the personal encouragement and help that those two historians gave us with this project. Margaret Gowing's lecture entitled 'Britain, America and the Bomb' from David Dilks' *Retreat from Power: Studies in Britain's Foreign Policy of the Twentieth Century* (Macmillan, 1981) was also invaluable. Further background information came from A. J. Pierre, *Nuclear Politics* (Princeton University Press, 1982); P. Pringle and J. Spigelman, *The Nuclear Barons* (Holt Rinehart & Winston, 1981); H. Macmillan, *Riding the Storm* (Macmillan, 1960); A. Moorehead, *The Traitors* (Hamish Hamilton, 1952); J. Simpson, *The Independent Nuclear State* (Macmillan, 1983); F. Williams, *A Prime Minister Remembers, Attlee* (Heinemann, 1961).

The authors also extracted information from contemporary documents of the Admiralty, Ministry of War, Ministry of Supply, Foreign Office and Cabinet Office held at the Public Records Office.

Chapter Five
'All the Fun of a Picnic'

The authors are indebted to the account of Britain's first A-bomb detonation in Gowing and Arnold's *Independence and Deterrence*. We were able to add to their version of the test eye-witness accounts from nuclear test veterans, some of whom had written to us direct and others of whom had submitted statements to the Royal Commission: these include in particular, Sidney Fletcher, now living in Liverpool; Raymond Jones, a British ex-serviceman now living in South Australia; Graham Mabutt from Devon; Michael Stephens from Southampton; Eustace Lamerton from Plymouth; Harry Carter from Hertford; Derek Parker from Hertfordshire; Harry Angwin from Cornwall; Keith Peck from Queensland; Maxwell Jellie from Adelaide; and Colin Bird from Queensland whom we interviewed at his home near Brisbane in 1984.

Additional details about the make-up of the bomb and the test operation came from the hearings of the Australian Royal Commission in London from January to March 1985. The documents submitted to the Commission by the Atomic Weapons Research Establishment were especially informative. Extra details emerged from our study of Ministry of Supply and Cabinet Office documents at the Public Record Office and from contemporary newspaper accounts.

Chapter Six
'Is There No Real Danger, Mr Menzies?'

Len Beadell's book *Blast the Bush* (Rigby, 1967) provides the story of his involvement in the test series, a story that he added to when he appeared before the Royal Commission hearings in Adelaide.

For the information on the bomb prototypes and the testing programme, we are indebted to John Simpson's scholarly research of the subject in *The Independent Nuclear State*. The details of the specific nature of the Totem trials come from contemporary Ministry of Defence documents. The official records kept by the AWRE provide an excellent account of the preparations and management of the test sites and details of the detonations themselves, which we added to from contemporary newspaper accounts.

Details of the 'Hotbox' mission come from a lecture given by Group Captain Wilson and Captain Dehin to the Royal Society of Medicine. The account of the RAAF air sorties and decontamination operations come from RAAF records submitted to the Royal Commission. Commander Wilson and former AWRE scientist, Dr Stevenson, both gave evidence to the Royal Commission. Once again, we drew from the recollections of test veterans, including Wing Commander Richard Nettley from Cornwall; William Turner, Bud Puxty and Rex Naggs from Queensland; Lance Edwards whom we interviewed at his home on the Gold Coast in 1984; and Bill Jones' widow, Peggy, whom we spoke to at her home in Melbourne.

Chapter Seven
'What the Bloody Hell is Going On?'

The account of the make-up and involvement of the Australian Weapons Test Safety Committee comes from documents and evidence given to the Royal Commission.

The background on weather conditions during the test series comes from the evidence submitted by British meteorologists, Robert Fotheringham and Albert Matthewmen, who were cross-examined by the Commissioners.

Details of the detonations come from Admiralty records and contemporary newspaper accounts.

We drew on the accounts of veterans Kenneth Black from Tyne and Wear, Keith Syder from Merseyside, John Perkins from Essex and Kenneth Stephens from South Australia.

The account of the misunderstandings between British and Australian officials over the Mosaic tests emerges from telegrams exchanged in 1956 between the Commonwealth Relations Office in Whitehall and the High Commissioner in Canberra, between the Australian and British Ministries of Supply and between the offices of the two Prime Ministers.

Chapter Eight
Black Mist

The accounts by Aborigines of their memories of Black Mist come from the Royal Commission hearings in Wallantinna, except for the story told by Yami Lestor whom we interviewed in Alice Springs in 1984.

The description of the Black Mist phenomenon comes from the report by AWRE scientists David Vallis and Bill Roach; the possible radiation danger emerged after their cross-examination by the Royal Commissioners in London.

We are indebted to Adrian Tame and F. P. J. Robotham for their account of the test effects on Aborigines in their book *Maralinga* (Fontana, 1982) and to Professor Robotham for his additional help, and to the Friends of the Earth Occasional Paper, 'Field of Thunder' by Judy Wilks. We must also mention David Leigh and Paul Lashmar of the *Observer*, who first made the subject of Black Mist known to the British public, which prompted the AWRE investigation.

The details about patrol officers come from Australian Ministry of Supply documents, and details of Aborigines who strayed into the test areas come from veterans who submitted evidence to the Royal Commission: Rod Kyle from Aberdeen; Barry Roberts from the Midlands; Clifford Tomlinson from Chester; John Hutton from Melbourne; and Patrick Connolly from Perth. Details of John Burke's confession were taken from ABC's 'Nationwide' and we interviewed Kevin Woodlands at his workshop near Brisbane in 1984.

The scientific documents on the possible effects of Black Mist include, 'A Survey of Diseases that may be Related to Radiation among Pitjantjatjara on Remote Reserves', SA Health Commission, 1981; 'High Level of Radiation Exposure Investigation', undertaken for the Pitjantjatjara Council by Dr B. W. Thomas in 1983; and the ninth report from the Australian Ionising Radiation Advisory Council published in 1979.

Chapter Nine
Field of Thunder

Details of the agreements reached on the protocol for the Maralinga test site come from the telegrams and documents exchanged between the Commonwealth Office in Whitehall and the Australian Ministry of Supply and from minutes of the Atomic Weapons Tests Safety Committee. Details of preparations at Maralinga and the detonations themselves come from Ministry of Defence and AWRE records and contemporary newspapers. Details of safety arrangements at Maralinga and at the other test sites come from the submission to the Royal Commission by William Saxby, formerly a Technical Staff Officer at the AWRE. Lord Penney's recollection of events was taken from the Royal Commission hearings. Information about the 'indoctrination force' comes from the reports of the Army Operational Research Group.

The descriptions of life at Maralinga were taken from veterans' letters and submissions to the Royal Commission, including those of Keith Therkelsen of Dunbogan, Doug Rickard and Edwin Bailey from Adelaide, Gordon Wilson from Hull, Robert Southwell from Hampshire, Alexander Sinclair from Newcastle Upon Tyne, Dennis Tilling from Shropshire, Terence Taylor from Lincolnshire and Brian Holbrook-James from Clywd. We interviewed Avon Hudson in Adelaide in 1984. We are grateful to Isabel Dovey for telling us about her husband's involvement in the 'minor trials' and his subsequent illness and death.

The description of the first air-drop in the test series comes from *Countdown* (Robert Hale, 1981) by Air Vice Marshal Stewart Menaul.

The official records of fallout over the Australian mainland come from Report 9 of the Australian Ionising Radiation Advisory Council published in 1979.

We are indebted to Adrian Tame and F. P. J. Robotham for their excellent account of the 'Marston Affair' in their book *Maralinga*. We were able to add to their account from evidence heard at the Royal

Commission. We were fortunate to interview Keith Lokan, member of AIRAC and Director of the Australian Radiation Laboratory, during our visit to Maralinga in 1984.

Chapter Ten
A Damp Squib

Very little has been published about the Christmas Island tests and most of the material in the two chapters on the 'Grapple Series' comes directly from conversations with the men who took part. The authors are grateful to Ken McGinley, Chairman of the British Nuclear Test Veterans Association for his help in locating participants in the Christmas Island tests.

Cabinet Papers revealing the decision to manufacture thermonuclear weapons were released in January 1985 to the Public Record Office at Kew, London.

Aubrey Jones, the Minister of Supply, outlined Government policy on the tests in the 'Christmas Island Handbook' issued to participants based on the island for the first 'Grapple' series.

Air Vice Marshal Steward Menaul is one of the few 'Grapple' participants to have written about his experiences of Christmas Island in *Countdown*.

The history of the island and its facilities for the tests are described in the official test handbook.

Roland Duck described the choice of Christmas Island as a location for the tests on BBC television's 'Panorama' programme – 'Cloud over Christmas Island', 19 September 1983.

Chapman Pincher's descriptions of his part in the H-bomb tests appear in his book *Inside Story* (Sidgwick and Jackson, 1978).

The shape and size of 'Red Beard', the hydrogen bomb, is described by Duncan Campbell in his book *The Unsinkable Aircraft Carrier* (Michael Joseph, 1984; chap. 4, p. 103).

The height of the bomb's detonation and its barometric fusing are detailed on p. 30 of *V-Bombers* by Robert Jackson (Ian Allan, 1981).

The authors are grateful to Nick Wilson for permission to quote from his diary.

Leonard Bertin's article appeared in the *Daily Telegraph*, 17 May 1957.

Chapter Eleven
'A Matter of String and Chewing Gum'

The nature of the work for the Royal Engineers on Christmas Island is listed in 'Christmas Island – Welcome to 36 Corps Engr Regiment, December 1958' a leaflet given to members of 36 Corps on their arrival on the island.

William Jones appeared on BBC television's 'Panorama' programme – 'Cloud over Christmas Island' – on 19 September 1983.

Clive Atkins described the 8 November test on BBC television's 'Nationwide' programme on 12 January 1983.

MP James Ramsden's comments about the diesel generator were made in a letter to Ray Gunter, the Marks' family's MP.

Air Vice Marshal Stewart Menaul describes the tests in chapters 5 and 6 of *Countdown*. The reference to radioactive Canberras is on p. 78.

The Prime Minister, Mrs Margaret Thatcher, revealed the doses of 30 rems in a written answer to Frank Allaun MP, recorded in *Hansard*, House of Commons, 3 February 1983.

Christopher Donne described his journey through the cloud on the 'Panorama' programme of 19 September 1983.

Bryan Young described the washdown procedures on the 'Nationwide' programme of 12 January 1983.

The transformation of Christmas Island into a US testing base was described in the *Daily Telegraph*, 26 April 1962.

All the other anecdotes, comments and descriptions of the Christmas Island tests were made in conversation with, or letters to, the authors.

Chapter Twelve
The Numbers Game

The authors are grateful to Dr Alice Stewart and Professor Joseph Rotblat for their help with this chapter.

The Prime Minister's figure of 12,000 servicemen was given in a written answer to Frank Allaun MP on 3 February 1983.

The University of Birmingham's study was published as a letter in the *Lancet*, 9 April 1983: E. G. Knox, T. Sorahan and A. M. Stewart, letter to the editor, 'Cancer following Nuclear Weapon Tests', *Lancet* 1, no. 8328, p. 815.

The Ministry of Defence's revision of the Prime Minister's figures was first publicized in the *New Scientist*, 'Defence Chiefs Juggle Figures on Bomb Tests', 14 April 1983, p. 62.

MP David Alton's comments on the revised figures and MP Geoffrey Pattie's statement appear in *Hansard*, House of Commons, 25 July 1983, cols 956 and 965.

The high incidence of young men at the tests later suffering blood cancer was publicized on BBC television's 'Panorama' programme – 'Cloud over Christmas Island' – on 19 September 1983.

The NRPB's study was outlined in a 'Protocol for a Study of the Health of UK Participants in the UK Atmospheric Nuclear Weapon Tests', ed. J. A. Reissland (NRPB, September 1983).

The Donovan Report was published as 'Health of Atomic Test Personnel', Commonwealth Dept of Health, Australian Government Publishing Service, Canberra 1983.

MP David Alton criticized the NRPB study in the House of Commons on 25 July 1983 (*Hansard*, col. 957).

MP Frank Cook's account of genetic damage was given in the House of Commons on 19 December 1984 (*Hansard*, col. 387).

Chapter Thirteen
The Crown's Defence

The authors are grateful to Michael Day, Head of Pensions Dept, Royal British Legion, and Mark Mildred, Solicitor to the British Nuclear Test Veterans Association, for their guidance on the complex area of compensation.

BBC Radio 4's 'Checkpoint' programme and the *Observer* newspaper have both investigated cases coming under Section 10 of the Crown Proceedings Act.

The DHSS explained the reasons for issuing the certificate to Mrs Pollard under Section 10 in a letter from Head of War Pensions, DHSS, N. Holt, 3 June 1983.

The Certificate of Attributability issued to Mrs Pollard was signed by Reg Prentice and dated 9 December 1980.

The justification for the Certificate in response to a letter to the Prime Minister from Mrs Pollard was made in a letter signed G. R. Tibbott for President, Claims Commission, 3 November 1980, Ministry of Defence Claims Commission.

MP David Alton's comment on the Crown Proceedings Act was made in the House of Commons on 12 March 1984 (*Hansard*, col. 189).

MP Frank Cook's comment was made in the House of Commons on 19 December 1984 (*Hansard*, col. 388).

Geoffrey Pattie's justification of the Act was made in the House of Commons on 12 March 1984 (*Hansard*, col. 193).

The Ministry of Defence's reasons for refusing to give Mrs Stephens an extra pension were made clear by Jerry Wiggins, Parliamentary Under-Secretary of State for the Armed Forces, in a letter to John Stradling Thomas MP, 12 May 1983.

The DHSS's explanation that rodent ulcers were caused by sunlight and not ionising radiation was made in letters sent to each recipient of an award in December 1983.

The DHSS's refusal to detail claims arising out of service at a specific place was explained in a letter to the authors by J. M. Bolitho, Deputy Director of Information, 12 July 1983.

Chapter Fourteen
Return to Maralinga

The Department of Resources and Energy collaborated with the Australian Radiation Laboratory to produce a document, 'Selected papers for background purposes – visit to Maralinga, 24 May 1984', which provides invaluable information on test chronology and current contamination.

Details of the cleaning-up operation and past contamination are found in the 1967 report by AWRE scientist Noah Pearce.

We are grateful for the information about the Australian veterans given to the authors by Harry Crosbie of the ANVA.

Our version of the history of the test controversy has been helped by the earlier account by Adrian Tame and F. P. J. Robotham, and by contemporary newspapers and parliamentary transcripts. Specific documents looking into the aftermath of the test series include the Australian Ionising Radiation Council's reports no. 4 and 9; the study, 'Health of Former Atomic Test Personnel', 1983; and the 1984 'Report of the Expert Committee on the Review of Data on Atmospheric Fallout Arising from British Nuclear Tests in Australia', known as the 'Kerr Report'.

We refer to opening statements delivered at the Royal Commission hearings in London by Mr Justice James McClelland and by Counsel acting for the Commission, Peter McClellan.

Index